Be a Great Step-Parent

This book is for all the stepfamilies over the years who have shared the struggle with me and shown how they can win through. Most of all, it's for my husband Vic who made me the gift of my stepson Alex. And for Alex and his lovely Kim, who rendered me speechless (not an easy task) when they announced I wasn't to be a stepgranny but a full granny.

And it's for Indie, from her Baba Ganoush.

Be a Great Step-Parent

Suzie Hayman

For UK order enquiries: please contact Bookpoint Ltd,
130 Milton Park, Abingdon, Oxon OX14 4SB.
Telephone: +44 (0) 1235 827720. Fax: +44 (0) 1235 400454.
Lines are open 09.00–17.00, Monday to Saturday, with a 24-hour
message answering service. Details about our titles and how to
order are available at www.teachyourself.com

For USA order enquiries: please contact McGraw-Hill
Customer Services, PO Box 545, Blacklick, OH 43004-0545, USA.
Telephone: 1-800-722-4726. Fax: 1-614-755-5645.

For Canada order enquiries: please contact McGraw-Hill
Ryerson Ltd, 300 Water St, Whitby, Ontario L1N 9B6, Canada.
Telephone: 905 430 5000. Fax: 905 430 5020.

Long renowned as the authoritative source for self-guided
learning – with more than 50 million copies sold worldwide –
the **Teach Yourself** series includes over 500 titles in the fields of
languages, crafts, hobbies, business, computing and education.

British Library Cataloguing in Publication Data: a catalogue record
for this title is available from the British Library.

Library of Congress Catalog Card Number: on file.

First published in UK 2008 by Hodder Education, part of
Hachette UK, 338 Euston Road, London NW1 3BH.

First published in US 2008 by The McGraw-Hill Companies, Inc.

This edition published 2010.

Previously published as *Teach Yourself Successful Step-Parenting.*

The **Teach Yourself** name is a registered trade mark of
Hodder Headline.

Copyright © 2008, 2010 Suzie Hayman

Typeset by MPS Limited, a Macmillan Company.

Printed in Great Britain for Hodder Education, an Hachette UK
Company, 338 Euston Road, London NW1 3BH, by CPI Cox &
Wyman, Reading, Berkshire RG1 8EX.

The publisher has used its best endeavours to ensure that the URLs
for external websites referred to in this book are correct and active
at the time of going to press. However, the publisher and the
author have no responsibility for the websites and can make no
guarantee that a site will remain live or that the content will remain
relevant, decent or appropriate.

Hachette UK's policy is to use papers that are natural, renewable
and recyclable products and made from wood grown in sustainable
forests. The logging and manufacturing processes are expected to
conform to the environmental regulations of the country of origin.

Impression number   10 9 8 7 6 5 4 3 2 1
Year   2014 2013 2012 2011 2010

Contents

Part three Working together

Meet the author

When I trained as a counsellor with Relate, over 15 years ago, 'stepfamily issues' were covered in a half-day session. As soon as I began counselling, of course, I realized that being in a stepfamily merited more deliberation than that (and now, of course, Relate puts it far more centre stage). For a start, stepfamilies are so much more common than we might think. I apply what I call the 1 in 10 rule – 1 in 10 is the usual figure for the number of people in a stepfamily. But try this test. When in any group of people, ask them to put their hands up if they are in a stepfamily – 1 in 10 are likely to say yes, they have stepchildren or a partner who is not the parent of their kids. But then ask if any of them, or their partners, were in stepfamilies as a child. Or do they have relatives who as children were part of a stepfamily, or even now as adults. Ask close friends and work colleagues the same. When you widen it out to include not just people who live with children not their own, or with an adult not the parent of their children, but also anyone directly touched by such a situation, you see what I mean by the 1 in 10 rule. Because it becomes more likely that only 1 in 10 can say stepfamily issues do *not* touch them.

I know this from personal experience as well as professional. I'm a stepmother. And that gives me particular insight into the other significant issue about being in a stepfamily – that it can have profound effects on your health and happiness. Hardly surprising, then, that a few years ago I was delighted to present my own series on BBC1, *Stepfamilies*.

I have trained as a teacher, worked for the Family Planning Association and Brook Advisory Centres as press and information officer, and then moved into being a freelance journalist. I became agony aunt of *Essentials* magazine, then *Woman's Own* and BBC Health Online and have written columns for the Saturday *Guardian* and *The Times*. I now write a family advice column in *Woman* magazine.

Not only have I trained with Relate to become a counsellor, but also with Triple P (Positive Parenting Programme) to become an accredited parenting educator. I am a spokesperson and trustee for Family Lives (formerly Parentline Plus), the major UK parenting charity, and a trustee of The Who Cares Trust, for 'looked after' children.

My particular interest in stepfamily issues meant I was an enthusiastic founding agony aunt in the Kids In The Middle (KITM) alliance, lobbying for increased support for children caught up in family breakdown, and I also edit the KITM website. I make frequent appearances on national and local television and radio, as a counsellor and agony aunt, on programmes such as BBC Breakfast, Woman's Hour, You and Yours, and am a regular on BBC 5Live, BBC Scotland and BBC Wales. I'm also an occasional presenter on my local BBC radio station, BBC Radio Cumbria. I am regularly asked to give expert comment in national and local media and to speak at conferences and to give seminars on a wide range of issues to do with relationships and parenting.

My personal and professional experience has led me to recognize the weighty and widespread effect stepfamilies have on our society and on so many individuals. It's not that stepfamilies are bad or wrong – so many are a wonderful second chance for everyone involved. In my own case, being a stepmum has given me a son and a granddaughter I would never otherwise have had. But I know only too well that there are issues you need to take into account if you're going to make it work. So often, it's not the people involved that make it hard but the situation itself. Understanding this, and that you aren't alone in feeling the way you do, can help you find solutions. Taking the blame out of the equation opens it up to an answer.

I wish I'd had this book when I started out on my journey as a stepmother. I don't think I did as badly as I might have done, but I'd have liked to have done better. With the benefit of my experience and training, I know you can!

Only got a minute?

Being in a stepfamily is neither unusual nor abnormal, but our lack of understanding or experience of them can make it difficult.

For you to be in a stepfamily, another family has to have ended and one or both of you will have suffered the loss of a partnership. More important, there will be children who have lost a parent, a family and the certain, safe knowledge that their family will always remain intact. Exploring and understanding everyone's feelings and reactions can help you manage what is likely to be a delicate situation.

To begin a stepfamily, you need to find the best ways of allocating space and time between everyone and of making sure that the newcomers have room for both their possessions and their traditions. You need to agree House Rules and to look at the importance of giving everyone in the home responsibilities and daily chores.

Where children live and stay, and how they may feel about such arrangements, contact with the non-resident parent and maintenance, can also be issues. You will need to manage holidays, festivals and family traditions in a new family, negotiate with exes, partners and children, draw up contracts between you and review ongoing arrangements.

You will need to find mutually agreeable approaches to discipline, behaviour and control from both the adults' and the child's point of view. These are all very important ways of building family bonds and producing mutual respect between family members.

Of course, school also plays a really important role in children's lives; it can be a haven but at the same time can also add to their problems. Therefore it is very important to bring the school onside, for both parents and step-parents. Finally, it is crucial to maintain and review continued contact with grandparents and other relatives, including relatives of the absent parent.

Introduction

Are you or your partner in a second relationship, with children from a previous one? Or perhaps your son or daughter or other close relative is in or is about to embark on just such a relationship. You can see it's a challenge and maybe you're looking for help. Look no further! This book will be your support, your guide and your prop. Most of all, this book will show you how you can create what everyone with a new family wants – not just a functioning stepfamily but a happy family.

Perhaps that name – stepfamily – feels as if it doesn't quite fit your situation. Plenty of people who could benefit from this book may not immediately see themselves as being in the step-parent zone. You may think it's a family shape or name that doesn't apply to you, or maybe you feel that just muddling on as you are will do.

You may be right. But think for a minute, because from my own experience, once I recognized I was a step-parent, I found it a lot easier to manage what became a very happy family.

For a start, it helped to realize I wasn't alone in the situation. The traditional family – two adults, married, living together and bringing up their own children – is no longer in the majority. Clearly, most families pass through this stage, but more and more people experience a range of family forms in their lifetime. You may find yourself a single parent, caring for your own children with their other parent no longer around or in touch for varying degrees of involvement and time. You may be a parent no longer in full-time connection with your children. And sooner or later, you may well pass through the family shape we call a stepfamily.

I hadn't thought I was in a stepfamily because we didn't call ourselves that. We weren't married and my stepson didn't live with us. But I soon realized stepfamily issues affect you whether or not a marriage is involved, and whether or not children live with you full time. You don't need to have been given the title 'stepfather', 'stepmother', or 'step-grandparent' for the issues to be real and close to home.

Insight

Not taking the family name does not insulate you from the problems. Recognizing you are a stepfamily, even if you see yourself primarily as a family just like any other, at least helps you understand why your situation may be difficult.

Stepfamilies come from all socio-economic groups and most cultures. You can be in, or join, a stepfamily at any age from becoming a step-parent in your twenties to seventies, or a stepchild from birth to late adulthood. It's not an unusual or abnormal family form to be a part of, but our lack of understanding of the issues that can affect people coming into a stepfamily can make it a difficult one to manage. At present, most people who marry and create a family stay there. Six out of ten couples who make those vows 'until death do us part' are able to keep them. However, four out of ten marriages end, which is not a minor percentage.

One of the statistics that brought me up short was that second-time marriages are more likely to fail – 50 per cent end in divorce. Once you get to third or fourth time around, you're even more likely to divorce. When it's a third marriage for at least one of the couple, the figures are the reverse of those for first-time marriages: six out of ten third-time marriages end in divorce.

And those only are the statistics for marriage. Relationships not regularized by a formal ceremony are even more likely to come apart.

There are all sorts of reasons why people in second or third-time relationships will find it harder to stay together, which is why I wrote this book. I know from both personal and professional experience that if you know the challenges and are prepared for them, if you see possible problems coming, you can do something about them. This book aims to help you look at the danger zones and chart your way through them so yours becomes one of the many stepfamilies that not only succeed but also thrive and bloom. There are a lot of us out there, and this book aims to normalize the situation and to help you overcome the sorts of problems that often arise.

The aim of this book is to help you *Be a Great Step-Parent*. You'll find information, issues to explore, consider and discuss, and plenty of tips. Here are five to start you off:

1 *Don't allow the reputation of stepfamilies to put you off.*
2 *Do some preparation – the more you understand the pitfalls, the better you can avoid them.*
3 *Accept that it may take some work, but if you put in the effort, a stepfamily can be as happy a place to be as any family.*
4 *Don't take sides or ask anyone else to do so. You're all in this together.*
5 *Make your motto 'Do praise, don't criticize'.*

Part one

Getting together

1

Early days and introductions

In this chapter you will learn:
- *what constitutes a stepfamily*
- *why stepfamilies may be difficult*
- *early days and introductions between children and step-parents*
- *how to tell the children*
- *how to have a family discussion.*

You've met someone and everything in the garden's rosy; you're special to them, they're special to you – enough for the two of you to be thinking about bringing your lives together. There's one problem – what do you tell the children?

If you or your new partner have children, even if they don't actually live with you, sooner or later they're going to have to know there's a new person in their mum's or dad's life. Because, whether or not it's the way you see it at the moment, putting your lives together makes you a stepfamily.

What is a stepfamily?

A stepfamily is any household that includes children who arc related to one partner but not the other. You may feel that partners have to be married for one of them to be a step-parent, or that children need to live with you full-time for them to be stepchildren. The truth is that all the emotional needs and problems that go with stepfamilies kick into play whether the adults concerned are actually married or not, and whether the children live with them full-time or visit part-time. In fact, the issues may be more difficult to manage if you don't define yourself as a stepfamily. In such a situation you get all the problems but may not realize why they are happening and what you can do about it.

So tip number one is this: if it looks like a duck, swims like a duck and quacks like a duck, it IS a duck. If in your particular relationship one of you has children, whether you're getting married or not, whether you see the children daily or not... you're a stepfamily.

When the time comes for a new person to be introduced, you need to recognize they will be part of the child's life as much as they are a part of the adult's life. To get your stepfamily off to a good start, how do you introduce the new addition?

Why early days may be difficult

Introductions are an important issue. You'll want to get off on the right foot, although it's reassuring to know that even if the situation turns sour, there is plenty you can do to redress matters. It's worth noting, before you even proceed to introductions, some of the reasons why this may be such a touchy moment.

Stepfamilies are so hard to manage because you cannot separate your present from your past. A first-time relationship may not be an entirely blank sheet, building as it does on your childhood and early personal interactions. Your past and your experiences inform your ability to make relationships – your expectations, your ability to trust and commit, your social skills. These may make you able to flourish inside the partnership you have chosen, or they may make it a hard place to be. Second-time relationships, however, add an extra level of difficulty. Every stepfamily exists on the foundation of the failure of a previous one.

> **Insight**
>
> For you to be in a stepfamily, another family has to have ended. One or both of you have suffered the loss of a partnership you might have had every expectation of being in for life, with the sadness and disappointment and feelings of failure that such a loss often causes.

You may be feeling sad or disappointed, angry or a failure. More important, there will be children who have lost the three things no child should lose: a parent, a family and the certain, safe knowledge that their family will always remain intact. The adults involved in this stepfamily may feel vulnerable and wary; the children will almost certainly feel so, as well as abandoned, cheated and powerless.

YOUR JOY CAN BE A TRAGEDY TO A CHILD

The new family, and the new partner, will be viewed by the adults as a joy, a triumph, a beginning. The urge to introduce them will be based on a need to rejoice and the perspective that this is something to celebrate about. The difficulty may be that any children involved – and, indeed, some relatives and friends too – may see it in a very different way.

As far as a child is concerned, this is not a beginning but an ending – the ending of the original family and the final end of any hopes that the old family may get back together. A new family may be the choice of and in the control of the adults concerned, but as far as a child is concerned, it's not their choice, it's well out of their control and possibly not at all what they want. Far from being something to be pleased about, it may be seen as the cue for anger, depression and bewilderment.

The complex and often contradictory emotions that adults and children may be feeling will be explored later in more detail.

For now, it's simply necessary to recognize that when you do announce the news, the way it's seen by the adults may not be the way it's seen by any children involved and so tread lightly and tactfully for that reason.

> ### Essential points to consider
> ▶ *Whether you're married or not, whether the children live with you or not, you're a stepfamily.*
> ▶ *A beginning for you is an ending for the children.*

Introducing the new adult to the children: the options

You could:

1 *Say nothing and let them gradually work it out for themselves.*
2 *Leave it for someone else to break the news – their other parent, a friend or relative.*
3 *Announce they've got a new Daddy/Mummy as soon as you begin to date regularly.*
4 *Announce it with your new partner.*
5 *Ask the children's advice, or permission, about having a new partner.*
6 *Talk it through before, during and after the event.*

OPTION 1

Saying nothing and letting them gradually work it out for themselves is what many people do. It often seems the natural way, since frequently we may not be able to put our finger on the moment a relationship slips from simply dating to being in love, to deciding to join lives. Or, you may feel embarrassed or unsure of what to say. You don't think of it as making a choice of how to tell – it just happens.

OPTION 2

Leaving it for someone else to break the news – their other parent, a friend or relative – is another option. Again, it often happens because you're not sure what to say or when to say it, so broaching the issue gets put off and, suddenly, the moment has gone and it's been done.

OPTION 3

Single parents often long to have a partner and someone to support them, day to day, in looking after their children, and can often feel that a new adult would be appreciated by their children too. So announcing, or implying, or allowing children to think they've got a new Daddy/Mummy as soon as you begin to date regularly is another very common way of introducing the new partner in your life. It feels less selfish to frame the relationship as something for the child's benefit rather than the adult's. And, of course, it's often hoped that if it's put that way, the child may see it that way.

OPTION 4

Announcing, with your new partner, to the children that you have a new relationship can be planned and prepared, but often happens out of panic. You're there, your new partner is there, and so are the children. You may have a speech prepared or it may all come tumbling out.

OPTION 5

Asking the children's advice, or permission, seems to be an inclusive, caring and sharing move that some parents will opt for. Parents can see this as a modern, thoughtful way of announcing the change in family arrangements that respects their children. They usually do it when the new partner isn't there, hoping to enlist the support and agreement of children, especially if they fear some opposition.

OPTION 6

Talking it through as you go along is the final option in my list. If you're someone who likes to plan ahead and be in control, this may be the option you choose. But even if you think it's the right thing to do, putting this into practice is often harder than planning it.

How to choose which option is best for you and your family

> **Insight**
> Coolly and calmly choosing your options may seem unrealistic. After all, life often doesn't give you time to plan. But the more you seize control, and believe you can, the better off you will all be.

So which of these methods is the best? There are all sorts of arguments to show one is the better in terms of fairness, inclusion, kindness. But the most important measure is which is the option that is most effective – effective in terms of helping you and your family steer the situation to the best, lasting outcome.

OPTION 1

Saying nothing and letting them gradually work it out for themselves is frequently the default choice. One day you're seeing each other, the next you're sleeping with each other and a moment after you're moving in. Each step of the way it might feel presumptuous or getting ahead of yourself to say 'Hey kids, this is what we're going to do...'. You may even feel it could prejudice a good thing if you talk about it openly too soon. And you may not be sure what to say and how to say it anyway. So you let it slide, and at least feel you haven't made a mistake in choosing the wrong option.

Being passive and letting things take their course is not usually seen as an act of decision making. But in saying nothing you are actually picking an action as much as deciding to hang up banners and announce it. Not only is this the most frequent option, it's one of the worst. Kids aren't stupid and even young children can pick up what's going on. But if you say nothing, silence breeds confusion and resentment. Children may begin to feel there is a dirty secret being kept – the fact that you avoid discussing the situation makes it forbidden and furtive, which makes it hard for children to ask questions or unload on you any anxieties and fears they may have.

If the situation is left unexamined until it's plainly obvious a new family has been created, all sorts of assumptions may have been made and left unchallenged. For instance, children may be convinced it means the non-resident parent has chosen to abandon them, or may be excluded in future. They may conclude that their position with one or both parents, or other siblings, is tenuous and in danger. Silence usually results in painful misunderstandings, which are difficult to tackle since avoiding questions and discussion becomes the pattern.

OPTION 2

Leaving it for someone else to break the news – their other parent, a friend or relative – is another option often used in default. Deep down, you may hope that the tricky business of explaining what is going on will be taken out of your hands by someone else jumping in. And if you leave it, it usually is. A child will come home and ask the question you've been avoiding tackling, or announce over tea that a friend of yours has been asking, or a friend of theirs has made remarks, or you or a family member has been overheard talking about it. Worse, children may say nothing. They may decide there is no point in discussing what they have heard since they have lost trust in your ability or willingness to tell them what they need to know.

OPTION 3

'So-and-so is going to be your new Mum/Dad – isn't that wonderful?' may seem a reassuring and exciting way to introduce someone, but it may be less than honest. A new partner may become a Significant Other to children, a co-parent, but that is not the way they should begin and is not their primary role. Parents need to beware of false starts before finding the person to share their life with, and potential step-parents need to be aware of the pain and confusion caused if they throw themselves into being a parent and then have second thoughts and end the relationship. My agony aunt postbag is always full of sad letters from parents left holding not only their own misery at being left but also their children's disappointment at yet another let-down. Adults may be able to deal with the sadness of starting and then having to finish a relationship that promised much but did not live up to hopes. Young people who have already lost a family and a parent will find such disappointment much harder to deal with. Single parents should not be hermits, but until they are certain this relationship is to be serious, the new person in their life is a date – someone to have fun with, to go out with, visit and stay over with and to introduce as a friend but no more.

OPTION 4

Announcing it with your new partner can be planned and prepared, but often happens out of panic. You're there, your new partner is there, and so are the children. You may have a speech prepared or it may all come tumbling out. Showing the sort of solidarity and mutual support you will expect to find in your future relationship can send a useful message to your family. If done with frankness and openness, this option can be the beginning of a dialogue in which children can question and comment and adults can explain and listen.

But equally, announcing the new family together can be seen by children as the two adults hiding behind someone else's skirts. Faced by one parent and one new partner, children may feel they cannot ask questions or express worries to their own parent. They may see it as the parent choosing sides, and not with them.

OPTION 5

Asking the children's advice, or permission, seems to be an inclusive, caring and sharing move. Parents usually do it when the new partner isn't there, hoping to enlist the support and agreement of children.

Asking for and listening, with respect, to input is vital. But asking permission is shifting the burden on to children in an inappropriate and unfair way. It's a dangerous tactic. If the child says no, and the parent accepts the veto, what is being said in that family? That adults are no longer in charge or capable of making decisions? That's actually a very frightening prospect for a child. It's one thing to listen with respect and attention to what children feel and need. Sometimes, children may assess what is going on better than their elders and 'betters' – an adult may be blinded by love while a child may have realized the partner has nobody's interest but their own at heart. But in most circumstances a child may be focusing on their own immediate needs, which in the long run may not do any of the family any good.

Insight
Sharing information with children and asking for impressions and opinions is an excellent idea. But decisions are for adults and parents to make. That's what being a grown-up is all about.

From the postbag

My partner wants to tell my children about us – we met six months ago and we really do think this is it. But I'm not sure. It's not that I don't think we're going to last, it's just that they've had so many disappointments in their lives I'd hate to get their hopes up until we're more sure of the future.

The problem with keeping quiet is that it's highly unlikely your children are entirely ignorant about your partner's

(Contd)

existence. Whether they have picked up hints from the fact you go out in the evening or whether they already have met, they will have drawn their own conclusions and have their own fantasies about this. You don't have to announce weddings or shared homes or anything permanent to let them know some changes are happening. All you have to do is tell them the truth – that you've met someone you like who is becoming important to you and you don't yet know what is going to happen but you'll keep them informed.

If you don't, they will go on spinning their own tales out of wishes and dreams but they won't be able to talk these through with you because they know talking about it is taboo. If anything does go wrong, if you say nothing, it will leave them even more confused than before, and if you announce it's over, they may be furious that you kept them in the dark and then sprang it on them. And if it goes right and eventually you tell them, they may be upset you didn't tell them beforehand – how can they trust you if you won't trust them? Talk to them as soon as possible. Good luck!

OPTION 6

Talking it through as you go along is the hardest option. It means being sensitive, tactful and on the ball. It means being flexible and honest, and being able to update children as time goes on. A series of parental updates could include: 'I've met someone I like. We're just seeing each other as friends', 'I had a really nice time. We're seeing each other again', 'I'm really enjoying so-and-so's company', 'I think this is becoming special', 'Yes, this is definitely becoming special', 'So-and-so will be staying over tonight', 'We're talking about moving in with each other', 'We're moving in with each other.'

Giving a regular debrief of the progress of a relationship also means having to think about it in clearer terms than you might otherwise have done for yourself. That's one of the issues of being in a stepfamily; in other relationships, things happen and develop and slide by under the radar. In a stepfamily, if you want to keep on top of it, you need to be analytical and aware.

> ### Essential points to consider
> ▶ *It's better to plan how you tell children about a new partner than to let them find out another way.*
> ▶ *Keeping children informed from the beginning is better than springing it on them as a surprise.*
> ▶ *When there are children involved you can't let relationships 'just happen', you have to be aware and analytical.*

How to communicate

It's never too late to begin talking to children honestly. It may feel difficult, and children may block initial attempts with scorn or indifference. In the long run, if adults communicate:

▶ *honestly*
▶ *clearly*
▶ *directly*
▶ *with respect*
▶ *and with a willingness to listen as well as talk*

both adults and children are far more likely to cooperate and manage introductions and what comes after.

Insight
Genuine communication is always a two-way process. As well as saying your piece, it means having a willingness to hear things you might find uncomfortable from children.

Listening to your kids may mean they rain on your parade, expressing feelings of anger and loss and grief at a time when you feel it should all be happiness and optimism. But acknowledging and accepting negative emotions does not:

▶ *Make them real. These feelings are real anyway. Hearing them makes them manageable.*
▶ *Make them stronger. Negative emotions actually increase if ignored and left under the surface. Bringing them out in the open allows them to be challenged and tackled.*
▶ *Make them last. Denying feelings is what makes them continue. Discussion and understanding can help them disperse.*

If your stepfamily has got off to a bad start, with children and possibly other relatives and friends feeling upset or alienated, take a deep breath and start again. Get in touch with those who are upset and say 'I think we got off on the wrong foot. This is what we have decided to do and we'd like everyone to appreciate it. How can we talk it through so we can understand the situation and cooperate?'

Case study: Carl and Leonie

Carl and Leonie started living together a year after they met. His children live with their mother, visiting alternate weekends and one night a week. For the first six months, Leonie did not meet them and then began joining them for some weekend events. She never stayed over when the children were there and was introduced as 'a friend'. She and Carl's two daughters got on really well – they thought she was fun and she thought they were sweet. She moved in on one of the weekends he did not have the children, and Carl put off telling them until the next time they arrived for a visit. When they realized she had moved in, they went ballistic – sulking, shouting and refusing to go to bed or eat. From then on they made life extremely difficult for both Leonie and Carl, until their mother said something would have to be done or she was going to keep them at her home. Carl was sure it was a discipline problem and all the girls needed was a firm hand but their mother disagreed. Eventually, their mother suggested the girls talked to a support worker at their school who in turn suggested Carl and Leonie, his daughters and her mother visited a family counsellor. When both children were helped by telling Carl how angry they had felt at being 'fooled' and left out, and Carl and Leonie took their feelings on board and apologized, a good relationship was restored.

How to introduce family round-table discussions

Perhaps the best way for a new stepfamily to communicate is for parent and partner to initiate regular round-table discussions. Family discussions can be effective and fun. They can not only be the place and time for introductions but also the place and time to settle many of the issues that will come up as a result of your new stepfamily.

A family parliament is an ideal way of making agreements in a family that are kept. It is also a way of keeping in touch and of pulling everyone together. In a stepfamily, it really helps to make time and space for family discussions regularly, not only with the people who live together most of the time but also with those who have a stake in the family but may only visit from time to time.

There are three main rules to make a family discussion work.

1 GIVE EVERYONE A CHANCE TO SPEAK

Everyone, from oldest to youngest, is to have an equal turn to speak and to be heard. You might like to go round the table letting each person say one thing, to start. Then, take turns to add to the discussion. You can use an object handed round to signify whose turn it is to speak – an ornament, a kitchen implement such as a spoon, a pencil. Ask everyone to keep the rule about only talking when they have had it handed on to them, and handing it on when finished. It helps to appoint one person to act as the 'Facilitator' for a family discussion, and to have each member of the group take it in turn to play this role. The facilitator ensures that everyone takes it in turns to speak and not interrupt.

2 HOW TO HELP PEOPLE SAY WHAT THEY REALLY MEAN

The most important rule is that everyone has to 'own' what they say. That means, everything you put forward has to be your own thoughts and feelings and you should acknowledge them as such, saying 'I think' or 'I feel'. No one can say 'So-and-so says' or 'Everyone knows' or talk about what other people do or what you think they think. You can talk about how other people's behaviour affects you, by saying 'When you do such-and-such, I feel...' but the aim is to put forward your point of view, not to criticize or attack other people.

Insight
The key to finding solutions to any difficulty is confronting problems, not people.

3 GETTING AGREEMENT

The eventual aim of your discussion is to create a space where everyone feels they have been heard and appreciated, and have heard and appreciated everyone else's point of view. There should be no winners or losers, but an all-round agreement on the outcome. To that end, no one is to be shouted down for what they say. Discuss the points rather than arguing with the person. Set aside time for the discussion and allow everyone a chance to speak, as many times as they like.

Essential points to consider
- ▶ *Every family should learn to practise communication skills such as family round-table discussions. In stepfamilies, it's vital.*
- ▶ *Getting off on the right foot is important but you can always retrieve the situation.*
- ▶ *Decisions are for adults and parents to make. That's what being a grown-up is all about.*

How to involve the wider family

When introducing a new partner, and a new family, you may see this as something that only has to do with your immediate circle – your partner and the children involved. But both you and the children may find it easier to manage the situation if you have the support of your wider family and friends. Grandparents and old family friends may be particularly helpful in encouraging children to see the advantages of change. After all, the fact that their support continues no matter what suggests that while some things alter, the fundamentals of family life go on. Enlisting the presence and understanding of other family members may make the difference between a stormy transition and one that is simply slightly rocky.

THINGS TO REMEMBER

▶ *Stepfamilies come in all shapes and sizes. Married, unmarried, with children living with you, with children visiting or out of contact. If your family is now a stepfamily, recognizing and acknowledging this fact and acting and planning accordingly will make life far easier for everyone.*

▶ *Every stepfamily is the result of a loss. To one person it may be a glorious new beginning. To another it can be an ending – a painful reminder of what has been lost or taken away from them.*

▶ *How you introduce your new partner to your children and others involved may be critical. Get this right at the start and the rest should follow more easily. Miss a trick and you can recover, but you will need to work at it.*

▶ *Ask and listen with respect to everyone, but do not ask for 'permission'. It is your decision and not one to burden children with.*

▶ *Give everyone regular updates on progress. In other relationships things often 'just happen' but in a stepfamily you need to be more analytical and aware.*

▶ *Communication must always be a two-way process. Develop a willingness to hear things from the children, and others involved, even if you might find this uncomfortable at times.*

▶ *Have regular family round-table discussions. They may take some getting used to, but once everyone is familiar and comfortable with the technique it does help.*

▶ *The support of your wider families and friends will benefit adults and children alike.*

IDEAS TO TRY

▶ *Look at and consider your family shape. Recognizing that you are a stepfamily is an important step towards making the situation easier.*

▶ *Have you chosen the best way to introduce the new adult to children? If you haven't done it yet, use this chapter to plan your approach.*

▶ *Has the introduction happened, and would you like to redress the situation? You can always go back and catch up.*

▶ *Introduce family round-table discussions. Use this chapter to give you the rules and the encouragement – there will be more about them in later chapters.*

▶ *Talk to your wider family. Enlisting their support can be vital.*

▶ *Recognize the importance of communication skills and review the tips in this chapter. Read on for more communication tips.*

▶ *Using this chapter, consider the different viewpoints of children and adults in a stepfamily. You may be seeing what is happening in a different light – read on for more help with managing that.*

2

Landmark days

In this chapter you will learn:
- *how to deal with landmark days in stepfamilies*
- *a good technique for gathering ideas together and choosing which one to use*
- *how to prepare children for a new partner moving in*
- *how to manage wedding days and the emotions that surround them.*

There are certain days in the life of a stepfamily that are special – landmark days that you look back on and that stand out as significant. There are some obvious ones: the day you moved in with each other, the day you cemented your relationship with marriage, your first birthday as a couple, the first family festival such as Christmas, Eid, Diwali or Hanukkah and the day you recognize as an anniversary. There may be other less public ones: the anniversary of the first time you met, dated or made love, the day you booked your first holiday together. My husband and I have one – the day we decided to live together. And another – the day we actually married, 20 years minus one day later! All of these say 'We're together' and some involve some actual activity and restructuring of your life. How do you make sure the events of such a day go smoothly for everyone? And how do you ensure the underlying emotions that everyone has about what is happening are acknowledged, understood and managed?

Some landmark days slide by unannounced and unnoticed and we only recognize them by looking back. Moving in can happen slowly and in stages. Your partner stays one night and goes home. A few weekends later they come, bringing a change of clothes and a toothbrush. Sometime after, they leave the toothbrush and then the clothes. And one day you agree it seems silly to keep two homes and you either let one go, or start looking for a new place that will be your shared home. When the actual day arrives when one of you moves all your belongings into the shared house, it might seem silly to make a big deal about it since shared living has almost become routine and accepted.

Landmark days may mean different things to adults and children

Whether it has become a done deal for you or not, it may not have become so for the children. Whether they live with one of you full time or are weekend visitors, the fact is that their parent's home is their home too. And someone moving in can feel like invasion and trespass.

When you are two child-free adults establishing a relationship, how you do it and what pace you choose is entirely up to you. If it works better for you to go slowly and be slightly in denial about exactly how much your life is becoming intertwined, that's your business. Yes, you can gradually increase the number of times one of you stays over until you've actually moved in together in all but name and signatures on the lease. You can drift slowly and imperceptibly into coupledom, since there's nobody there to see it but the two of you. But when one or both of you have children, that's another situation entirely. If there are children, you have to consider the profound effect your behaviour has on them.

The new relationship isn't just a case of an additional adult in their lives. The new addition might have been very welcome in the early days – someone to cheer up their parent, someone to take them on treats, someone to take on a few parental duties such as reading a book at bedtime or checking homework or running them into town to meet their friends. Or, of course, to lift off their shoulders some tedious household chores such as taking out the rubbish! But once the new person becomes a fixture, all sorts of emotional issues come to the surface.

> ### Insight
> We don't like to recognize that adults can feel jealous of children or that children might feel in competition with a new adult in their lives. But these emotions are natural and normal in stepfamilies and need to be acknowledged in order to be dealt with.

A new adult is in competition for the child's share of their parent. What frequently happens in the wind-down of a failing relationship, and in the aftermath, is that children come to occupy a larger and different space in their parents' lives than they might have otherwise. Single parents often lean on their children, both for practical help and for emotional support. Non-resident parents, when they do see their children, give them undivided attention. A new adult not only takes up some of the available time but they also commandeer a proportion of available concern. You can insist that love is unlimited and that no matter how many times it is divided everyone gets an equal share. You simply can't say the same for the time and the attention that is free to spend with them. Children used to being supportive and caring can feel diminished, patronized and robbed of responsibility. You may think they should be relieved to have such a burden lifted off them, but instead they may feel rejected and cheated.

And new adults can feel in competition, too. They come late to the scene, may struggle to keep up with the strong and established relationship they see between parent and child and resent the fact they have to share someone they newly love with people with prior claims.

Children may also be seen, and see themselves, as representatives of the missing parent, and as such be fighting a rearguard action on the part of that parent. Children, after all, are living, breathing proofs that someone was there first; that their parent has loved before. Children often resemble their parents, either in looks or in behaviour and mannerisms. Their own parent and the new adult may find this acutely uncomfortable and find themselves acting towards the child as they might otherwise act towards the other adult – competitively, aggressively, jealously. The child may also react in ways that may not be personal but by proxy. Children who like, admire, even love the new adult may reject them from a conviction that any sign of acceptance would be disloyal to the missing parent. In effect, they feel that as the absent parent's representative they should and must be hostile. Ex-partners who feel continuing anger about the new relationship may exploit this and goad children into behaving badly.

From the postbag

My eldest son Paul really doesn't get on with my new partner. They fight over everything – who feeds the dog, where each of them will sit on the sofa, even what cereal to have in the morning. It's driving me crazy and I can't understand it, especially since he's always been such a kind, quiet helpful boy. When my husband left us he was a rock to me and his younger sister. He and John seemed to get on at first – why is he being like this?

When a new partner is just a date, they do not upset the dynamic of a family. Once they become partners and have a place in your home you need to look at who has to shift around to give them room and what they feel about that. Eldest children often feel they have to take the role of a missing parent, caring for, looking after and over the parent they live with. When a new partner comes along he or she takes over, in effect supplanting the child and pushing them out of the place they have come to assume is their own. Your son feels like a rival and so he and the new partner bicker over all sorts of territorial issues and issues that the head of a family may usually decide.

(Contd)

It's understandable, so the best way to deal with it is to acknowledge it. Say 'It must feel odd to have someone come in and be a responsible adult when you felt you were doing that job. I'm really grateful for how much you did when we were alone. How are we going to sort things out now so you and John don't argue so much? I really hate it when you quarrel.' Simply bringing the issue out into the open sometimes does the trick. One tactic may be to agree specific responsibilities, and to thank him when he does them, so Paul doesn't feel he has to fight to be recognized as his role is accepted. Another is for John to find something such as fishing or football they can do together, so making Paul an ally rather than a rival. Good luck!

So you need to recognize that landmark days aren't only yours. 'Whoopee! The Day We Decided to Become a Couple' may have another title for the children involved, such as 'Oh Woe! The Day I Realized My Parents Were Never Going to Get Back Together'. And this is why it is so important for you to be aware of landmark days and acknowledge them. You need to observe each landmark day so you can manage how it feels for everyone concerned and not let negative emotions get swept under the carpet. Unresolved grief or anger do not go away by being ignored; they fester and multiply.

Your private landmarks may indeed be something you want and need to keep quiet about. It's not appropriate, to say the least, to draw your children into celebrating the first time you slept together. But, it's worth noting that children – even quite young children and certainly teenagers – may well be aware that something momentous has happened, something that does impinge on them and their future. For that reason, it may be advisable to be prepared for a child to ask, 'You seem different. Anything happen?' or 'You and so-and-so seem to be getting on. What's going to happen?' and to be able to say, 'We had some special, private time together and it felt important,' and 'Yes we are. I don't know yet but I'll let you know.'

But public landmark days are in the public domain and need to be brought out as such. This means that rather than letting it slide, you need to recognize how much the children involved will notice and react to someone moving in, even if they don't live full time in the home in question. Moving-in day becomes momentous, and should be set aside, planned for and heralded.

Moving-in day: how to prepare children for change

The moment clothes or toiletries start being left, or if you have the conversation about it being sensible to pool your resources and live together, call a family meeting and let the children know. If you find the idea of this awkward, embarrassing or scary, then think how awkward, embarrassing or scary it may be for them to have to realize that changes are going on but not be able to talk to you about it. If you don't raise the issue, they may well feel it's not something they can come and discuss.

Consider beforehand what emotions may be going around. Indeed, get paper and a pen and do an 'ideas-storm' about them. Ideas-storming is a technique for gathering all the ideas and information about a situation and then sifting it to find what you need. When you ideas-storm, you and the people you storm with write down *everything* that comes to mind – even the things that seem silly or wrong. Ask 'What do we feel about moving in? What might the children be feeling?'

Write down every single thing that comes to mind. If you do this on your own or with your partner, you may find you put down a range of both positive and negative emotions. You may be feeling excited, nervous, relieved, on the threshold of a whole new life. You may have some regrets and mourn some losses from your past, as well as hoping to enjoy the future.

Insight

Change is always hard, even positive or planned or longed-for change. Anything that involves a loss or an alteration is painful and difficult.

If you do this with children, you may need to be prepared for some different viewpoints. And if you don't want to ask them at this point, try doing the exercise once you've done it for yourself but this time putting yourself in their shoes. What you may discover is that while they may agree on the excitement and nervousness, and feel some relief that their parent is happy and past conflict may now be over, their overriding feeling may be of a door closing rather than one opening. They may express many regrets and mourn many losses from their past, and feel particularly hurt at the idea that their old family is never coming back. They may have what appear to be entirely selfish and apparently silly concerns such as whether they still get to go to some after-school activity or see certain people. It isn't trivial – it's a genuine fear that some changes may bring about other irrevocable and painful losses.

If you have already ideas-stormed, you can call a family meeting with some idea of what you may be saying but also what the other people in the family may be feeling. The best way to deal with unhappy feelings is to bring them out into the open so you can talk them over. Talking them over does *not* mean:

- ▶ *Arguing them away – 'I won't put up with this behaviour. You'll do as you're told.'*
- ▶ *Minimizing or trivializing a child's concerns – 'Oh don't be silly, it's not going to be as bad as that!'*
- ▶ *Trying to put your spin on the situation – 'Won't it be fun? You're going enjoy living with Sam, aren't you?'*

Denying unhappy emotions doesn't melt away reservations or hostility. It makes a child bite their lip, knowing they can't tell you how they feel. But they will show you, in tantrums, arguments and moodiness.

So once you know moving in is on the cards, start preparing. Tell your children, 'We're planning to live together.' Invite them to say what they feel, what they'd like, what they'd not like. Be prepared for a child to say, in effect, 'Over my dead body and I'm gonna make you pay if you go ahead!'

The key is to tell them, *not* as an exercise in democracy but in consultation. A democracy is where you put it to the vote and first past the post wins. Two adults against several children are likely to lose. The difference with consultation is that you are the adults and you are the ones who are in charge and are presumed to know best. You are choosing to make this family – this stepfamily.

But in order to make it work, you need to allow everyone the opportunity to say what they think, to take those feelings on board and to work towards a situation where everyone gets at least some of what they want.

Essential points to consider

▶ *You can go at your own pace in a first-time relationship, but when children are concerned, you have to consider the effect your new arrangement has on them.*
▶ *Children may see themselves as 'standing in' for a mum or dad and feel in competition with a new adult.*
▶ *You need to acknowledge and observe landmark days because they have different meanings to children and adults and should be handled carefully.*
▶ *Preparing children for change is an exercise in consultation not democracy. Everyone needs to have their say but adults need to take the decisions.*

How our territorial instincts make it difficult

There are a variety of new living arrangements you may be contemplating. You may be moving in with your partner. Your partner may be moving in with you. You may both be leaving your previous home to move in to a new place together. You may have your own children, who either primarily live with you and visit an ex-partner or who live most of the time elsewhere and visit you. Your partner may have children, who either primarily live with them and visit an ex-partner or who live most of the time elsewhere and will visit you. Whatever the format, the most important issue you should consider is territory.

Children are like cats. They mark their territory, not by spraying but by leaving socks and trainers, empty cans and mugs, toys and gadgets scattered around. Their rooms are important to them, as their own space, their own base. Consider what a cat will do if you suddenly walk in with a new kitten or a dog. They'll spit, they'll fluff up and they may well attack. And then they may rush around laying claim to their territory and trying to repel boarders. Sooner or later, they may settle down and play and could become best of friends. But even eventual sworn buddies begin by being totally hostile.

The new members of your family may have been slowly and stealthily making inroads for some time. You may already have had spats and disagreements. When it becomes official, that may be the signal for open warfare unless you take steps.

STEP 1

Acknowledge a new era is about to dawn. There will be new people in the house, or you will be going to a new house. Raise this with everyone and let people give their reactions.

STEP 2

Taking your actual situation into account, devise a new house plan. You will have several, possibly competing, needs to take into account.

On the one hand, new people in the house need to feel at home and that this is as much their place as everyone else's. One pitfall for stepfamilies is when people feel as if a home isn't actually theirs and they are interlopers. It can mean that they feel as if they have no stake in this place and thus this family and so no incentive to put effort into making it work.

On the other hand, anyone living there already can feel invaded
and pushed out. They can feel as if the new people, whether
living there full time or visiting, are getting special treatment and
allowances. They can resent the invasion and find themselves
taking up a position of resistance, both emotionally and physically.
Especially when space is at a premium, children can become
aggressive and defensive.

On the one hand, everyone needs to know that this is a new
situation and that you are moving forward into it, leaving the old
behind. On the other hand, children need to retain links with the
past and so, in fact, do adults.

Even when the only new face is an adult, and even when children
will be staying over rather than living full time in your new home,
planning to make this acceptable is crucial. When there are two sets
of children concerned, it is even more important. Children desperately
need to feel they have a place, even if they visit sporadically.

How to share out the territory

So – look at what you have. Important memorabilia and items
important to all of you should stay. Children need to see photographs
and items that remind them of their original family and the other
parent, and the new adult has to accept this. But the new person will
bring stuff of their own which should be given room in shared areas,
and a private spot too.

Children who come to stay need a locale they can call their own. If
you're lucky enough to be able to give them a room of their own,

even if this is generally used as a spare, visitors' room, allow them to decorate it as their own room and feel they can leave items that will be safe and untouched until the next time they are there.
If they will have to share a bedroom with resident children, negotiate how this will be managed. If they visit regularly and frequently, it will be reasonable to see this room as a full-time shared room in which the resident child or children are lucky enough to be in sole charge at some times. But they need to agree that the room is seen as a shared one with all the rules of a shared room. That is, that decoration should be agreed between them or divided down the middle. That neither child touches, takes or uses property that isn't theirs without first asking. That each respects the other's right to private property and privacy.

WHY HAVING TVs AND COMPUTERS IN BEDROOMS IS NOT A GOOD IDEA

Stepfamilies may need to seriously consider their use of technology in bedrooms. There is a lot of evidence to suggest that children having TVs, DVD players and game machines in bedrooms is less than desirable. It disrupts bedtime routines and sleep patterns, exposes children to material of an adult nature and in shared bedrooms can provoke arguments and resentment. It can also cause enormous disturbance with children moving between houses which have different rules and different equipment. If you want to keep an eye on what children are viewing and how much time they spend in front of a screen, the best way is to locate all such technology in shared areas, however much you may not want to have it there. Indeed, your desire for occasional peace and quiet or the programmes you enjoy should force you to discuss, negotiate and ration viewing. Which is no bad thing!

If a child visits occasionally, dividing a room into equal shares may well be seen as unfair by the resident child. But the visiting child still needs to feel they have some claim to belonging. Set aside a wardrobe, a dresser or a box that contains items of theirs that will stay untouched while they are not there and that can be taken out and used to make their presence felt and legitimate when they come to stay.

To minimize feelings of being invaded and avoid the very natural, human impulses to defend our territory, plan beforehand. Set out the situation to everyone involved and invite an ideas-storm on how it can be handled. Point out that everyone is to feel at home, nobody is to feel hard done by, but to achieve this you need to acknowledge that initial feelings may well be hostile.

Insight

One really useful tip is to ask the family to see the situation as a puzzle posed in a board game. The goal is not to rule the world or own all the hotels and take everyone's money; the goal is to take a home with two, three or four (or more!) people, add another one, two or more people full time or part time, and help everyone deal with it.

On the moving-in day

On the day new people move in, make as much of a change around for everyone as you can. You could get everyone to swap bedrooms, so instead of having to go into a bedroom already occupied by a child who may feel their hackles rise at the invasion, both children move into a room new to both of them. If this isn't possible, redecorate the house so it feels different and thus new for everyone. Be flexible and acknowledge that room allocation may not remain the same for long – as children grow older you may want to suggest new configurations. Be prepared for the day to be exhausting, exciting but also argumentative. People may react to stress, disappointment, loss and regrets by hitting out at seemingly inappropriate targets. An argument about curtains or posters on the wall may actually be about a child's extreme discomfort at recognizing their world will never be the same again. Be prepared to say, 'It sounds as if you're finding this a bit hard. Shall we take a time out and relax for a moment? Want to talk about it?'

How to manage a wedding

A wedding day is probably the pinnacle of landmark days – a celebration of two adults' commitment to each other and to a new life and a new family. Wedding days are often the stuff of fantasy, and some children can seem to throw themselves into the planning and the day itself, leading you to believe all will be fine, both on the day and after. You may need to recognize what might be going on under the surface to understand their initial, positive reaction and their possible sudden about-face.

Everyone loves a party and children of both sexes and all ages may look forward to fun and games, food and drink and a good excuse to stay up late. Girls may be delighted at the excuse to dress up, transforming themselves in their own minds into princesses or brides for the day, and boys may relish the opportunity for presents and treats. Both may be pleased at the chance to show off to their friends. But at some point the bubble may burst. And for some young people, right from the moment you announce it, a parent's wedding to someone other than their other parent will be a signal for depression, rage or mixed feelings.

Preparation is all. Not just preparation for the wedding – the seating plans, the special clothes and food and decorations – but for the emotional response to the wedding, and thus to the marriage. Discuss beforehand with all the adults concerned:

- *how you feel about the day*
- *how children may be feeling about the day*
- *how you will understand and make allowances for conflicting feelings and displays of anger, hurt or resentment.*

Resolve among yourselves how you will address 'bad behaviour'. Children never act up simply for the hell of it, to make your life miserable. They act out what are their own sad and bad feelings. Bad behaviour is always an attempt to externalize and show you how dejected or hurt or outraged they may be feeling. For that reason:

- *Don't make light of or dismiss negative feelings. Accept them, understand them and promise to address them.*
- *Don't react with anger to 'bad behaviour'. It may be disappointing and you may feel it's an insult to you but it's both understandable and normal.*
- *Tread the fine line between totally ignoring the children and putting the spotlight on them in an embarrassing way.*

Insight

Children do not 'act up' simply for the hell of it. Bad behaviour is a statement – of sadness, desperation, anger. You deal with it best if you look for, address and resolve the reasons rather than simply trying to banish the symptom.

WHY FLEXIBLE PLANNING IS SO IMPORTANT

Discuss with children the involvement they might want on the day. A wedding day is the preserve of the couple involved, but when there are children from a previous relationship it would be wrong to leave them out. Once you decide to marry, the first people to hear should be the children and they need to be part of the discussion and planning from then on.

Essential points to consider

- *Weddings are joyful days for the couple but can be fraught and distressing for children.*

(Contd)

> ▶ *To ensure a happy day you may need to be prepared to alter arrangements at the last moment as children change their minds.*
>
> ▶ *Bad behaviour is about sad feelings. Be prepared for it and forgive it.*

Some couples put children at the heart of the celebrations. A step-parent may make a commitment to the children of the new partner along with the vows they make to their spouse, and some children may choose to have their say too, or serve as pages and bridesmaids. Children may change their minds, wanting to be front of house right up until the day itself when they suddenly refuse to be in the spotlight. Or wanting nothing to do with proceedings and on the morning, asking to be an integral part of the ceremony. The only way to manage is with good humour and understanding of the emotional ups and downs they are likely to be going through, and a flexible plan that can be chopped and changed to fit the moment.

Case study: Sue and Les

When Sue and Les married, Les saw the wedding as much about a celebration of gaining a stepson as gaining a wife. He and Sue wrote their own vows to exchange but Les also wrote a commitment to Kai, where he acknowledged how important Kai had become to him, promised to always be there for him and to respect his opinions and cherish the times they shared together. Kai in turn read out his own lines, saying how much happier he and his mother had been since Les joined them and promising to listen to and respect him.

CASE STUDY

On the wedding day

Make provision for youngsters to be able to go off and have quiet or chill-out time in a safe place and so have time to themselves on the day. Some children may be grateful to have a friend or two along, to be their guest and their support. Select and brief a caring adult to keep an eye on each child so they can pick up on quietness or rage or tears and offer a shoulder to cry on, protection from other enquiring bodies or distraction. For the day to be enjoyed by the celebrating couple, the children should not be swept away as an inconvenience or an irrelevance. However young, children should always be at a parent's wedding.

Insight

Above all, remember, it's just a day. It may be an important day and one you'll remember, but the years of marriage afterwards are more important than the wedding day itself.

If one or several people act up on the day, they won't be 'spoiling' anything but simply expressing feelings that are better out in the open than hidden away. If you acknowledge that their feelings may be different from yours and that they have every right to feel that way, the chances are they won't have the need to make a public demonstration. After all, most public tantrums and strops are about getting you to take something on board. Acknowledge it beforehand and the job is done.

Honeymoons – should your children come too?

And what about the honeymoon? If your children should be at the wedding, should they go along with you on the honeymoon as well? For a clue, consider what honeymoons are all about. Traditionally, they were the bride and groom's first taste of their future – presumed to be the first time they would live and sleep and have sex together. Privacy and being on their own would be important because it may have been the first time they had that opportunity.

But is it yours? Have you lived together? Have you slept together? Have you had sex? Indeed, have you holidayed as a couple or a family already? There is a good argument for couples being able to have some time alone as an adult couple and the first holiday after a wedding may well be the time to have that luxury. But equally, one of the vital aspects of a stepfamily is that you aren't just a couple; as well as marrying an adult, the step-parent marries the kids too. If you want to start the way you mean to go on, taking the children on your honeymoon may be the very best beginning. It would mean the children will know they are welcomed, included and an integral part of the unit, not simply also-rans. And this is as important in stepfamilies where children visit as it is in which children live full time. If you want to send the message – the message they want and need to hear – that they are part of your lives, coming along with you to your honeymoon as well as your wedding may be what has to happen.

Clearly, this is something you need to talk over with the kids. Depending on their ages, they may be happy for you to go off for part of the break on your own while they have a special treat with family or friends, and then join you, or wave you off on a honeymoon while they have some alternative holiday. If you make a big deal of the next break, following on fairly quickly, as the first family vacation this may be ideal for all concerned. But be prepared to recognize that they may feel cut to the quick if you leave them behind. It could confirm all their deepest fears – that this wedding and this marriage is the beginning of the end for them, that they will be excluded and left behind in your life as well as on this holiday. Just as 'Kids Come Too' is the motto for stepfamily life, it may well be for stepfamily honeymoons!

Plan the honeymoon carefully so you and the children have a share of the best times – doing things together and having some opportunity for you to go your separate ways too. Accept that there may be times when they will act up and behave 'badly'. Be sympathetic and sensitive – the tears and tantrums are more about the momentous family changes that are taking place than whatever it is that triggers the quarrels. In the end, it is likely to be a holiday to cherish and remember, and all the more so for having them along.

THINGS TO REMEMBER

▶ *Landmark days are particularly important to a stepfamily. Try to recognize them and plan ahead if necessary to make them go smoothly for everyone.*

▶ *How you pace your new relationship is up to you but if children are involved you must consider the effect your behaviour will have on them.*

▶ *Any adult coming into a new family will be in competition for the child's share of their parent. Recognize this and be aware of any resentment from the people with prior claims.*

▶ *Have family meetings regularly and let the children know what is happening at all times. Have ideas-storming sessions so that nobody's feelings or views or requests or needs get missed out or overlooked.*

▶ *Prepare your children before you and your new partner actually start living together. Remember, this is not an exercise in democracy but in consultation. You and your new partner alone are choosing to make this new stepfamily, but everyone needs the opportunity to say what they think and feel.*

▶ *Try to have your plans for personal territory in your new stepfamily home sorted before 'arrival day'. Those coming in will need to establish their place, while those already there will need to retain some links to how things were.*

▶ *If you are going to get married, plan beforehand for the mixed emotions and feelings this will almost certainly create. Your day of joy may be welcomed by the children, but they may react with depression or 'bad behaviour'.*

▶ *A child's bad behaviour is never simply for the hell of it. Bad behaviour is the acting out of sad or bad feelings. Don't react but act, with exploration, understanding and sympathy.*

IDEAS TO TRY

▶ *Sit down and make two lists – what you have gained and what you have lost in the new arrangement.*

▶ *Put yourself in the children's shoes and consider what might have changed for them with a new adult in their parent's life. Consider whether the children might agree with your lists or come up with different assessments.*

▶ *Ask the children to consider what they have lost and gained in the new arrangement and explain it to you.*

▶ *Practice ideas-storming. Try it out on an unimportant but enjoyable issue before tackling something significant.*

▶ *Ask the children to draw up a new plan for their home with different rooms for different people or uses than now. Might it work better than the original arrangement?*

▶ *If you are planning a wedding, review your plans in the light of the suggestions in this chapter.*

▶ *Plan an adult-only break, and ask the children to plan a break somewhere they'd also feel was a treat – a sleepover with friends or with indulgent relatives.*

3

Practical issues

In this chapter you will learn:
- *how to decide where children live*
- *how to decide on arrangements for contact visits*
- *why non-resident parents lose touch and how to overcome these problems*
- *how to manage different routines in two different households*
- *how to make House Rules and keep them*
- *how to tell other people about the separate households.*

When a family splits up and parents go their separate ways, new families are formed. From one family with two parents and their children living together they become two families of one parent and their children, living with them full or part time. Sooner or later, however, one or two new adults are likely to come on the scene and stepfamilies are created. The common assumption may be that children will still be based in one 'home' – the place they live with the parent who has them most of the time. Which home, and with which parent children should live may not be an easy decision to make. One home may seem 'better' than another and one set of adults may feel their claim to have the obvious place for the child overrides the other.

As far as the adults are concerned, the feeling may be that the child has one base – usually the home both parents shared before the break up – and a place they visit, which is the new home of the non-resident parent. One 'Home', one 'Dwelling'. But as far as the child is concerned, they may see it as having two 'Homes', even if the second is one they visit on a weekly, monthly or less regular basis. Home, after all, is where the heart is. In making decisions about where a child resides, for how long and under what conditions, you need not only to take your own views on board as well those of your ex and anyone else involved, but also most importantly your children.

Basic rule no. 1

The bottom line is that children have the right to see both parents, to grow up in contact with both their birth parents, knowing that their Mum and Dad love them and are there for them.

But, in fact, continuing contact is also a question of what works best. When children know both parents and feel they are loved by, accepted by and approved of by both parents, they thrive. Children who feel a parent doesn't love them, has abandoned them, and isn't there for them, tend to feel not only rejected and deserted but also alienated and judged. They tend to feel they were left behind because they deserve no better, that they are worthless and lacking. The resident parent and step-parent can work very hard at undoing and managing such feelings, and children left without one parent can manage very well. But it is an uphill struggle. If you know you are having to redress, you can do so. But if there is an option, if by making the effort you can keep the contact, it is far better for the children and thus for the stepfamily.

There are various arrangements you can opt for and each have their advantages and drawbacks.

Seeing the non-resident parent for the day

When children are very young or when the non-resident parent does not have a home at which children can stay, contact may be for a day and not overnight.

PROS

Young children can find it frightening to spend a night away from home, separated not only from their primary caregiver but also from their familiar room, belongings and routine. Short, regular contact may be better than long stays, and if it can be arranged, having the non-resident parent visit where the child lives may be better than taking them out.

An advantage of a day visit, when contact is a point of contention between the parents, is that children still get to see their other parent even when parents find contact difficult to accept or manage.

Insight

If contact is a difficult issue, meetings can take place at a Child Contact Centre, where children can be dropped off and collected without face-to-face contact between exes, and children can be safely monitored before and after resident parents are there and while the visit takes place.

CONS

With older children, day visits can become treats and treats only. Children and non-resident parents do not get the chance to live a 'normal' life together. Children do not have the opportunity to be part of their other parent's day-to-day life or see and become familiar with their non-resident parent's new partner or family.

Parents and children may take a day visit less seriously and be less committed to keeping arrangements than they might for a longer stay. One or two cancellations could add up and eventually visits may become irregular and subject to cancellation if one parent chooses to renege on the deal.

Staying for weekends and during school holidays

Perhaps the most traditional and seen to be the easiest solution is that children live with one of their parents, seeing the other parent at weekends or alternate weekends and during school holidays. This may be the only option possible if parents move some distance from each other after a separation.

PROS

This is a simple arrangement. Children keep their own rooms and homes – the family may have splintered but the home remains intact. Continuity is important for children, so continuity of living arrangements can help them weather new family formations. They can retain a support network from neighbours, friends and school which stay the same as before the break-up and before the stepfamily.

Even when a new person moves in, there is some predictability in being in a place they know and recognize.

Visiting their non-resident parent and their new family or being taken out for days from their known base can seem manageable, especially if they return to the familiar home at the end of weekends or holidays and so return to school from what they consider to be their own household, which holds all the clothes and equipment they need. Children know where they 'live', with their primary family, and 'visit' their other parent and family.

CONS

Seeing a non-resident parent each weekend means the resident parent and their partner gets all the work and none of the play, only seeing these children on work days except in holidays.

Children seeing a non-resident parent infrequently – and for a child, once a week is infrequently – puts enormous pressure on them. They feel the absence more than the contact and may become moody and fractious around visits. Not because the visit causes grief but because it only serves to remind them that visits are temporary and their family has split up.

Children living apart from a parent they love may feel out of control – they may have little choice about timing as the adults arrange visits, often around times that suit the adults not the child. Children can be upset by visiting a much loved parent who lives some distance away if it means they miss out on something important to them – a friend's birthday party, a sleepover, a school sporting event. They may feel guilty at wanting to attend that instead of seeing people they only see infrequently, and act out their conflicting emotions in sulks and arguments.

If one set of children in a stepfamily sees non-resident parents more often than others, the set going away can feel the set left behind is getting preferential treatment; the set left behind can feel the ones going away are getting treats and experiences they are denied. Both may be upset at the issue of who gets to see their own parents more often.

Insight
Children can be devastated by the fear that someone else's child is spending more time with their own parent than they are.

If, as is most likely, the non-resident parent has a new family with a new partner, whether their own, a stepfamily or a mixture, children who visit infrequently can struggle to make a place in their parent's life and home. They may feel like outsiders and be resentful of any resident children. Living in the original home and only seeing the non-resident parent briefly and at some time apart, such as weekly or fortnightly or even monthly, children may harbour the fantasy that this is a temporary arrangement which may change at any time. By not being able to fully join in and become part of the non-resident parents new life, it may seem remote and unreal.

Staying for weekends, holidays and an extra day a week

Children spend weekends (sometimes alternate weekends), time in the holidays and one day a week with the non-resident parent. This works especially well if the two families live nearby.

PROS

The more contact children have with both parents, and with the new families their parents have formed, the better as far as their emotions are concerned. Having an extra day somewhere midweek as well as weekends helps kids feel far more settled and 'at home' with the parent who has left, and they have far more of an opportunity to lead a normal, ordinary life together.

More regular contact helps adults to spend some routine time with children rather than just 'leisure time' at weekends and holidays. This allows you all to develop a more natural relationship – one that deals with the day-to-day routines and indeed the nitty gritty and even negative aspects of life rather than just play and down-time. This allows both parents, both families, to establish habits and routines – bedtimes, homework, chores – that are the stuff of every home and homelife.

CONS

Children spending one night in the week away from their main residence, and main family, can feel disrupted and distressed. It can lead to confusion and difficulties with school and with friends and family. They either need to have two sets of clothes in the two places or to be organized in making sure they have everything they need when starting out in the morning from one and ending the day in another, only to then go on to school from that base.

Everyone needs to be on the ball as to where children are, and how they may keep in touch with friends and family when they are in one place one night, another the next night and back to the first the following night.

If the two households have different styles and rules, switching from one to the other at such short notice can become confusing and demoralizing.

Children living full time in the stepfamily may find it hard to have other children popping in and out at such frequency but for such a short time.

_____

Spending equal time with both families

Children spend an equal amount of time in both families; either one week with each, or seven days out of fourteen in three-day followed by four-day blocks.

PROS

Both families get to share the days off as well as the days at work and school equally. Children spend a longer stretch of time with each family, giving everyone the chance to develop relationships, ground rules and routines, and to live what feels like a normal family life.

Each family gets an equal amount of time either to be on their own (weekends off without needing a babysitter!) or with the children.

Children get the chance to build their own friendship networks at both homes and to establish with friends that they do have two bases.

Children can negotiate with both parents that they need chances to see other people and attend events – something not possible when they only have a day or so a week to see a non-resident parent and their family.

CONS

Parents may find it stressful to have their children away with the other family for such long stretches.

Children may find it distressing to become accustomed to one family being 'home' only to have to move to the other for a week or three to four days.

Children may organize events based at one home only to find they will be in the other home at that time. Parents may arrange something that they would like to share with their children only to find it falls in the middle of their time with the other family.

A novel approach – communal living

Parents live in very close proximity – next door or even in the same house with their own separate living quarters but a connecting door – so that children can see both families as much and when they please.

PROS

In this arrangement, even young children can regulate contact, not needing parents to manage a timetable and be gatekeepers or facilitators to their relationships with both families.

This eliminates the need for two wardrobes in separate houses or the situation of forgetting gym kit or homework – it's just next door.

Being next door means children can both develop their close relationship with each family and have free access to their own social network – friends, neighbours, family – and not have to miss out on events and occasions that happen from one household while in the other.

Both child and parent have the opportunities to contact each other on the spur of the moment without it intruding on the other family – calling the other family while on a visit can often be seen as breaking the rules.

Both child and parent have the opportunities to contact each other for very short but important moments – to see something brought home from school, to say goodnight or simply say hello, to check out an invitation or request for an outing together.

The child can maintain one bedroom in one house. Another room may not be needed if the child and the 'non-resident parent' can come and go as they wish, for example, to read bedtime stories, put kids to bed or chill out watching TV together.

CONS

Can be extremely stressful for parents to live nearby an ex and their new family. If there is still continuing conflict or resentment or hurt or jealousy, it may be stimulated or reinforced.

If children rather than parents are regulating contact, parents may feel the children spend more time with the other family than with them.

Parents and children may feel there are no boundaries and no ability to close their own door and have their own family life.

Insight

It's helpful to recognize that there is no one ideal solution. There may well be hurt or conflict with someone in the mix whatever you do. Don't expect perfection but strive for something that works for all of you at some level.

How to decide where children stay and who decides

Parents may assume that it is up to them to make the choices, and the parent 'left holding the baby' may feel they should have the major say. In most cases, this is the mother. Of course, more and more men are taking on primary care for their children, either because of losing their original partner through bereavement or illness, or because it was the woman in that partnership who left, or because the new family arrangements are such that it is agreed he takes the lead. But in the main, it seems to be assumed 'Kids Go With Mum'.

That may not, however, be how the children actually want it, or what may be best for all concerned. Families can fall into what seems like the traditional and assumed role because everyone is worried about how other people may see it, or how they may feel if they 'let down' their children.

Sometimes we make decisions for less than perfect reasons, not only for our children but also for ourselves. As separated parents, especially when there is a new partnership or stepfamily involved, we sometimes fight for sole control over our children and against contact as a way of punishing or getting back at the ex-partner, with whom we may still be angry. 'Reasoned' arguments why a child should stay in one place and have limited contact with the other parent – the other parent let them down and doesn't deserve contact – or with their new family – the new partner is a bad influence and a horrible person – may actually have roots in our own feelings of rage, loss and pain, and may not be in the best interests of the child.

CHILDREN NEED A SAY

So when it comes to making decisions about where children should live and how much contact they should have, the children should have their say and input, as well as the adults. If they are too young to do so, or if they may be swayed by their need to please an upset and angry parent, it's up to adults to do the grown-up thing and put themselves in their child's shoes and answer for them. When making these decisions, it helps to consider:

▶ *your or your partner's need to have a continuing, healthy and loving relationship with children*

- *your or your partner's need to 'finish business' with an ex and move on from being partners to co-parents*
- *your need to feel loved and secure in the relationship with a new partner and in your new family*
- *your need for contact to be as easy and streamlined as possible*
- *your children's and stepchildren's need to be in contact with both their parents*
- *your children's and stepchildren's need to make good relationships with new family members*
- *your children's and stepchildren's need to keep their social networks going with friends, neighbours and other family members such as grandparents*
- *your children's and stepchildren's need for continuity in school*
- *your children's and stepchildren's need for contact to be as easy and streamlined as possible.*

What is at stake is that 50 per cent of fathers lose touch with children within two years of separating from their ex. Very few of those fathers are 'deadbeat dads' who don't care. Most are overwhelmed with the difficulties and the pain of keeping contact. Making it easier can only benefit the children.

Insight

An angry, non-cooperative parent is almost certainly a hurt parent who is struggling to understand and communicate their feelings. Professional help for one or both of you in the form of counselling or mediation is often a real help.

Second marriages are more likely to split up than first-time marriages, and the reasons for that are many and complex. But I would argue that one reason is the stress and strain of managing everyone's emotions, needs and anguish around the fact that children have two parents who live apart, whom they may only see for short periods or irregularly and who may still be at war with each other. The solution is not to try to win the war, but to negotiate a settlement that satisfies everyone – adults and children too.

Case study: Joe, Martin and Sunita

Joe would stay with his father, Martin, and stepmother, Sunita, one weekend a month and during school holidays. Soon after he started secondary school, Martin and Sunita began to find these visits difficult. Joe would often arrive in a bad mood, might cheer up as the visit progressed but invariably go back to being bad tempered and sulky for the last two days. Things came to a head one visit when Joe didn't cheer up and Sunita was reduced to tears. Martin blew up with Joe's mother, saying it was really hard on them, especially as Joe asked for that trip at the last moment and Martin and Sunita had cancelled a friend's birthday party to be with him. Joe's mother at that point confessed she was the one who had wanted the break, to go out with a new date, and that Joe had actually not wanted to come as he too was missing an event with friends. Once Martin had a chance to talk to Joe, he realized that the real problem was that he didn't see his son nearly enough. That was why Joe would go quiet towards the end of every visit; he hated having to leave knowing it might be a month or so before being in contact again. Martin made an effort to call and write more often, and he and Joe arranged to be in touch themselves in future about when Joe would come. This resulted in fortnightly visits, and a far happier Joe.

Insight

When it comes to contact arrangements, you're not trying to win a war, but to negotiate a settlement that satisfies everyone. But the most important people in the mix are the children.

Finding outside help

Arranging contact can become very complex. That's when you might benefit from some outside help.

A solicitor may not be the best first port of call when contact and living arrangements are on the table. Many modern solicitors do see their role as being able to minimize conflict and broker agreements rather than win at any cost and increase conflict. But some still see their job as representing their client no matter what. If you do want to use legal advice, find a solicitor through Resolution, the Solicitors Family Law Association (www.resolution.org.uk). Resolution gives advice on family disputes, separation, divorce and new families, and its members encourage mediation and agreement rather than confrontation.

The courts would far rather you discussed and agreed arrangements between you instead of leaving the situation to develop into what can become an angry legal confrontation. If you're finding it hard to get over your own angry feelings, a counsellor may be the first and best person to turn to.

If you have arrangements that need to be settled between yourself and an ex-partner, or parents and grandparents, or any other family members, mediation may help. When you're finding it hard to come to an amicable agreement, mediation is a way of taking the sting out of those difficult yet very important discussions.

Whatever the reason for your dispute, when there are children involved it's really important for the adults concerned to put their own arguments aside. If your dispute is with an ex-partner, you may no longer be partners but you will always be co-parents and your children really need you to work together.

WOULD MEDIATION OR COUNSELLING HELP?

Mediation is not the same as counselling. Counselling is about looking at yourself, your emotions and reactions. It helps you understand why and how you feel and why and how relationships break down. Counselling can be anything from two- or three- to 21 hour-long sessions to help you deal with the situation you need to resolve and is entirely confidential. Your own GP may have counselling available in the surgery or you may need to find a counsellor through Relate or privately through the British Association for Counselling and Psychotherapy (see the Taking it further section at the end of this book for contact details) and the costs may vary from a token few pounds to £25 to £65 ($50 to $130) a session depending on income and area.

Insight

Counsellors are objective and do not take sides, supporting both parties to communicate and come to an agreed conclusion.

Children also often need support and help in the aftermath of a family break-up and when a new family comes together. The stepfamily may be a positive move for them and may be seen by them as such, but there may still be issues from the past that they'd welcome help in sorting out. You can ask for specific help for them through your own GP or through some schools. Or you could consider family therapy so all of you could get some help together (see the Taking it further section for details).

Counselling often involves painful heart-searching and a willingness to be open and honest with yourself and the person with whom you're being counselled. You may not want to submit to such a process when a relationship has broken down, but you and your ex-partner need to at least agree certain things between you. That's when mediation can come in. A mediator can help all of you see eye to eye over contact arrangements, money and any other disputes involved in your situation. A mediator may suggest you go on to see a counsellor, if they think you may benefit from talking through your feelings. And a counsellor may suggest you go to mediation to hammer out the practical arrangements once you have come to terms with the emotional issues.

You, the person or people you're wanting to reach an agreement with and the mediator will get together for between one and five sessions, each lasting an hour or an hour and a half. The mediator will help you listen to the other parties, understand each other's concerns and needs and help you find a solution that suits everyone involved. Mediators do not take sides and do not push their own solutions. They may well put forward ideas and suggestions, but the aim is for you to find a resolution that is acceptable to and workable by you.

Mediation is confidential. Nothing disclosed in these sessions can be used in court, apart from anything said that suggests that someone is or will be at risk of being hurt or if a crime has or is to take place. Mediation can help you agree issues such as:

- ▶ *where children will live*
- ▶ *contact and holiday arrangements*
- ▶ *how you will communicate*
- ▶ *maintenance and money*
- ▶ *education*
- ▶ *parenting styles and family rules.*

At the end of mediation, you'll usually write down the main points you've agreed so you can check it's working for you and return to this document if there are any later problems. If your dispute is with an ex-partner, you may find a Parenting Plan helpful (see Taking it further).

Mediation is free if you are on a low income or is charged on a sliding scale depending on how much you can afford. You can find a mediator through the Family Mediators Association, National Family Mediation or UK College of Family Mediators (see Taking it further).

Essential points to consider
- ▶ *Children have a right to see both parents.*
- ▶ *There is a range of ways children can be in contact with their parents. You need to find the one that suits you, the child and the other family.*
- ▶ *What works for one child may not suit another. You may need to let different children in your family have different contact arrangements.*
- ▶ *What works now may not next week. Be prepared to be flexible.*

(Contd)

How to cope with different routines and rules in the separate homes

One of the flashpoints surrounding children dividing their time between two homes can be how you manage routines, tasks and chores. One family might have a household where bedtimes are strictly laid down and kept to, where homework is done as soon as children arrive in from school, where everyone has their set task – to feed pets or lay the table or fill the dishwasher. The other family may do it differently – allowing children to stay up later, not asking them to do chores, leaving them to monitor their own homework. Children may find it hard, especially in the period when new families are becoming established, to go from one routine to another. They may become confused and see this variation as destabilizing and a source of anxiety. They may find it a point of conflict, arguing 'Dad doesn't make me do this', or 'Mum says I have to…'. Parents may find themselves using the differences to attack or carry on conflict with an ex, sending messages through their children: 'Mum says I don't have to do it', 'Dad says I should tell you I can.'

And, of course, one parent may be manipulating the routines and rules in order to get at the other parent, to cause them problems without realizing how much it also troubles and hurts the children. Children may seem to delight in mischief making, in setting parents off against each other. But at heart, they find the situation frightening – it makes for extreme insecurity.

HELPING CHILDREN DEAL WITH DIFFERENT RULES

However, two families do not have to run their homes in the same way for parents and step-parents to be singing from the same songbook. Children are perfectly capable of managing and understanding different styles and different rules. They understand the difference between school rules and home rules, for example. In one, you can run around, fetch food from the fridge almost whenever you want, can answer back (in moderation!), wear your own clothes, laugh, sing and chill out. In the other, you have to sit at a table and work for set periods, must address adults in certain ways, have to observe rules and regulations and usually wear a uniform.

Insight

Children know when they pass through one door, one set of rules applies and when they exit it, another comes into play. They know when they go to town and enter shops they should act differently than when on a playing field, that a visit to an elderly grandparent may require different behaviour than the visit to a friend.

To manage two separate households, the best option is twofold:

1 *Discuss the situation with the adults involved, either all together (the two parents and new partners) or the separated parents together.*
2 *Discuss House Rules with your own family.*

HOW TO PRIORITIZE THE RULES YOU FEEL ARE NECESSARY

It really, really helps to raise the issue with the other household, either by having a discussion with all the adults involved, or at least between the two parents. The first issue to thrash out may be what each parent thinks is important. Consider using a traffic light system: Red for 'vital and must be agreed on', Amber for 'fairly important but we can negotiate' and Green for 'that's a matter of style'.

Under Red you may want to include:

- ▶ *basic safety – at all times kids must wear seat belts in cars, be safe on roads, not smoke*
- ▶ *education*
- ▶ *contact with family members.*

Under Amber you may want to discuss:

- *religious observance*
- *where parents live*
- *whether all internet access should be monitored*
- *what sort of films or programmes or games they can access*
- *what they eat and mealtimes*
- *doing homework*
- *pocket money*
- *bedtimes*
- *discipline and sanctions*
- *risk assessment – school trips, sports and activities.*

Under Green you may want to discuss:

- *whether you take shoes off at the door*
- *who feeds the cat*
- *who lays the table.*

There may be Red issues that you feel are non-negotiable. But consider everything as something to discuss; the most important aspect here is the child's happy contact with both parents and some compromise may be necessary. It's up to you to decide what fits in which category.

From the postbag

When my stepchildren come to stay, the way they leave stuff all over the house infuriates me. I think it's so bad mannered but I can't say anything because we do get on quite well and I don't want to upset anything. My husband and I argue about it all the time though because I want him to make them tidy up and he won't. What can I do?

You see it as untidiness and bad manners. They may see it as feeling at home and, without realizing it, this may be a

56

way of saying 'This place is mine!' If it really upsets you the best tactic is to say so, calmly, directly and clearly but without any criticism. So, you don't say 'This is such a mess!' or 'You're so untidy!' What you say is, 'Could you please pick up your socks and put them in your room? Socks belong in bedrooms! Thanks!'

The other point to consider is picking your battles. In the end, what is more important – that the house is nice and tidy when they come to stay, or that they come to stay willingly and you have a good time? There are more important issues you may want to put your foot down on another time; save the fight for them.

Setting your own Family Rules

Once you have thrashed out what you agree on and what you may differ on, it helps all of you to set out your own House Rules, for your own family and household.

For example, here is a list of ideas for Family Rules:

- ▶ *Take your shoes off at the door.*
- ▶ *Don't throw coats on the floor – hang them up.*
- ▶ *If you have a snack, put plates and mugs in the dishwasher and clean the table.*
- ▶ *Feed the cat before feeding yourself.*
- ▶ *Do your chores with no arguments.*
- ▶ *When you're out, your mobile must be on.*
- ▶ *Talk with each other instead of shouting at each other.*
- ▶ *No kicking, hitting, shoving, biting, swearing or shouting.*
- ▶ *Be kind, be positive, praise often and always say 'Please', 'Thank you' and 'Well done'.*

- *If you want someone to hear you, you have to listen to them.*
- *Help people do better instead of criticizing them to bring them down.*
- *Have a family talk at least once a week.*
- *Go out as a family at least once a month.*
- *Go to bed at agreed times.*
- *Do homework at the beginning of a night or weekend.*
- *Pocket money to be given every Friday night.*
- *Say what time you'll be home and keep to it.*

Every family has rules they live by. Sometimes, these have been discussed and everyone knows them. Sometimes, they're 'sort of known' and 'sort of agreed'. Often, they do exist but people aren't always sure what they are exactly and they do change from time to time. Putting together a set of Family or House Rules means you have to discuss them, agree them and learn what they are. Then there's no excuse for not realizing what you should or shouldn't be doing.

Discussing House Rules is particularly important in a stepfamily. One reason, as already discussed, is that rules can be different in different houses and it helps to be clear about what is different.

The second and most important reason is that when people in the stepfamily want to make a point or kick off or be uncooperative, the first thing they usually say is 'You can't tell me what to do, you're not my Mum/Dad!' Having House or Family Rules bypasses that. There should be no rudeness, no disrespect, no hitting or shouting or slamming doors or whatever you have all agreed. And that's not because some big bad adult has tried to usurp a parent's place and is telling you what to do; it's because that's the House Rule, and you all keep it.

ENCOURAGING YOUR FAMILY TO 'BUY IN' TO THE RULES

By talking the rules through and allowing everyone to have their say, you get two results. One is that everyone should 'buy in' to the rules. If everyone sets them, they had a chance to make them or alter them and now they should keep them. And this means all members of the house get a say – kids too. For every rule that the adults would like to impose, there should be one the children put forward. So rules can be negative: no swearing and shouting or hitting. But they can also be positive: one night a week must be games night when children can choose a game to play – Monopoly, Cluedo, Scrabble, whatever – and the adults have to take part.

Another result of talking through the rules is that setting them helps young people as well as adults think about why they are needed and what might be the effect of having – or not having – them. Sometimes, it helps adults realize priorities. After all, does it really matter if a child's room is untidy? Surely having sensible times for them to come home, or go to bed, are more important. And you'll be surprised how sensible young people can be, given the responsibility and the option.

Insight

Discussing rules allows you to choose your battles. If you kick up a major fuss over the less important things, you may find it hard to insist on something that really *is* important – you've used up all your arguments and sanctions on something less important.

But perhaps the number one result of allowing everyone to have a say is that it allows you all to feel a part of this house – to have a place and a stake in it. This can be vitally important in a stepfamily household.

HOW TO DECIDE YOUR HOUSE RULES

You set House or Family Rules by all getting together round a table with a big sheet of paper and some pens. This is the preliminary stage – you're not looking for perfection or neatness at this point. Appoint someone to be the note taker, and then ideas-storm.

Ideas-storming is putting down every single idea that comes to mind. Ask 'What House or Family Rules do we think we already have? What House or Family Rules do we want?' You might also ask 'What problems do we have and how could we do something about them?'

Write down every suggestion. Even if you think them unworkable, silly, too difficult to manage. The only thing you should exclude might be rules that anyone suggests with the intention of 'getting at' another member of the family. So, 'No coming in and messing up my books' would not be acceptable. But 'Everyone to ask before using anyone else's belongings' is fair – it applies to all.

Having written everything down, go to the second stage; look at and consider all the ideas. Think about what you all want to achieve. Some of your rules may be about getting on with each other – about being nice and helpful. You might put in a rule about not swearing, hitting, fighting, shouting. Some may be about running the home smoothly – you might have a family rule about always taking shoes off at the door or always hanging coats up when you come in or always washing up your own coffee cups. Some may be about big and important things such as teenagers always carrying mobiles when they're out at night with friends and never getting into a car with a driver who's been drinking.

The third stage is agreeing which rules you will choose to be your House or Family Rules. You might like to rewrite the rules to make them as constructive as possible – use Dos rather than Don'ts. Be as specific as possible – a vague rule about respecting people is less helpful than saying people should listen to each other, not shout them down, interrupt or call them names. You may find you have some overlapping rules – prune or combine them. You may have some you don't like, and some the children don't like. Make your case and listen to theirs. Do some 'horse trading' – you'll accept one rule they request if they accept another you champion.

Then, write the rules out neatly and agree you will all keep them. You might like to draw up a contract that says so, and have everyone (adults included) sign it.

How to draw up a contract and why it's a good idea

The idea is to write down exactly what everyone has agreed:

▶ *what you've all agreed to do*
▶ *how you agree to do it*
▶ *when you agree to do it by*
▶ *for how long you have agreed to do this.*

Everyone should sign the contract. Hang up the House or Family Rules and the contract somewhere you can all see them.

> **Insight**
> Once you have agreed House Rules, revisit them regularly – maybe once a week. Are they working? If not, why not? What needs to be changed so they can work?

If you can, share your House Rules with the other family, suggesting they may want to set their own and acknowledging that every home is different. Explain you're showing them yours so they have an idea of what you expect of the children when they are with you.

> **Essential points to consider**
> ▶ *Every family manages rules and routines in their own way. As long as you agree the basic essentials, children can go from one to another with ease.*
> ▶ *Every family would benefit from discussing, agreeing and setting out their Family Rules.*

What to tell other people

When a family separates and new units form, you may feel embarrassed and ashamed of what has happened, or simply too raw to want to discuss it. You can imagine that if you do draw other people's attention to the situation, you all may be singled out and made to feel unusual or even abnormal or criticized for the way you are managing (or not managing). But people need to know, for all sorts of reasons.

It doesn't need explanations or excuses or shame or embarrassment. It only needs a simple explanation:

▶ *So-and-so and so-and-so are no longer living together.*
▶ *So-and-so and so-and-so are now living together.*
▶ *The children will be seeing both their parents and will be staying here and there.*
▶ *Both parents will continue to be fully involved in their children's lives.*

Or:

▶ *Sadly, one parent is unable to be part of their children's lives and we shall do our best to support the children through that and will appreciate your help too.*

Ask them:

▶ *to respect the way you are handling it (you are trying to be as amicable as possible and to negotiate constructive contact)*
▶ *not to criticize the child's other parent*
▶ *to help and support contact*
▶ *to stay in touch themselves*
▶ *to be sympathetic to the child's feelings.*

Other family members need to know, but they need to be helped to be supportive and not divisive. Family often see their role in family break-up as being protective and defensive – to be on the side of their relative and thus against the other parent. The big problem with that is that the child is caught in the middle. They need to know about what has happened and what you plan, but above all they need to know their constructive and non-confrontational aid would be welcome.

The parents of your child's friends need to know, so they can understand that arrangements for the children to see each other may be complicated and affected by contact visits. They also need to understand that children may be upset about issues to do with family and parents – seeing a happy family playing together may set off an apparently contradictory reaction. Any illness or changes of plans may have to be dealt with by the non-resident parent if the resident one is away, so make sure as many people as possible have both sets of contact details.

The child's friends need to know, for all of the reasons above. But the person to tell them should be the child, so help them explain it. You could offer to rehearse by taking the role of the friend as the child practises what to say and how.

Your friends need to know, so they can be supportive and sympathetic but not defensive and divisive. Explain the situation to them and help them see that any criticism of other people in the loop is not helpful but encouragement is. Friends may take the brunt of any stress you are suffering, and of broken dates as something comes up or arrangements changed as a day suddenly becomes free. They need to be flexible and considerate and the more honest and upfront you are about what is happening and how you feel about it, the more they will be so.

The child's school and teachers need to know, for a range of reasons. One is simply practical – the school and all teachers should understand when children may have barriers to arriving with homework completed and in hand, materials with them or letters having been delivered, signed or acted upon and returned. Children may have gone from one to another house several times in a week or fortnight, and the parent dropping the child off that day may not be the one to whom a letter was handed a few days before.

The school also needs to know of the changes in the child's life so the staff can understand and appropriately deal with behaviour. Children who have experienced the loss, pain, guilt and confusion so often surrounding the breaking up of one family and the making of a new one can frequently act out their anger or pain in 'bad behaviour' at school.

Insight

It makes no sense to punish a child for behaviour that may seem irrational or naughty when in fact it is a cry for help or of protest. Schools need to know what is going on so they can make this assessment, and so you can protest if they treat the child unfairly.

Youth club workers, doctors, dentists and anyone one else who has contact with the child, where health, where they live or where their behaviour may be an issue, should be told. They need to know not only so permissions can be sorted out and where any reports should be sent – and if duplicates are necessary – but also to be sympathetic and encouraging if the child displays behaviour that may seem challenging but is actually a reaction to what is going on.

THINGS TO REMEMBER

▶ When deciding where a child is going to live and when a child 'visits' in a stepfamily, take everyone's views and needs on board. This means your views, those of your ex and anyone else involved but, most importantly, those of the children.

▶ The possible arrangements can vary from occasional visits through equal shares to communal living. Don't rush to a decision. Examine and discuss all the possibilities before making the choice. Be prepared to be flexible and adjust or change arrangements as needs and suitability fluctuate.

▶ All children need some form of contact with the non-resident parent. Few of the 50 per cent of fathers who lose touch with their children within two years of a separation actually want it that way, and even fewer of the children welcome no contact. You owe it to everyone involved to work to retain contact.

▶ Mutually satisfactory arrangements are best obtained by conciliation not confrontation. The courts would far rather you made your own arrangements and you can be helped greatly in this by the professional skills of solicitors belonging to Resolution. Solicitors who are members of this association are pledged to encourage mediation and working together rather than conflict and are the experts in helping stepfamilies managing their situation.

▶ Counselling or mediation will support everyone in a stepfamily. Counselling can help you understand why and how you feel the way you do and to manage your emotions. Mediation can help all of you to see eye to eye over practical arrangements.

▶ Routine is important in a child's life but they can manage variation and difference. A child's two family homes need not necessarily be run in exactly the same way, but all the adults involved should cooperate to ensure that certain basics are *agreed and that the two sets of House Rules involved do not produce conflict, confusion or unhappiness in the child.*

▶ *Help everyone 'buy in' to House Rules by ideas-storming them, discussing and agreeing them, and all of you signing a contract to confirm what you have agreed.*

▶ *People who deal with you need to know of your stepfamily status. It's far easier for you and the children if family, your social circle and all officials (schools, doctors, etc.) know as soon as possible.*

IDEAS TO TRY

▶ Are you and the children happy with contact arrangements as they are? Ideas-storm an agreed, preferred plan.

▶ Looking at the preferred plan, what would be different from the way it is now? What changes would you need to make?

▶ How might you make changes? What would help, what would hinder? Check out this chapter again and read on for ideas.

▶ Would you need help to make those changes, or to come to terms with not being able to do so? If so, consider the pros and cons of counselling or mediation. What would help or hinder you accessing it?

▶ Look at the routines and rules in the different houses the children stay in.

▶ Discuss your own rules as they stand at present and talk them through with the adults involved. Do they work? What might be different?

▶ With the children, ideas-storm a new set of House Rules.

Part two
Coming together

4

From partner to step-parent

In this chapter you will learn:
- *how to move from being a partner to being a step-parent too*
- *how to find your place in a stepfamily*
- *how to build bonds between step-parent and child*
- *when a stepfamily can be a second chance for adult and child*
- *the skills of communication.*

The transition from partner to step-parent can be a difficult one, and one that some partners of people who have kids from a previous relationship don't want to make. After all, you fall in love with a person. You may not want to take on a family too. Even if you know about them from the beginning of your relationship, you may still not accept that they will be an intimate part of your life. In effect, it's a package deal from the beginning but we don't always recognize it as such.

If the kids live with their other parent, you may assume that they will at worst be weekend and holiday visitors, and at best have a small percentage of your and your partner's life. In fact, even if the amount of time the children spend with your partner is limited, or even non-existent, a parent remains a parent and children occupy a full-time place in their lives, if not their diary, for ever.

Problems in how you may view your partner's children

Some step-parents concentrate on their relationship with their partner, seeing children as something to be tolerated or endured or allowed to tag along as occasional, optional extras. The reason for putting them in this box may be that accepting these children can be painful. While it may be easy to acknowledge, theoretically, that the relationships and experiences your partner has had has made them what they are today, it's far less easy to welcome into your life living, breathing remnants of that relationship and those experiences.

We all want to be the centre of our partner's life and love. Our own children come later and are part of that. But someone else's children are a different thing. They are proof that someone was here before us, and proof that to a certain extent they are still here and always will be. Taking on the package deal requires us to be selfless, understanding and very adult. One part of you will be screaming 'Tell me you love me best! Show me I come first!' It's a hard task to be the grown-up in such circumstances.

We have become accustomed to a pick-and-choose society – one in which we can design and select a lot of aspects. This mobile phone or laptop with those add-ons, a car with certain added extras, an outfit in particular colours. Cherry-picking is a part of modern-day society, but not in stepfamilies. You can't have a relationship without or even in spite of the children. Children are always going to be an integral part of a stepfamily and of a relationship where there are children from a previous partnership.

How to make space in your life for the children

Whether the children live with you or not, they are a part of their parent's life and the step-parent's life too, and both adults have to make space for that fact. And that means both partners taking on the realization that each had a past, a history and that sometime in this history along came children. In addition, you both need to accept that this past is not dead, gone and forgotten. It reaches forward into the present and the future too, in the shape of the ex, the children's other parent, and the links this parent continues to have with their children. The missing parent may not even be on the scene, but their existence and their influence on the children affects your stepfamily even so.

Insight

An invisible, non-existent parent is still a parent and plays a significant role in a child's life, if only in the imagination, desires and hopes of that child.

Some non-resident parents will walk away from their children, particularly if keeping contact is made difficult by the other parent or a new partner. But not only is this a damaging decision for the children involved, it doesn't do any of the adults concerned much good either. The missing parent may feel relieved to have sloughed off responsibility or to be out of an angry, painful and complex situation, but mixed with that will be guilt and longing. Ultimately that means the stepfamily and the new relationship suffers too, as it starts with unfinished business and baggage and continues with guilt and pain.

WHY PARENTS LOSE TOUCH WITH THEIR CHILDREN

Would you want to put your trust and invest your love in someone who could abandon their children? Could you, as a step-parent, ask your partner to put you first or accept that you want nothing to do with their children? Very, very few people would really wish to go to those lengths even though many are tempted, wondering if it would be the solution to their difficulties. It actually seldom is. Non-resident parents lose touch because of the barriers put in the way of keeping contact, not because they want to. And step-parents find it hard to make contact with their partner's children for a range of complex and difficult reasons, but rarely because they don't want to make some connection.

Why is it so hard? Often it is because of the grief, pain and anger felt by both ex-partners and children around the loss of the original family. When families break up, it is because adults have found they cannot maintain the relationship at the core. Few of us, however, walk away from that with confidence and surety. We may feel angry and cheated, we may feel failures. We are often convinced it is our own inadequacies that have led to the breakdown and that leads to a very human reaction – the need to place the blame and the anger elsewhere. Ex-partners go from being the love of our lives to monsters.

From the postbag

I'm not sure I can get on with my fiancée's children. The older boy looks just like his Dad, and the girl acts like him. They see their father every weekend and one night a week and those are the only times I relax. I know he would like them to stay longer. Should I persuade her to agree?

It's not the children you object to but the fact that they so strongly remind you that someone was there before you, that she loved and lived with and had children by. That's a difficult thing to swallow, I know – but you're going to have to come to terms with it if this relationship is to last. Even if they went to live half the week with their father, their visits would still ram this fact home. Even if you saw them once month it would still be a sticking point. So the only way you're going to overcome it is to face up to your feelings and deal with them. It might help for you to talk over your entirely understandable jealousy and pain with your partner and maybe a counsellor. But trying to edit out the children won't work. Your feelings are normal and you can't help them. You can help what you do about them; getting rid of the children is not the answer.

HOW TO MAKE EMOTIONAL BONDS WITH YOUR PARTNER'S CHILDREN

There can be no doubt it is difficult to love your stepchildren in the same way as you might your own. As soon as your own children are born, you usually feel some bond. For some parents this can take time to develop, but for others it is instant and powerful. Even if it does need to develop, you have the time to do so, as you and they grow together. A new stepfamily means everyone is catapulted immediately into having to deal with a multiple extended family and all that goes with it. The fact that the step-parent doesn't feel as strong a love for their stepchildren as they do their parent, the new partner, can have everyone feeling there is something wrong. Maybe, you think, it's the child's fault – they aren't lovable, they are bad and hostile. Or maybe it's the step-parent's own fault – there must be something missing in you that you can't summon up feelings for these children. What then often happens is that the adult withdraws and gives up. If you can't feel love at once, you believe it stands to reason you never will. So step-parents may concentrate on the love they feel and the relationship they have with the adult, or with their own children – or, indeed, for one particular child for whom they do feel some emotion or bond.

Insight

It takes time to build a relationship and establish ties between step-parent and child. Don't expect it to happen overnight. Given time and patience it will come, eventually.

How to find your place in the stepfamily

Step-parents have to find their place in stepfamilies, something that often causes problems. As adults we are used to the idea that children fit around us – that we set the rules, the agenda, the boundaries. The natural progression in first-time families is for you make your relationship with your partner and then children arrive; you're there first. So to a certain extent the idea that adults come first and kids fit in around you is both normal and indeed appropriate. It's not good for children to run households, to have their needs and wishes overriding all else. Children who have all their needs instantly satisfied grow up demanding, selfish and endlessly discontented.

But it is necessary to know about their wishes as well as their needs and to accommodate them as much as is suitable and realistic. Children who never have their needs satisfied at all grow up with little self-worth, convinced they are never going to have what they require. Neither extreme is good. For healthy development, children require a mixture of satisfaction and having to learn they must wait or occasionally not get what they want. The balance is important, so it is vital to recognize that it's a whole different ball game when you have a stepfamily. Children may be more demanding and needy because of what has happened to them in the break-up of their family. They may be less so, having sadly learnt that they don't get what they want. When it comes to moving a new partner into an existing family, it is essential for the adults concerned to recognize that the step-parent is the new face on the block. The children were there first, and have every right and every reason to expect you to be aware of and make allowances around that.

HOW TO BE A SIGNIFICANT OTHER RATHER THAN A SUBSTITUTE PARENT

A stepfamily can be a second chance for everyone concerned, in lots of different ways. It can be a second chance for children to have a father-like figure who would do all the things they hoped and expected a dad would do: support and love their mum, play with them, show an interest in them and their pursuits. Or a second chance to have a mum who will love them and be there for them. It can be an opportunity to have a family when otherwise that opportunity might not have existed. It can be an opportunity for the adult to be a better step-parent to a partner's children than they might have been first time round to their own first family and a chance to try again at being a good parent to their own too.

These opportunities – to get it right, to make it better, to have something you might otherwise not have had – are all available if the step-parent accepts that children are an integral part of the relationship they have with their new partner.

Some step-parents throw themselves wholeheartedly into the role. They adore their new family and are passionate about being a parent to them, so much so that they wish the other parent would go away. Some may believe it would be a good idea to block access to the other parent since they feel they could fulfil that role so much more lovingly and efficiently. Or they may see their task to strive to be the best Mum or Dad, so that the children, and their partner, may come to see that they are the preferred person for the job.

And some children appear to agree with this point of view. If the non-resident parent has let them down or been violent and physically or emotionally damaging, children may be relieved to never see them again and embrace a step-parent as the real thing. Even if the non-resident parent has done no more than be one side of a sad separation, the child may take out their disappointment on them in rejection and withdrawal, turning to the step-parent as a substitute.

But more often, what children need from a step-parent is for them to be an addition; to be a 'significant other' rather than a replacement for a parent, no matter how inadequate that parent may be. And the truth is that often people can be poor partners but good parents. Or, that their failures in parenting are not due to lack of love but lack of a good role model in their own lives as to how to do the job acceptably. The step-parent's role may be to help and support their partner and the ex in becoming a better co-parent and non-resident parent than they were a full-time parent.

> ### Essential points to consider
> ▶ *You can't pick and choose when it comes to stepchildren. If one of you has children, they are part of your relationship.*
> ▶ *You don't fall in love with stepchildren the way you fall for your partner or your own children. But given time, love can grow.*
> *(Contd)*

How to deal with stepchildren

When one partner in a relationship has children the step-parent has three choices:

1 *To ignore them – they're not yours and you don't want or need to make a relationship with them.*
2 *To set out to take them over – what's your partner's is yours and you will be a better parent to them than the ex.*
3 *To embrace them and make a relationship of your own with them, but to do so with tact and care as an additional caring adult but not as a substitute parent.*

Many people opt for the first choice. Having affection or love or even tolerance for children not your own isn't easy. You grow up with your children; many parents don't fall instantly in love with their own, but many do or at least find that a bond grows in the first few hours, days or weeks after having them. It's gut-deep and you have very little choice about it. Even when you don't like what your children do, you can't help loving them.

Another person's child is a different thing. You don't have that bond, and you may even have primeval reasons for actively disliking, fearing or being wary of them. After all, their existence proves that the person you love was loved by, and loved, someone before you. The children will have their own reasons for finding you an intruder or an affront and it can all lead to hostility at worst; indifference at best.

Insight
We are programmed by nature to find it difficult to accept children who are not our own. Lions, when they take over

a pride, kill the offspring left behind by the previous male. Some humans understand the impulse and in fantasy wish they could do the same!

In the second choice, the step-parent sets out to annexe this family as their own, setting rules and trying hard to be a perfect parent to win the loyalty and love of their stepchildren. They may try to limit access to the other parent or criticize and demean them in an attempt to change the child's view of them.

Neither of these choices is easy to live with, either for the adults involved or the children. It sets up tugs of loyalty and confusion in the kids. It can trigger conflict and guilt in the adults. You may feel the other adult or adults are all to blame, are horrible people and that you're justified in belittling or insulting them. Whether this is true is irrelevant. The result is going to be miserable children, and a bad taste in your mouth; anger and conflict tend to distress everyone involved.

The final choice is the best. Not the easiest, but the best. Making a relationship between step-parent and stepchild benefits everyone. The couple relationship is a gift to the two adults involved, but involves loss to the children. If in addition to struggling to deal with the changes in their family they also fight with the new person in their parent's life, it's a lot to take on. You can help them turn it from a burden to a pleasure and something that will be to their advantage. A good relationship between step-parent and stepchild is also of great benefit to the adults. The parent will be relieved, especially if their relationship had become difficult. The step-parent may gain children in their life they never felt they needed and may never otherwise have had. A step-parent with children of their own may gain skills at relating to children that will stand them in good stead. All in all, it's a win–win situation. So how do you achieve it?

TAKE YOUR TIME

You may fall in love with your own child immediately, you may even have fallen in love with your partner at first sight, but it's highly unlikely anyone would feel anything approaching love when first meeting stepchildren. Liking, maybe. Tolerance. A desire to make friends. Or jealousy, suspicion, resentment, competitiveness. Don't blame them or yourself for this. It's a natural reaction. But don't assume first impressions are for ever. Give it time, give both of you some space and both liking and love can and will develop.

DON'T TAKE IT PERSONALLY

Stepchildren may behave horribly to newcomers and those around them. They may be argumentative, moody, arrogant, demanding and generally tiresome. They may accuse a step-parent of the most awful things and do their best to stir up trouble and rows. They may refuse to listen to or cooperate and constantly repeat 'You can't tell me what to do, you're not my Mum/Dad!'

Don't take it personally. They'd say the same whoever was their step-parent, whatever they did. They're not protesting about or getting at the step-parent him or herself. They're protesting about the fact that their parents live apart. The step-parent is in the firing line because they're the final proof that parents are never getting back together and things never will return to the way they were. Grit your teeth and be pleasant. Bite your lip and be understanding. The worst thing that could ever happen to anyone has happened to them – their parents have broken up and their family has come apart. Of course they're angry and the step-parent is the one to take the flack for it. If a step-parent can understand it's not about them, it's about the situation, they can bear it. You can allow them to get all that bad feeling out into the open, and let it wash off like water off a duck's back. Don't minimize or trivialize the feelings but recognize it's not the step-parent, personally, that is at fault. Accept their feelings, recognize their pain and wait for the storm to be over.

Insight
Don't take it personally. It's not about you but the situation.

KEEP TRYING

Small children will want to hear the same story again and again and again. And when you're furious with someone, you may need to hear them apologize more than once, or at least need to let your feelings die down before you're ready to be friends again. In the same way, children may need to see a step-parent make repeated efforts to woo them before they're ready to set aside their initial feelings and connect with them.

You may have found them happy to share treats when the new adult was fresh on the scene or simply a date for their parent. However, once the step-parent becomes a part of their parent's life, their attitude may change. At that point, the newcomer becomes a rival for their place with the parent and a rival for their other parent's place in their lives. A step-parent will have to be patient, persistent and prepared to repeat offers, olive branches and overtures of friendship. And with each couple of steps forward they may have to beat a one step retreat. Two steps forward and one step back is progress; keep trying.

How to make your stepfamily house a home

The fridge door

Most families with children use the fridge door. You may have magnetic letters on it, use it to display the drawings and certificates your children bring home from school and exhibit magnets which are presents or souvenirs from holidays. Stepfamilies can use the fridge door as a way of pulling everyone together.

One way to make it clear that everyone in your family has a position and a role in your household is to make use of some place as a message board. It can be the back of the kitchen or a cupboard door or even a message board you stick up in the hall, but the fridge door is an obvious place.

If you have a chore rota (and you should!), you can post it here. You can also keep a calendar in clear sight – a big one, so all of you can keep track of who will or should be where

(Contd)

when, and everybody can have access to it. You can leave messages and reminders to each other.

But it's also where you can pin all sorts of material to celebrate and pull your family together. Stick up photos as well as the school certificates and drawings. You can invite any member of your family to stick up anything they've seen that they'd like to draw to the attention of other people – cartoons, magazine or newspaper cuttings, letters. It's a way of making a mark and of providing continuity. It's a way of keeping in touch. It says that everyone who contributes has a say, even if they're not there all the time or haven't been there very long.

You might decide to divide the board up into sections – one for each member. Alternatively, stick things all over, higgledy piggledy. You may pin up an envelope for each person so others can put messages to that person in it. In fact, you can arrange your fridge door or other type of message board to suit your home and your family.

When the children are with you, it's tempting to make life as much fun and as easy as possible. A step-parent could curry favour by buying things, taking the children out on treats, relaxing rules and letting them get away with staying up late, watching films they're not supposed to see and eating food that's bad for them. Sometimes we do this with the view that they've had such a tough time, they need some compensation. Sometimes we do it because it seems to avoid conflict and make it a smoother ride. But constant treats don't make for happier children. For a start, it can destabilize the other home, as children go there saying 'Why don't we do this?' or 'We don't have to do that!' You or your partner may feel some satisfaction that the other home is taking flak but it rebounds on you eventually, if for no other reason than it makes for unsettled, miserable children.

The most important reason, however, is that for children – and adults – to manage in a stepfamily in a way that supports everyone, each household has to feel like home. What children want and need, and what you profit from, is knowing they belong and are at home in both households, not visiting one or being cosseted unnaturally in the other. Children may demand entertainment, may try to dodge chores or get out of tasks but the bottom line is they crave, push for and need boundaries. They want to be with you, but not to go to theme parks or play areas – though that's welcome too, thank you very much. What they wish most of all is to chill out like any normal family and to be expected to play a part, like any normal family. To stay in, maybe watching a DVD or playing a game, but to do it as a family. And that also means sometimes being able to go and see friends, to have them round, to spend time in their rooms. Far from being a dereliction of duty, when a non-resident father and new partner have children for a weekend and take them to visit their grandparents, maybe leaving them there while they go shopping, that's the sort of thing families do. The more stepfamilies and separated families 'act like normal', the better everyone manages the situation. What children in any family – and a stepfamily is 'any family' too – need is to *sometimes* have special attention paid to them, to *usually* be given ordinary consideration and to *often* share experiences.

Insight

Recognizing and accepting that what you may believe is abnormal is actually normal in stepfamilies is the key to making it work.

Case study: Jessie, Jeannine and Tèa

Whenever Jeannine came to stay with her father Jessie and his partner Tèa, they would go out – to the park, on trips, to cinemas and events. Jessie and Tèa would make great efforts to find things to do with Jeannine and sometimes felt quite disappointed and upset when she didn't seem to like what had been arranged or appeared ungrateful. It wasn't until a friend suggested that Jeannine might like simply being at home with them, in their home which she might want to share, that they recognized the non-stop
(Contd)

whirl of activities they always offered her. The original reason had been that their first home was very cramped and they felt Jeannine might not like it after her mother's larger house. Eventually they recognized that Jeannine didn't really care where they lived – she just wanted to be part of it. The next time she came, they did nothing – just stayed at home being together. Jeannine pronounced it the best visit ever.

How to use communication skills

For step-parents to make good relationships with children, the most important key is communication. And communication doesn't just mean talking – it means listening too. You need to listen in order to learn what it is that is really bothering the child, or to find out what they actually need. You may think you know the answers but unless and until you ask, and are prepared to take on board what they say, you won't. Respectful, concerned, concentrated listening has another effect – it helps the other person listen to and hear you, too. Communicating is an art and a skill – it needs to be learned and practised – but once you have the trick, it works. And it's a 'transferable skill'. Learn to communicate fully with children and you can find all sorts of adult-to-adult situations where it puts you at a distinct advantage.

Turn an argument into real, two-way communication with these five tips:

1 **Confront problems, not people.** *When you feel upset, take a deep breath and pause a moment to work out exactly what is bothering you. Instead of shouting at the person, explain what your anger or upset is really about, then find a way of agreeing on a resolution.*
2 **Accept that you can't help what you feel.** *Anyone in a second family is likely to have a complex and mixed range of feelings about themselves, the other people involved and the situation. Perhaps one of the most important messages we need to take*

84

on board is that those feelings, however destructive they are and however much they may distress you, are likely to be natural and normal. If you want to become comfortable with yourself and to reach a working arrangement with everyone else, the first step is to recognize and understand why you feel the way you do. So accept your feelings, even if they are sometimes ones you would rather not own up to. Be honest about what you are feeling and why. You are not to blame for your emotions.

3 **Accept that you can help what you do about your feelings.** You're being dishonest if you say you can't control your actions. Having gained some insight into why your circumstances might be so difficult, you can pinpoint your own fears, angers or anxieties. You can understand how the other people involved might feel, and then work on strategies for making a change. Sometimes a 'pre-emptive strike' can nip problems in the bud before they really begin. Many families that experience change go through difficult periods but come out the other side, so don't despair. There are many things you can all do to improve your life together.

4 **Make it honest and personal.** When we want to drive home a point, in discussion or argument, we often say 'Everyone' or 'All my friends' or 'Your mother' thinks such and such, rather than taking responsibility for those feelings ourselves. Many of us were brought up to think it was arrogant or selfish to use the 'I' word so we tend to avoid it, or we put the responsibility on the other person by saying 'Look what you make me do'. One important step to constructive arguing is owning, or taking responsibility for, our own feelings. There is a great difference between saying 'I'm angry because when you talk about your past I feel second best to your ex' and 'You make me feel second best'. The main difference is that the other person may rightly object to the second statement because it may not be their intention at all, and once they disagree you will find yourself stuck in a circular argument. But no one can disagree with an honest explanation of your own feelings. And once they are explained, you may be well on your way to dealing with them.

5   **Use active listening.** *This helps you to hear the other person. You can ask them to do the same to hear you. Active listening is when the other person shows they're really listening, wanting to understand and to help without taking over. It doesn't mean they have to agree. It does mean what they say and what they do shows us they care about us. Using active listening can help in any exchange, whether it's a child telling you about their pain at their family breaking up or your partner saying what they want to do on holiday. When you're actively listening, you:*

   ▷ *care for, trust and accept the other person and their feelings, want to understand but don't want to sort it out for them*

   ▷ *concentrate on this person and this problem,* now

   ▷ *use your body – leaning forwards, facing them – to show you're paying attention*

   ▷ *ask open questions – 'So, tell me about it'*

   ▷ *check out what's been said – 'Have I got this right...?'*

   ▷ *acknowledge feelings – 'That must feel hurtful'*

   ▷ *identify needs – 'What you want is...'*

   ▷ *move them on – 'So what can we do to make this better?'*

Having an AIM

When facing any issue in a stepfamily, the best tactic is to have an **AIM** in mind. **AIM** stands for Acknowledge feelings, Identify needs and Move on. When you talk:

▶ Acknowledge feelings *– 'I can see you're angry with me.'*

▶ Identify needs *– 'You wanted to be able to stay with your other family and we made other arrangements.'*

▶ Move on *– 'What can we do to satisfy both of us?'*

How to make agreements by negotiating, compromising and agreeing contracts

When children know you are prepared to listen and take on board their feelings and requests they will trust both their parent and their new step-parent. When they trust you, you are more than halfway there to building a relationship. It need not be a loving, parental relationship, not at first. It just needs to be one of mutual respect and of give and take. The best decisions are always the result of negotiation and compromise – when one person does not get all they want but everyone gets some of their needs met. And the best agreements are made when, at the end of the discussion, you draw up a contract.

There are several very good spin-offs of getting into the habit of negotiating. One is that if anyone in your family has a disagreement, it's up to the ones involved to settle it, not the role of one adult alone. This puts a stop to a parent feeling they have to mediate between step-parent and child or between stepsiblings. It means 'steps' have to have their own dialogue between them.

Insight

Negotiating doesn't mean losing control or giving up. The buck still stops with you as the adult. But it makes for far more efficient discussions – kids are more likely to do what is agreed when they've had a hand in crafting that agreement than when you simply tell them what's what.

When you're faced with a disagreement, ask everyone to sit down and talk it through. Work out a fair exchange that you can all agree on. You may have to conduct some horse trading – 'you can have that if I can have this'. When you've thrashed it all out, write it down. Include:

▶ *what you've all agreed to do*
▶ *how you agree to do it*
▶ *when you agree to do it by*
▶ *for how long you have agreed to do this.*

Everyone should sign the contract, and have a copy for themselves. The original should be pinned up in your kitchen or hallway.

Review the contract and the agreed changes regularly. If the terms are not being met, discuss why and whether the contract needs to be redrawn or whether something needs to be adjusted.

How to build relationships with stepchildren

How do you build a relationship with your own children? We don't always start with that rush of affection or have an instant bond. And even when we do, as time passes and the children grow and inevitably change, we sometimes have to revisit and renew our connection with them. You build a relationship with your stepchildren in exactly the same way.

Accepting them for who and what they are. They may do things we hate and may irritate the hell out of us at times, but deep down, our children are ours and we love them unconditionally. Stepchildren may not be yours, but by loving their parent they become yours by proxy. You build a relationship by accepting that, and them.

Spending time with them. We don't always feel we have enough time for our partners, our own children and ourselves, so stepchildren may come some way down the list of priorities. You need to prioritize children because, unlike partners who (you hope!) are with you for life, children grow up and leave. The few years you have full-time with them set the standard for the whole of their life – and set a flavour for the rest of yours. There's a well-known song called 'Cat's in the Cradle' by Harry Chapin which starts with verses about a man who can't play with his son because he's too busy. The last verse is the now-adult son fobbing off his father, now old, with exactly the same excuses. Having stepchildren who value and feel affection for you and want to continue seeing you will be something you prize later on. It starts with you valuing and wanting to spend time with them, now. Ask them what they did today and don't interrupt or comment – simply listen. Sit on the sofa and watch their favourite programme and don't sneer. Take them to the movies, take them bowling, take them to the park. Doesn't matter if you hate doing these things – if they like it, they'll like you for doing it with them.

When it all goes wrong

There may be times when a stepchild either suddenly becomes moody or argumentative or hostile to a step-parent, or steps up previous dislike to active warfare. It's very easy to wonder 'What did I do?' and become riddled with guilt. Or, to search your mind, come up with nothing and become furious with the child for being so unreasonable. That's the time to wonder what is happening in the other family.

Perhaps there are arguments going on elsewhere which upset the child, who finds it hard to protest or put their own case forward. They may be anxious that disclosing their emotions would make an already fragile situation even worse, so conceal their feelings out of a wish to protect others. But the feelings have to go somewhere so they may resort to taking out frustration and distress when with you. Children often hit out and kick back at the adults in their life who seem safe and steady rather than risking alienating those they feel are vulnerable or unreliable. Or maybe some change is going on – the other family may be under strain, or conversely being strengthened by a marriage. Or maybe there's a baby on the way, or step- or half-siblings may be changing their pattern of being in that home.

Insight
Children are more likely to act out their anger, pain or confusion than to state it. Bad behaviour is always about bad feelings.

Whatever, changes in the other family are not something that happen in isolation from you. Because the child lives with a foot in both camps, they are intimately affected by changes in both, and bring their reaction to such events from one to the other. A child who seems balanced and quiet and well-behaved may be playing merry hell elsewhere. If the other family come to you saying the child is acting up, it may be worth honestly examining what is happening in your life and your family that might be driving them to act out distress or anger or pain in another arena.

Children may have managed to forge a good relationship in one home. Difficulties with the matching relationship in the other may rebound back, affecting the one that has so far seemed to be positive. Remember the psychoanalyst Freud's description of couple dynamics – that in any bedroom there are always six, not two people; you, your partner and both sets of parents sitting in your minds making judgements and tut-tutting! In any stepfamily the extra four are joined not only by any children you have between you and those you bring to the relationship but also by each ex, their parents, their children, the cat and the hamster. It's a crowded situation and it's as if you're all balanced together on a see-saw. If one person moves, everyone's balance is affected. You may be able to manage this when it's happening with people in your own home who you see every day. But when it's people you see every so often or not at all, you need to be quick and light on your feet to keep from falling off.

THINGS TO REMEMBER

▶ *You are only a partner for as long as a relationship lasts, but you're a parent (and can be a step-parent) for ever. Children occupy a full-time place in your life, even if they cannot do so in your diary, for all time.*

▶ *All stepfamilies start with unfinished business and baggage, and with parents and children having different views. What is a beginning and a joy for the adults is an ending and a loss for the children. Adults need to make the effort to understand and accept the child's feelings otherwise the stepfamily or any new relationship will suffer.*

▶ *What most children need from a step-parent is for them to be an addition – a significant other rather than a replacement Dad or Mum.*

▶ *Don't expect instant results or acceptance. Take your time, keep trying and don't take things personally if children are argumentative or uncooperative. It's not about the step-parent, it's about the fact that their parents now live apart and that some of their old life is gone forever.*

▶ *Communication is the key to everything in a stepfamily. This doesn't just mean talking, it means listening too. Respectful, concerned and concentrated listening helps the other person to listen to and hear you. In turn this can lead to negotiation and compromise – the solutions to so many stepfamily problems.*

▶ *Building a stepchild/step-parent relationship is not an instant thing. Patience, acceptance of the child for who or what they are and spending as much time as possible with them will help as will having realistic expectations. There is no such thing as a perfect parent or step-parent. What you aim for is being 'good enough'.*

IDEAS TO TRY

▶ *Consider how often you see the children in your stepfamily. Daily, weekly, twice a year? Do they live with you or stay with you? Ask yourself if you consider your house their home, whatever the frequency of contact? Would the children agree with that?*

▶ *Is contact too much, not enough, too little for you? Your partner? The children? The other parent? Sit down and write out your preferred plan of contact. Ask your partner, the other parent and the children to do the same. Is there consensus? Can you all agree on a schedule that achieves some if not all of what everyone would prefer?*

▶ *What activities and interests do step-parent and stepchild have in common, or might enjoy together? Can adult and child(ren) come up with a list of things they could do together, time they could share?*

▶ *Think about issues you'd like another chance at getting right – revisiting relationships between parent and child you might like to do better from your own childhood or past life? How might you do that now, in your own family or stepfamily?*

▶ *Practise the communication skills outlined in this chapter, at first with your partner and then with any children involved. Confront problems not people, accept you can't help what you feel but can help what you do about your feelings, make it honest and personal and use active listening. Have an AIM.*

▶ *Spend time with the children in your stepfamily.*

▶ *Listen to messages, but don't take anything personally!*

5

Emotions

In this chapter you will learn:

- *how to understand the complex and mixed emotions in a stepfamily*
- *why we think some emotions are 'good' and some 'bad'*
- *what to do about bad behaviour and bad feelings*
- *how to manage emotions and behaviour.*

When anyone sets up a first-time family – a family where neither of you have been married before – the overwhelming emotions in everyone involved are likely to be joy, hope and eager expectation. Whether the couple is at the stage of deciding to live together or marry, or when a child is on the way or has just made its entrance, each person is probably going to be celebrating and feeling optimistic. Of course, there may be some dissenting voices; a disgruntled old flame, a worried or controlling parent, friends who disagree with the choice of partner. Nobody starts a relationship or a family with an entirely clean sheet. Baggage from your childhood and unfinished business from your past may well be hovering over you, affecting your choice of partner and your ability to make and keep good relationships. But on the whole, everyone is of a similar mindset and looking forward.

When you and your partner embarked on your relationship, you may have assumed that the above rules apply. Especially if you are an adult without children, you may be focusing on your own emotions of uncomplicated anticipation and assuming everyone else feels the same. Even if you have children of your own, you may suppose this is a new beginning for everyone and one that they will welcome.

But if first-time families are at risk from unfinished business and baggage, that's absolutely nothing compared with the complications almost certainly simmering under the surface when a stepfamily gets under way. Recognizing this may be tricky. After all, if the children have their primary home elsewhere and visit but do not live with you, you may feel that what their parent and you decide may be central to your lives but not to theirs. If they are to live with you, you still may assume that what is good for you will be good for them.

It may be. But don't assume they will welcome it, like it or accept it. What makes it complicated is not their objective understanding and acceptance of the situation but their emotions. The one thing always to remember about emotions is that we simply can't, ever, help what we are feeling. We have control over our actions. We don't have control over what we feel.

What they may be feeling: the new step-parent

The new step-parent may be seeing this as a joyful beginning. If they don't have children of their own, they may simply be focusing on the couple relationship. If the new step-parent is thinking of the kids, they may assume the children will be looking forward to having a new parent, and hoping they'll be good in the role. Or, they may be assuming they won't have much to do with them so it won't matter. If the new step-parent has children of their own, they may be hoping the children will accept the new partner as a step-parent and that all the children will get on. The new step-parent may be feeling nervous about this, recognizing that there are various viewpoints and needs to balance and that it might be complex.

A new step-parent may be struggling with anxieties about the place the ex-partner and children have in their new partner's life. They may feel jealous and resentful that the children were there before them and that the link with the children pulls their partner back to their former life and family. They may feel these ties could be a threat to their relationship and the family they want to establish. They may see the ex and the children as rivals, in competition not only for time and attention but also for love. If they have their own children, they may see their partner's children as a threat to their own, demanding not only the love and attention of their partner that they might want for themselves or their children, but also diverting their own love and attention from their own kids to their partner's.

Insight

You can't help what you feel – feeling jealous and in competition with stepchildren is entirely natural and normal. You can, however, help what you do about your emotions. As an adult, you need to deal sensibly and sensitively with the situation, not blame the child or yourself.

What they may be feeling: the parent

The parent may also be seeing this as a new beginning, and want to put the past behind them. But the one outstanding fact about a stepfamily is that while it is a beginning, it is also an ending. A stepfamily cannot exist unless something has finished. A relationship, or a person, has to have died for your stepfamily to be there. So the parent will be having to deal with emotions around what they have left behind as well as what they have before them. A death and the ending of a relationship brings grief. It can also create anger, guilt, resentment and feelings of failure. When a relationship ends, through death or separation, one way of dealing with it is to draw a line and move on – to leave it, and the emotions that went with it, behind. But when there are children from that relationship this simply isn't possible. Even if those children do not see the other parent, a child's very existence is still a daily reminder they were there. And in most cases, the other parent is still there, in regular contact. So all the emotions around the break-up may

continue to be played out between the ex-partners, and to affect
any new relationship.

What they may be feeling: the child

But it is the children's emotions that are really the most important,
simply because they are likely to be the most complicated and also
the ones that can derail the best intentions. Children may seem quiet
or remote from what is going on during the end of one relationship
and the setting up of a new stepfamily. They may seem to go along
with what adults want and decide, even to throw themselves into
plans and changes. But the reality is that however young they may
be, they will have their own feelings and reactions and these may be
very different to those of their parents and step-parents.

YOUR NEW BEGINNING IS THEIR END

Children may have had to watch their parents argue before a
separation and may well feel relief that it is over. But if they had
had the choice, children will always prefer the arguments to go
away and the family to stay together. They may nurse, for years,
a fantasy of their parents getting back together. The presence of a
step-parent, the existence of this new family, is the final nail in the
coffin for those dreams.

That is the key to the difference between how adults feel about a
new stepfamily and how children feel. Even if they like the new
step-parent, even if the end of the old family is a relief as it means
no more arguments and conflict, a new stepfamily is a beginning
to you and an ending to them. However much it may open up
their lives, it still closes down something that was there from the
moment they could understand. The adult can remember what it
was like before the other parent came long, and so can imagine
what it will be like to live without them, and with someone else.
Children cannot remember or even conceive of life before their

parents were there, and so find it hard accepting life without them. And however much you may be promising them that both parents love them and will continue to be there for them, the beginning of a stepfamily feels like a final separation. As, indeed, in some families it is.

The end of a relationship for adults can come out of the blue, or it can be the culmination of some period of dissatisfaction and misery. An adult may see it as the worst thing to ever happen to them, or a solution to a nagging problem. Whether you or your partner (or you and your partner) were the ones left or leaving, you will feel a mix of the same emotions – rage, pain, humiliation, crushed pride and failure. There are many reasons why you may find it hard to move on from this, but most adults eventually do so. Children find it far harder. A new partner may enable the adult to bridge from loving and relying on their ex, to loving and relying on the new partner. You may expect children to do the same – to learn to rely on the step-parent to fill that gap. But that's not how it works. You can divorce or separate from a partner; you can't completely excise a parent.

Insight

An adult can replace one partner with another. You cannot do the same with a parent. When people try to do so, it tends to result in profound hurt for both the child and the adult.

From the postbag

My ex is the most selfish, immature man possible. I finally gave up on him and divorced him and I did hope he might grow up and treat his children right but he shows no signs of doing it. He's late on visits and often cancels or changes the arrangements. My new husband is a total contrast – loving, caring, totally reliable. So why on earth does my

(Contd)

son refuse to accept him? He idolizes his father and it is like having an enemy soldier in the camp – he spends the whole time battling with my husband, who's just bewildered by it all. He tries so hard and my son just throws it in his face.

The contrast may be what baffles your son so much. Children love their parents, come what may. But they can also be angry with them. The problem for your son is that expressing the anger he might have for his father is very risky. The man has shown graphically what he does when things get uncomfortable – he leaves and avoids coming back. So your son's negative feelings have to go somewhere and it sounds as if some of it doubles back on himself – he sounds both depressed and lacking in self-worth – and the rest is dumped on his stepfather. The best strategy is twofold. One would be to tell your ex that his behaviour, while understandable in that he's avoiding pain and loss himself, is severely harming his son. If he needs help he should get it, but since he's the adult he should pull his socks up, stop only thinking of himself and think of the effect he is having on his boy. The other strategy is to focus on your son's behaviour as a way of expressing needs. He needs love, attention, affirmation. Give it to him, from both of you. Acknowledge, openly, how painful it must seem to him that his father lives away from him, how much he must miss him and how disappointed he must be when his father doesn't see him as much as he'd like. Be positive and don't criticize his father – your son is his representative and it may be that it's criticism he has overheard that makes him take such a stand on his father's behalf. Good luck!

WHY CHILDREN MAY BLAME THEMSELVES

Children may well have raging feelings of anger, anxiety and self-blame over what happened to their family. You may understand that the quarrel was between the adults and not to do with the children; children assume it is all about them. They often blame themselves, believing if they had been better behaved or more obedient, the family wouldn't have broken down. The anger and guilt they feel for themselves is often directed outwards, towards the person they feel best able to hate – the step-parent. They can hate the step-parent because they perceive this newcomer as disposable, and not their responsibility. They may be hampered at letting loose to their own parents out of an anxiety that the force of their emotions could be devastating. Some kids find it frightening to show their feelings to the parent they live with, in case they 'up and leave' as did the non-resident parent. Some find it hard to show anger or pain to the non-resident parent, in case they go one step further than leaving by cutting off all contact. But, if letting fly at the step-parent actually achieves those results, it may be seen as a positive result.

They may fear that if they accept or love a step-parent, it may disappoint or even harm the other parent or damage the relationship they have together.

Insight

Showing anger or resentment at the newcomer may become a test of loyalty, a way of showing solidarity with the other parent, even if this is not what the parent wants at all.

Essential points to consider

▶ *Every stepfamily is a new beginning for the adults but an ending for the child.*

▶ *Stepfamilies always have unfinished business and baggage left over from the end of the previous family.*

▶ *Step-parents may be jealous and resentful of a stepchild because they remind them of their partner's ex.*

▶ *Children often think the failure of their parent's relationship was their fault and that they weren't good or lovable enough to keep it together.*

Are there 'good' and 'bad' emotions?

Children often do take out their understandable grief and pain on the people they love. But they often find it hard to express these feelings clearly. For a start, they may not be able to recognize what they are experiencing.

We tend, in this society, to divide emotion into good and bad. Good emotions are feelings such as love, happiness, excitement, gladness, calm, cheerfulness, pleasure. Bad emotions are anger, jealousy, resentment, depression, rejection. When we feel the former, we know not only that we feel good but also that other people are going to approve of our emotions. But when we feel the latter we not only feel terrible, we also suffer the burden of knowing other people are likely to disapprove and even look down on us for experiencing them. It's often very hard for us to put such emotions into words, to know that it's anger or jealousy or the fear of rejection or abandonment that is driving us, because our guilt at feeling like this can obscure the real feelings. So not only may children be feeling differently from the adults, they may be finding it very hard to put those feelings into words, and parents and step-parents may be finding it hard to see or accept that the children do feel differently and what they feel.

When children are struggling to understand and manage powerful emotions such as anger, grief, resentment and pain what often happens is that they act them out. They aren't able to say 'Oh, I say, mother and father, stepmother and stepfather, I'm feeling really angry and upset about all this.' Instead, they 'kick off'. They pick arguments over silly things, such as being given a food they don't like or one person in the family being allowed to watch a TV show or allowed some privilege when they weren't there. Doors will be slammed and voices raised. Or they may embark on a slow war of attrition, never doing what you ask, talking back, nitpicking at every opportunity.

If they're behaving badly, are they bad children?

Bad behaviour is never about being bad. It's about feeling bad. Behaviour is a way of showing emotions, of asking for needs to be met. Children have the same needs as we do – for love, security, approval. What can happen in a stepfamily is that some of those needs become buried. In the rush of having our own wishes fulfilled, adults can assume children are being pleased as well. Or, we take our eye off the ball and forget about them. Rather than remind us in words, they remind us in actions.

It may not be very hard to find the source. It may be a new home, a new school, a new member of the family, especially if the child had expressed concern or opposition before. But sometimes you have to dig a bit and be imaginative. Children often react late. They may appear to weather the event itself, even to be in approval. But later, doubts may arise. Or, a small event will bring home feelings and memories of something they may not yet have been able to process. Most people can go through difficult situations on automatic pilot, numb or in denial about their emotions, but children may continue to put on a cloak of indifference for some time. Only when the second, or third, hammer falls do they react, not only to that event but also to the ones preceding it. So, a child who has seemingly accepted a family break-up and a new person coming into their lives will only go off the rails when that person moves in, or when the situation is formalized with a marriage or when a baby comes along or when other children from the step-parent's family begin to visit. Or, indeed, when something else such as an argument with or the loss of a friend or other member of the family, it can become the proverbial straw on the camel's back.

Insight

When a 'good' child suddenly, or gradually, starts behaving badly, always ask yourself 'What happened?' A recent change in their life – or the recall of one years previously – is likely to be the trigger.

Case study: Clare

Clare had been a model student until Year 10 when all of a sudden she had a string of detentions for talking in class and ended up on report, having to carry around a booklet to be signed after every lesson by the teacher. Her mother, Kate, was in despair because Clare simply couldn't explain why she had suddenly lost it, playing around in class rather than concentrating on the work she had done so well until that point. Her tutor finally suggested she take the opportunity to talk things through with the school counsellor, but Clare was reluctant until Kate burst into tears and said she couldn't cope with what was going on. The counsellor waited patiently through several sessions of Clare being either silent or insisting nothing was wrong before she finally began to talk about what she felt about several unrelated issues that bothered her. Her mother had recently married Clare's stepfather – a man she was very fond of, so she saw no problem there. But it also emerged that her grandfather and grandmother had died in the last year. Clare's mother was still mourning her mother, but she and her new husband had rather passed over Clare's grandfather's death since they didn't have much to do with him. But Clare did, and he was the last link with her father, who had died when she was eight. To cap it all, two months previously the family dog had gone missing. Once the picture was put together, the counsellor suggested that Clare's behaviour was an understandable reaction to grief and loss. Not so much one particular loss but the accumulation – her father, two grandparents, her dog – and all of them highlighted by an event she actually welcomed, the marriage of her mother and stepfather. Once the school, her family and Clare herself realized what was going on, her behaviour improved. All she had needed was to have her losses acknowledged properly.

How to manage bad behaviour

Whenever a child starts behaving in ways that displease or worry, there are two questions to ask:

- ▶ *What has recently happened or changed that this child may not be happy with?*
- ▶ *What might this behaviour be trying to say?*

Bad behaviour is a way of making a point. However trying or upsetting it might be, the best tactic is, whenever there are arguments or there is tension, to ask yourself what this is really about. A row over 'Who moved my books?' may really be over 'Why has my family changed?'

Hard as it might be, the best way to deal with it is:

- ▶ *not to take it personally, even when it seems targeted at you*
- ▶ *not to get drawn into arguments or slanging matches, no matter how tempting it may seem*
- ▶ *be sensitive to changes in behaviour or mood and deal with them when they arise*
- ▶ *dive down under the behaviour to try to identify the real reason for it*
- ▶ *take a few steps back, recognize that unresolved emotions may lead to outbursts and plan to head them off before they happen.*

Young people in stepfamilies are bound to be feeling fragile and vulnerable. It helps to be positive and reassuring. Parents and step-parents can:

- ▶ *be calm and confident*
- ▶ *be sympathetic and understanding*
- ▶ *be firm about behaviour but flexible about what causes the behaviour*
- ▶ *be willing to listen and hear*
- ▶ *be willing to negotiate and compromise.*

How step-parents cope with hostility is key to how you may later get on. If you are willing to make allowances for how children may feel, by saying things like 'I can see this must be upsetting for you.../I understand you must be missing.../It feels like you're angry...' but not compromise on drawing boundaries, 'But that doesn't mean we shouldn't be polite to one another.../Please don't slam doors.../We don't swear in this house...' the mutual respect this displays will sooner or later pay off.

Insight

Deal with bad behaviour by addressing the cause. Bad behaviour is a symptom – of loss, pain, anger – and best resolved by managing the reason rather than the result.

Essential points to consider

▶ *Children often 'act out' their bad feelings.*
▶ *Bad behaviour is a way of showing how unhappy, angry or confused they are.*
▶ *Since bad behaviour is a way of trying to get needs met, understanding the underlying need is the first step to managing the behaviour.*
▶ *When a child behaves badly, ask yourself what has happened or changed recently and what the behaviour may be trying to say.*

Should you ask for help outside the family?

When you are trying to establish a new family you may feel it's desirable, and shows both resolve and competence, if you manage everything yourself. So, you may feel inclined to rely on your own emotional resources. However, far from demonstrating your expertise, refusing to ask for or accept support can lead to everyone in your immediate family being thrown back to their own devices and struggling. There is no shame in using all the help you can get. Children particularly may benefit from knowing they can go elsewhere – to their friends, relatives such as grandparents, to teachers they trust or other professionals such as counsellors. It is a difficult situation – there is no point pretending otherwise. And anyone in this situation may need help. So it does not show disloyalty, incapability or indecisiveness to lean on other people for guidance and encouragement. Friends who might have been through similar experiences are often enormously supportive of young people – the more you can help them feel they can go elsewhere, the better. In the Taking it further section at the back of this book you will find addresses of organizations that can help you or the children.

The key is to understand the following:

- ▶ *Everyone will have their emotional reactions to the changes in this family.*
- ▶ *Adults and children may have very different reactions.*
- ▶ *Feelings are powerful but no feeling is 'bad'.*
- ▶ *You can't help what you feel but you can help what you do about it.*
- ▶ *It shows maturity and self-confidence to ask for help.*

THINGS TO REMEMBER

▶ *There will always be unfinished business or baggage even when starting a first-time-for-both relationship. There will be even more when it's a case of second time around and it is likely to be more complicated.*

▶ *Don't assume that any children involved will necessarily like or even accept the new situation. They may not have the ability to be 'adult' and objective but they do have adult-sized emotions. They may see no reason and no incentive to accept what you feel is desirable or right.*

▶ *No one can control what they feel, but everyone can control what they do about it.*

▶ *Your new beginning with your stepfamily may be seen as an ending by the children involved. The arrival of a step-parent and the existence of the new family can put an end to any dreams they may have about their life going back to the way it was before.*

▶ *Children can think the break-up of their parents was their fault and take out their pain and guilt on the people they love. They seldom express these feelings clearly and often cannot recognize what they are experiencing.*

▶ *Bad behaviour is a way of expressing bad feelings.*

IDEAS TO TRY

▶ Ideas-storm, with your partner or a friend, all the emotions you might have felt when your new family began and those you're feeling now, and talk them over.

▶ Ideas-storm, with your partner or a friend, the emotions you think the children might feel or have felt when your new family began, as well as their feelings at present. Talk them over.

▶ Talk to the children about these emotions you all might have had or are experiencing now. Acknowledge they almost certainly would be different and discuss why.

▶ Ideas-storm emotions – negative and positive – with adults and children in your family and discuss whether there are 'good' and 'bad' emotions. Discuss what to do about them.

▶ Look at all the examples you can recall of the children's 'bad' behaviour. For each instance, see if you can work out what had recently happened or changed that the child might not be happy about and what the behaviour might have been trying to say.

6

Chores, rules, traditions

In this chapter you will learn:
- *why traditions can be difficult to manage in a stepfamily*
- *how to plan family events*
- *how to manage day-to-day living, chores and rules*
- *about control and responsibility within the family.*

All families have a variety of rules and traditions. In some, there is an insistence on 'shoes off at the door', in others homework has to be done before the evening meal, and in yet more there are penalties for swearing or fighting. Some families mark gift-giving celebrations such as Christmas, Eid, Hanukkah, Diwali, New Year or birthdays with a flurry of present opening first thing in the morning, others ration them out over the day. In one way, stepfamilies are no different. But there are two ways that issues such as chores, rules, traditions and festivals can be difficult for stepfamilies – far more difficult than for first-time families.

One is that stepfamilies have some events that simply don't happen in first-time families. First-time families don't have to contend with contact visits and all the planning and negotiation that go around them, especially at key times in the year such as birthdays and family festivals. First-time families don't have to struggle with some unofficial anniversaries – anniversaries that cause pain rather than happiness such as the last time your original family was together, the day you knew your parents were never going to get together again, the last time you saw a relative who now is not in touch.

The other is that in stepfamilies, adults and children have to cope with change in routines, both when a new family is established and each time children travel from one household to another. For your stepfamily to thrive, you need to recognize the significance of such changes and how they can affect you all, and how you might manage them to best effect.

Why traditions can cause problems

Traditions can be a flashpoint for children in a stepfamily. There are two types of traditions: public and private. That you celebrate a festival such as Christmas, Eid, Hanukkah or New Year – and, indeed, people's birthdays – may be considered public. They are public holidays and everyone in your immediate circle probably enjoys and takes them for granted. Clearly it might cause offence and confusion, and feelings of being cheated, if children suddenly find themselves in a family that either doesn't celebrate the festivals they're used to, or celebrates others.

But more important are the ways we privately enjoy such events. One family may take it for granted that presents are opened at a certain time, with such-and-such ceremony; another may have entirely different expectations. One family may set the table a certain way and offer particular foods, in particular order, for each event. Another may offer different foods in a different order, or be casual and *laissez faire* about the whole thing. One family may have certain games or activities associated with certain days – Easter egg hunts, spin the dreidel – and others may not. What matters is how you all view such changes and how you manage them.

Insight
Family celebrations can be the time when children most acutely feel the loss of their original family.

Logically, you might expect children to enjoy having a family celebration at two or more separate places and times. If a child has Christmas or Hanukkah or Eid, Easter or Passover at several homes they get to enjoy the food and the jollifications twice and probably get more presents and treats too. And that's the way some adults would see it, but emotions aren't logical. Several celebrations underlines the fact that their family is different. It emphasizes the fact that sometime in the past the family was one shape and now it is another. Dad lives in one place, Mum lives in another and they don't have the opportunity to share this family time with their original unit. Far from being an advantage, separate celebrations can be seen as a source of hurt and embarrassment, and children may act up not only at the time but also for a period before and after. Children being unable to see the other parent and family, for whatever reason, far from solving the problem, only intensifies it.

Why you need to plan ahead for special events

For the adults concerned, managing the logistics for separate festivals or holiday periods can be a nightmare. You may view it as work, and damn hard work at that, trying to agree and then coordinate arrangements, liaise over travel arrangements and dovetail commitments. You may be juggling your own or your partner's desire for children to be with you, with not only the other family but several sets of grandparents and wider family too. Children may throw in their own requests, to see friends or attend events, which also have to be taken into account. Travel may not only be exhausting and time-consuming but expensive and hard to synchronize.

One of the first and basic arrangements that needs to be sorted out in a stepfamily is how and when, and how often and where, children will be spending time with both their parents and their family. It's a basic issue, but one with many different strands that need sorting (see Chapter 3). Once you have the rights issue sorted (that children have a right to see both parents and a right to have free access and a say in contact) and have sorted out the rules issue (again, more in Chapter 3), the issue of special events and family celebrations is bound to follow.

So what do you do about Christmas or Hanukkah or Eid, Easter or Passover and birthdays? How do you manage school holidays? There are several options:

▶ *Leave it till the last moment and see who is free – or who demands loudest, or has 'possession'.*
▶ *Having set up your timetable of contact – every weekend and Wednesdays, or every other weekend and three days midweek on alternate weeks, or an alternate week in each household, or whatever – let the child spend the special event with whatever family they're supposed to be with when that event happens to fall.*
▶ *Plan a timetable of contact but set aside events and make special plans for them.*

Simply because it's often hard to grasp the nettle and make plans, the first option is often the one we find ourselves lumbered with, by default. Needless to say, it's the least desirable. If that's where you are at the moment, with an event coming up fast, make emergency plans *now*. Take the suggestions I make below but do them just for the immediate event, for the present. But in the long run it may be best to put longer-term arrangements into place.

If you opt for the second point above, you may find over a period of time children do end up spending the same number of special events with each family. But this isn't guaranteed and it may cause grief and bad feeling if it turns out, for instance, that the special spring festival – the one that tends to move around in the year – is with one family two or more years running. You may want to consider making specific plans.

The third option seems to work best. It is, however, often hard work to put in place as it involves long-term planning and discussions with everyone – children, partners, ex-partners and even wider family members. You may need to take on board wishes and feelings you simply don't want to hear. You may need not only to negotiate but also to compromise – and we don't always wish to do that. And, of course, you can't be spontaneous and if you're someone who prizes spontaneity that may be hard.

But the carrot that goes with this stick is that more work now means far, far less work later. When everyone has been consulted and their needs and wishes taken into account, arrangements tend to go more smoothly.

Insight
When people have had input and 'buy in' to an agreement, they have an incentive to keep it.

From the postbag

I have such a complicated family. Two children by my previous marriage and two with my husband. We tend to get on well but the problem is always Christmas and Easter and birthdays and anything when their father or his parents want to see the kids and so does my Mum. And so does my husband's parents. Oh – and I almost forgot – my husband has a son too so he wants to see him and then there's his ex and her parents. So we have so many sets of grandparents wanting to see all or some of the kids it just makes my head spin. We seem to lurch from year to year – I can't remember a Boxing Day that wasn't spent on some motorway somewhere. Any time one of those dates comes up I just want to scream. I can't cope!

The only way you're going to bring some sort of order to this and get back to enjoying these days is to get organized. What seems to be happening is you're trying to please everyone else, and forgetting you have needs and deserve to have something for yourself too. The result is actually nobody gets what they want because you're rushing about, frazzled and stressed. Take a deep breath, calm down and sit down with your family. Write down a list of everyone you think wants to see who, when and where. Then talk through it with your family – your four children and your husband – what you all want. If there are any 'duty' visits – visits you think you should do but nobody enjoys – ditch them. You have too much to do to service any demands that don't please you too. Then, draw up a list of the festivals and events in the next year and apportion them out. Take travel and distance into consideration. It might be far better to see people who live some way away over an Easter or Summer break than dash there for one day at Christmas. Offer a long chat on the phone or via webcam on the day to keep contact. Then, liaise with the other families to make sure they understand your concerns and the competing demands. Once people know the situation, they tend to be helpful. Good luck!

How to make plans for family festivals

Sit down with your immediate family and ideas-storm what each person would like for the special events over the next year. You need to look at the whole picture because you may be able to 'trade off' certain events with others, i.e. 'Yes of course you can spend *that* time with them. We'd like to spend *this* time with you – can we agree to make that a fair swap?'

Remember to take the following into account:

▶ *Your partner and you need and desire to spend time with the children, sometimes in the company of other relatives such as grandparents.*
▶ *Children need and desire to spend time with not only your partner and you but also their other parent.*

- *Children need and desire to spend time with their grandparents and other relatives (from both sides).*
- *Grandparents (from both sides) need and desire to spend time with the children.*
- *The other parent needs and desires to spend time with the children, sometimes in the company of other relatives such as grandparents.*

Everyone wants their share and this can take effort, time and expense to arrange. And sometimes, it takes time, effort and indeed expense to cope with the fact that family celebrations can become uncomfortable if certain relatives are antagonistic or simply unwelcoming, not accepting that new people are part of the family.

Balance it all up with the practicalities – finances, travel expenses, planning and coordination. Do so with the intention of looking for solutions so that visits can go ahead, not excuses to put barriers in the way.

Listen to what children are saying and pay attention to their reactions. Sometimes children say they 'don't care' when they care very much but are afraid of being let down or rejected. They may refuse to see the other family more out of anxiety or because certain issues haven't been addressed than because they really don't want contact. Sometimes, they have a right to object if someone in the mix is making a visit difficult or unpleasant. It may be necessary to address the emotions and what is really going on and look for solutions to that as well as discussing the practicalities. Children shouldn't have to endure bullying or exclusion, and the other parent or other family members may need to have behaviour challenged if visits are to go ahead.

On the same level, listen to your own and your partner's objections or insistences. Don't forget that children from a previous relationship are the painful proof of a former love. When there is only weekend or the odd weekday access, the kids may be seen as an optional extra to one partner's life, which can be tolerated. Once the children become part of festival and holiday planning, it becomes far more intrusive and far more real and final. There can be arguments over money, whether over presents or travel or living expenses when you go away. Whatever the apparent topic, the arguments aren't really about the cash, they're about the need to make room in your life for other people who are also loved and important to you or your partner.

How to come to a consensus

Insight

Of course you may like the plans to go entirely your way and suit you. Just remember, the more your arrangements have consensus and have everyone involved on board, the more likely they are to go through with everyone adhering and no one making last-minute and inconvenient changes.

When your family unit has some ideas of what you'd all like, communicate with the other family (or families). Explain what you've done, suggest they do the same among themselves and get back to you for a joint planning session. You could suggest a face-to-face talk – with a mediator if that would smooth things over – using all your notes. Alternatively, do it by mail or letter, or by phone when both parties have the notes in front of them. And be prepared to be flexible. That doesn't mean being at the beck and call of one or two people's whims; it means being prepared to change plans if necessary, with the understanding that it goes two ways.

Essential points to consider

▶ *Family festivals can upset children because they are reminded of their original family.*

▶ *Family festivals can be a nightmare to arrange in a stepfamily with competing demands for the children.*

▶ *To plan a family event you may need to balance everyone's needs and wishes as well as the practical issues of time and money.*

▶ *The more you have consensus on the arrangements, the more smoothly they will proceed.*

How to arrange summer holidays

Summer holidays are often the most contentious, especially if there are several children at different stages in a family and even more if there are several sets of stepsiblings. Having two families able to take children on holiday or have them for a period during the summer break may seem desirable and the answer to the problem with providing childcare during school holidays. But if one set of children have one home to go to, and stepsiblings or half-siblings have two, or if stepsiblings both have different homes to go to which have different timetables or contact patterns, conflict can soon blow up. You may find one child saying 'I only have one lousy visit to Spain and you get to go to Florida too!' The real complaint, however, may be 'You have another parent who wants to see you and I don't.'

Different children may find special affinity with members of one of their families. A holiday that is built around their tastes may bore or scare another child who can feel left out. In any family, that can happen and lead to accusations of favouritism. But the additional problem in a stepfamily is that the child may rightfully feel their few precious moments with a parent were hijacked and spoilt. Adults may need to be sensitive to the moods of children, and be prepared to tease out and discuss issues affecting them and make particular efforts to be fair and equal. But fair and equal may not be the same as spending the same amount of money or even the same amount of time. What matters is that children have their say and get what they need, at that time and stage in their lives.

WORKING OUT WHAT IS FAIR AND EQUAL

So it's vital to work out with the children concerned what they might see as 'fair and equal'. Adults and older children may be aware of the price tags attached, and feel hard done by if one child has twice as much spent on them than another. Young children tend to assess gifts by the yard, or by how popular a brand or object is among their friends. So when a five-year-old gets a mound of inexpensive presents for Christmas but his 12-year-old stepsister gets two or three expensive gifts, rather than recognize the same amount has scrupulously been spent she may well feel slighted. Other children may not mind about the money – a well-chosen and precisely targeted gift or treat may make up for any other deficiencies. But assessments are likely to be made. Children in any family may be sensitive to whether there is favouritism. Children in stepfamilies may be especially susceptible to what they interpret as a slight and rebuff.

Breaking the cycle of family festival rituals and sorting difficulties

As well as planning the where and the when of family celebrations such as Christmas, Eid, Hanukkah and others, you also need to pay especial attention to the little traditions you take for granted that go to make up such a time. A new family may seem like the perfect time for adults to review how you manage certain routines. Each family has their own way of marking special days, with presents at certain times in the day, particular decorations that come out year after year, specific rituals revolving around food and drink or games and activities. Two adults merging their lives may mix and match the traditions from their own families of origin and come up with a hybrid that suits them both and fits their tastes and lifestyle. Two adults merging their lives when one or both of them have children from a previous relationship may think they can do the same: 'My family always had their main meal at one – yours had theirs at six? Yours sounds a much better idea – let's do it!' But trying to impose that on children can lead to difficulties.

Special events are the time when everyone concerned may be remembering previous occasions. All families play 'Remember when...?' on such occasions. For stepfamilies, this can be painful because this Christmas, Eid, Hanukkah emphasizes that sometime in the near or distant past, things were different. Clinging to old traditions, to the ways things were done before the family split up or before the new adult came on the scene, can come to represent, to children, a way of keeping a link to the past. Letting go and accepting change can feel like abandoning and rejecting not only the past and all that was good about it but also the other parent.

> **Insight**
> With so much changing in their lives, keeping family traditions may seem to children a last desperate attempt at holding back the tide.

Special treats that a step-parent may offer may be rejected, not in fact because the person is being rejected or even because the treat is being turned down, but because accepting it and enjoying it would mean accepting that this situation is here to stay. The new regime will have taken over and if you cooperate, you'll have given up on those dreams and fantasies of your parents getting back together again that all children have. Children may dig in their heels and resist against all blandishments, even when it's clear that the new idea may be preferable. They're not defending a ritual, they are defending what it represents – their old family, right or wrong.

MAKING FAMILY DISCUSSIONS WORK FOR YOU AND YOUR FAMILY

One good way of breaking the cycle and sorting the difficulties around managing family events is using family discussions to find out what people want and how they can have it. Look back at Chapter 1 for details on conducting round-table discussions and ideas-storming sessions.

We sometimes use family discussions as a way of telling children what we have decided to do. They're a good way of getting everyone together and being clear about what the adults have determined. But family discussions can be even more effective – and fun – if they become a time and place where everyone has a say. Where, in effect, you work together rather than have adults simply lay down the law.

If young people are given as much space and respect to have their say as adults, the result may be that they get some of what they want and you get less of what you would choose. But when young people have an input into decision making and are heard, they usually 'buy in' to what has been decided, being far more cooperative than when a situation is imposed. In the long run that means less work and more fun. A family parliament is an ideal way, not just of making agreements that stick and keeping in touch, but also of pulling everyone together. In a separated family, it really helps to make time and space for family discussions regularly. You can do it with the family members that live together. But it also helps to make room for those that have contact but may not live together full time.

Use a family discussion to hear what everyone feels is important to them about the family events that are coming up. Listen to the emotions about little things and big things. Get everyone to ideasstorm on what they feel is really important, and not so important, about the upcoming event. Ask everyone to input:

- *What I really like about (Christmas) is…*
- *What I really want to keep is…*
- *What I'd hate to lose is…*
- *What I don't like is…*
- *What I don't mind is…*

Encourage everyone to be inclusive and extensive about their lists, down to what they like or dislike for breakfast at such times. It's all those little routines and traditions that actually are the 'deal breakers' – the things that they may not realize are so important and make them either feel safe or exposed when these events come around. What you're then looking for is to broker a deal that gives everyone some of their favourites.

Children may want to ask that as little as possible should change. They may fight to keep the little things the same, but even if you do try to recreate what they initially demand, it may not bring satisfaction. This is because the one big thing they may want to retain has already gone – their original family. Talking over what is and isn't possible is an opportunity to listen and accept their feelings about this, and reflect on it. Going through the lists with them is a chance to suggest that you cherry pick the best elements and dump some of the less good ones, and that you combine everyone's views to make something that is uniquely theirs and yours.

> **Insight**
> Help children accept change by recognizing their need to keep links with their past.

Are Mother's Day and Father's Day the most difficult family events?

Most events and anniversaries have the potential to upset, because they highlight the fact that your family exists on the foundation of another family's dissolution. Each time that particular event rolls round again, people may be thinking 'This time last year/ x years ago, Mum and Dad were still together.' Public holidays may be fairly obvious times of stress and tension and once you realize they can be sources of sadness as well as times of enjoyment, you will be able to manage them with sympathy and tact. Private anniversaries may be more difficult to spot since, unless you know about them and mark them in your diary, they may pass you by – such as anniversaries of the day something changed. The two days in the year with the potential to upset everyone in the equation are Mother's Day and Father's Day.

Parents set great store by these days. It's the one day in the year you could be guaranteed to receive a thanks from your children and hear that they love you and think you're doing a good job. In separated families, both days can be fraught. Parents may expect a card and be hurt if one is not forthcoming. Children may give cards to a parent their ex feels doesn't deserve it at all, causing anger and jealousy. The child might actually be doing it more as a way of asking for attention than as a recognition of a job well done, but the other parent may not see this. Children may give cards to a parent who has done well by them but who did a lousy job of being a partner – again, the result may be tension and upset on the part of the other parent. Children may not give a card to a parent who has struggled and strived to do their best in a difficult situation. The child may be hitting out at the situation, or delivering a sideswipe really felt towards the non-resident parent whom they dare not upset in case they withhold favours. Kids tend to blame the parent they feel most secure with rather than the one to whom they feel anger or resentment. Or they simply may forget to send a card because nobody has reminded them to do so. Children can be delightful and loving and caring, and still simply forget. Sometimes it needs a Dad or Mum on the spot to be managing the card, the breakfast on a tray, the little treat. If parents live apart and have no incentive to make the other look good, and there is no one there to take on that responsibility – or the step-parent doesn't realize they need to – the event may be passed by.

SHOULD WE HAVE A STEP-PARENT DAY?

But above all, while some children do, many will not see it as either necessary or appropriate to give a Mother's or Father's Day card to a step-parent, however well they are doing the job of parenting, however much they may be loved or however much they deserve it. Even if they are the only mother- or father-figure these children have in their lives. The reason may be twofold. One is that a step-parent isn't their Mum or Dad. Some stepchildren will give cards because it is expected and they know it will cause offence if they don't – but they wouldn't do it without pressure or urging. Or, they don't give a card because they know the parent whose place the step-parent has taken will be furious or hurt. So how can you manage Mother's and Father's Day in a stepfamily?

▶ *Make it the subject of a family discussion. Give children a chance to explore what they feel about it, explain your own emotions and what the other parent may be feeling.*
▶ *Give children the right to make their own decisions with no apparent or hidden pressure.*

- *Don't take it personally if they choose not to send you a card. It doesn't mean they don't appreciate you – just as sending you a card may not mean as much as you'd hope!*
- *Don't take offence if your children give their step-parent a card.*

Essential points to consider

- *What is 'fair and equal' in one person's eyes may not be so in another's. Make sure you hear what people really value, need and want.*
- *Children can insist on doing things the same way it's always been done, not because they actually like doing it that way but because of what it represents – a link to the past.*
- *Using family discussions may be the only way to get everyone to 'buy in' to the plans.*

Why are chores so important?

Nobody likes doing chores. Kids will complain about them, forget them, fight over whose turn it is and generally make it so difficult that, in many families, adults give up and do it themselves. It seems less work and a way of guaranteeing work gets done, and properly, with the least conflict. But doing chores is important in any family, and even more important in stepfamily.

Insight

Doing chores says 'This home is mine, this family is mine.'

Chores are a vital part of children's lives for these reasons:

- *Mum or stepmum isn't a slave or a servant, put on earth to look after everyone else. When children do chores, they have a respect for their parents and appreciate what it takes to keep a home running.*
- *When children and every adult pull their weight it means everyone can have some free time. Having an adult do it all*

means that one person is tired and sometimes resentful. Shared responsibility means more time for fun for all.

▶ *Delegating chores means sometimes things aren't done to your exacting standards. It's a valuable learning experience for everyone. Plenty of people bemoan not spending enough time with their family; nobody ever says on their deathbed that they wished they'd cleaned the house better.*

▶ *Sometime soon, children will leave to run their own homes. It comes as more of a shock, and can end in disaster, if they haven't acquired the skills to look after themselves, and a recognition of what it takes.*

But the most important reason for handing out a chore roster in a stepfamily is this: if you do chores, you live and belong there. It's your home. Stepchildren are frequently let off chores, for several reasons:

▶ *When children visit or when they spend some time away from your home you need to give them some leeway.*

▶ *Since they're not with you all the time it may be difficult to keep to a chores rota.*

▶ *If the other family doesn't ask them to do chores, they may feel resentful if you do.*

▶ *It would be too difficult – there's enough bad feeling to cope with as it is.*

However, if children are feeling rootless and confused by switching from home to home, then being treated like visitors, and privileged ones at that, only worsens the situation. Being handled with kid gloves underlines that this is a difficult and odd state of affairs, not like 'normal' life, and that they are guests in your home, not people who live there. However much they may complain or object, whatever arguments they put up against it, it would be of benefit to you all if you insisted that chores are done. Explain the reasoning behind the chores:

▶ *Everyone who lives in this house pulls their weight and does their chores.*

▶ *Since this is their home, they should do their share.*
▶ *Living somewhere brings privileges and duties. The privilege is having a say. The duty is mucking in and doing your bit.*

Of course, that does mean you have to hand out both privileges as well as duties, which is why family discussions are so important.

How to draw up a chore chart

Children need to do chores, even very young children and children who live with you part time, as a way of claiming their place and being involved. And adults should share the work equally too, even if they go out to work all day or one of you is a stay-at-home, full-time parent.

How should you draw up a chore chart? For it to be something that everyone 'buys in' to and agrees, it's best to make it a cooperative effort. But it does help for one person in the family to take responsibility for managing it and making it run. That doesn't have to be one of the adults; you can delegate this to a child, as a way of further enlisting their cooperation and sense of ownership. To forestall arguments you could rotate this, asking each child to take responsibility for a week or a month at a time.

Sit down, as at a family discussion, to agree the following:

▶ *What are the routine chores that you all concur need doing. These could be washing up or filling the dishwasher, loading the washing machine, laying tables, vacuuming the living room, etc.*
▶ *Decide which chores have to be done, come what may. Different families have different ideas of what's important, so come to your own agreement.*
▶ *Decide which chores are quick and easy, which are long and hard.*
▶ *Draw up a list of chores and assign them. You might like to give everyone a mixture of easy, medium and hard chores for each period. Or you might opt for each person having easy,*

*medium or hard weeks. You might opt for everyone having
their set chores from then on or rotating so everyone gets a
go at all of them, with some allowance for age, height and
weight. Whatever measure and scheme you decide, share
out chores equally. That's the essence of being in a family;
everyone pulls their weight and does their part.*

▶ *You might also want to agree on what might be 'extra' chores,
such as washing cars or mowing lawns, and negotiate whether
these can be done as paid-for chores. Some families may want
to tie chores into pocket money – you get it if you complete
your chores, or the amount you get is dependant on chores.
You may want to consider whether this introduces an element
of 'Shall I, shan't I?' into the equation. Children wouldn't be
very amused if Mum or Dad felt it was optional and depended
on how they felt that day as to whether they got their evening
meal or not. In the same light, whether or not you do your
chores should be approached as similarly non-negotiable.
Everyone does chores.*

Agree what you're going to do, and then draw up a written
agreement or contract setting it out. Ask everyone to sign the
contract: 'We, the undersigned, agree…'. Review the contract
regularly, and if it's not working go back to the table to discuss
why and what you'd like to do to make it work in future.

It may help to let the other family know what you are doing, to
forestall any arguments about 'We don't have to do this with Mum/
Dad'. If you're doing it and they don't, they may like to consider
instituting it too. Even if they don't, deal with objections very
simply: 'Your Mum/Dad has every right to run their home the way
they do and that's fine. But in this house, we all do our chores.'

Eating together

There are many apparently very good reasons why families no
longer eat all their meals sitting round a table together. In some
families, different schedules make it hard to get everyone in the

same place at the same time. Adults may come home from work too late for young children to be able to wait, some children may have clubs or after-school commitments. Many families have got into the habit of having mix-and-match meals that can be prepared plate by plate, as family members want them. Even when people do eat together it's often from plates or trays on their laps while watching television.

All families can actually benefit from making a point of regularly eating together around a table. It may mean extra effort and extra planning, it may even mean extra expense – but the benefits of sitting round a table and sharing food, and the drawbacks of not doing so, are so great it is something every family should reconsider. When it comes to stepfamilies however, a family meal is probably one of the issues that you should be making a top priority. Simply put, it's essential. Taking meals together:

- ▶ *promotes discussion. Facing each other with no other entertainment or distraction, people talk – and when you talk and listen you get to know each other.*
- ▶ *encourages inclusiveness. It promotes the feeling that you are a family unit.*
- ▶ *is a basic, ancient way of building bonds. When you 'break bread' together you lay aside hostility or reservations and get close.*

If this is not something you have already made a daily habit, bring it back and tell your family from now on, it will be the default – you'll only accept other arrangements when absolutely necessary.

Insight
Change timetables, amend working or study patterns, alter the times you will eat in order to bring everyone together round a table at least four times a week. Preferably, every night.

When you get together:

- ▶ *Ask everyone to contribute to the meal by laying places, preparing or cooking or taking something to the table.*

- ▶ *Help everyone to talk. Go round the table asking everyone to tell the family about something they did that day they enjoyed, something they were pleased and proud about, something they could have done better.*
- ▶ *Use mealtimes to discuss plans to spend time together – outings, nights in playing games, shared time on the computer.*
- ▶ *Don't harp on about table manners – at first. You can encourage chewing with mouths closed and holding cutlery properly once everyone has begun to enjoy having shared meals.*

Case study: Sasha, Tim, Joel and Naomi

When Tim came to live with Sasha and her son Joel and daughter Naomi, he found it really difficult to build a relationship with the children. They weren't antagonistic – their father was in regular contact and he supported Sasha having a new partner. But he just felt he and they continued to be strangers even after he had been there for almost a year. If he suggested they did something together – go to a film or a sporting event – they tended to make excuses. Sasha worked from home and Tim had recently begun a new job which meant he was often late home. It was only when they had a big meal together to celebrate Sasha's birthday, and had such a good time, that Tim realized they usually never ate together. The kids often had after-school clubs and would eat on the run before or after. Sasha might wait for him and they would share a meal, or eat with one of the children. So Tim rearranged his work patterns, negotiating being able to go in early and bring work home. He announced he would be home for an evening meal every night and would everyone please try to do the same. Sasha was delighted – she and Tim began preparing the food together and enjoyed doing so. Joel and Naomi said it was one of Tim's 'funny turns' and joked about it. But gradually Tim noticed they would appear in the kitchen around cooking time, and graduated from chatting during the preparation to helping too. They'd chat and laugh and soon Tim and the children were doing things together and they were treating him like one of the family instead of the lodger.

How spending time together can help a stepfamily

New friends tend to get to know each other by doing things together – going out, exploring each other's pursuits, interests and hobbies, learning each others tastes, likes and dislikes over activities, meals and cups of coffee. First-time families don't have to do that because they grow up with each other and bond and learn about each other over changed nappies, bedtime stories, bathtimes, games and simply being together. Stepfamilies often fall into a 'friends getting to know each other's pattern because they don't have the advantage of long, slow years to learn all about each other. Instead of two adults building their relationship followed by the arrival of first one then two or more children, you're straight into an instant family – and often, they're beyond the nappy-changing era. But feeling the need to be forever doing things can unbalance and destabilize your new relationship. In 'real' families, children can spend times with their friends, can go to their rooms and be alone, can visit other relatives, can simply chill out with other people in the house. If you want your family to come together, it's important to:

▶ *Take it slowly. It takes time for people to get to know each other – first-time families take years. Give all of you some time.*
▶ *Be relaxed. You don't have to be doing something for you to be building bonds. Chill out.*
▶ *Let go. You don't have to spend every minute together to be a family. Cut all of you some slack.*
▶ *Respect children's support systems. Their relationships with friends and other relatives doesn't take anything away from you. The more secure and supported they feel, the better able they are to bond with you. Step back.*
▶ *Build relationships. Make a point of having some sort of one-to-one contact each day with each child when they are with you – as simple as a chat about your day while washing up. Get to know each other.*
▶ *Build a family. Make a point of having some sort of family time at least once a week – a family games night, a family-chosen DVD when everyone is encouraged to heckle and join in. Get in touch.*

Insight

Children 'act up' to try to get some control in their lives, if only to have the power to refuse or to be out of control in their own time. Temper tantrums or bad behaviour are powerful expressions of loss and distress.

Should you give children more control?

One of the issues that particularly affects stepfamilies is that of control. Adults may be fighting each other for actual control – where children live, who is responsible for them, who pays what. They may be clashing and struggling over emotional control – who children believe, trust and listen to. Children, however, may feel spectacularly out of control. It isn't their choice for their original family to have split up and it frequently isn't their choice for a new one to be formed. They may pick a variety of ways to make a protest about this and to try to gain some say over their environment, their family and themselves. But one important way of heading off some problems is to make a point of giving them a measure of control from the beginning. For example:

▶ *Make them responsible for some aspects of the house. When children know chores are their responsibility they feel some measure of ownership in this house, which becomes a home. That doesn't mean make them skivvies – ask them to do their share along with everyone else living there.*

▶ *Make them responsible for themselves. As parents, we often run around after children long after they need it or benefit from it. A child constantly nagged to do homework, tidy up, be on time in the morning may never acquire the skills to manage their own lives because they depend on you to do it for them. By the end of primary school and certainly by secondary school, children should know that they need to manage themselves. You can offer support and discuss how they will plan and schedule and how you might build in reminders, such as a call to get up and a call to breakfast. But they need to know it's up to them and if they miss a bus or forget their lunch or homework, you won't bail them out. Step-parents often try even harder than parents to look after and protect the children in their charge. You need to recognize when and where that may be counter-productive.*

▶ *Make them responsible for their finances. Different families have different ways of managing money. In some, up to quite a late stage, young people get pocket money with which to buy treats, can save from money given at birthdays or other occasions for presents to give other people or special items, and otherwise must ask for and individually negotiate things they want. In others, young people are given an allowance from which they must pay for fares and lunches and special items such as clothes other than school uniform. If you incline towards the pocket money model, it might be worthwhile considering broadening this approach. It's a good idea for any child, to help them learn about budgeting and get a measure of respect for money and skill in managing it. In a stepfamily, anything that helps children feel they're in the driving seat helps.*

▶ *Consider what happened before you joined this family. Often, when families break up, children find themselves responsible for much more than they might ordinarily take on, in an intact family. When the situation changes you might think they will feel some relief at no longer having to be relied on or having to act above their age. And to a certain extent, they may well welcome another pair of hands around. But they may also feel resentful and cheated, especially if as well as extra work they felt they were taking on some status. Review, perhaps with them, the way it was and ask them what they may prefer to retain as their tasks or areas of concern.*

THINGS TO REMEMBER

▶ *Family traditions, whether public or private, can be a flashpoint in a stepfamily. They can underline the difference between the old and the new families.*

▶ *Plan ahead for each special event, not only to streamline the practicalities but also to predict, understand and manage the emotions and reaction it may evoke. Ideas-storm with each member of the family and find the optimum arrangement using 'trade offs' and 'swaps'.*

▶ *The best situation is when everyone feels arrangements are fair and equal in everyone's eyes. Since one person's idea of what is 'fair and equal' is not the same as another's, you will need to listen to and involve children, often by having family discussions, to achieve consensus.*

▶ *Children should be involved in the running of the home for them to feel it is 'theirs'. Use a family discussion to ideas-storm and agree a chore chart to get consensus on this.*

▶ *Eating together on a regular basis can be the glue that binds a family together. A family meal includes everyone, allows family discussion and can give the children a sense of being part of this unit.*

▶ *Children need some control over what is happening to them. Chores may mean work but they also mean responsibility. The more children feel they have responsibility and a say, the less they need to sound off or act out.*

IDEAS TO TRY

▶ *Consider the flashpoints in your family for conflict. Do they increase around family festivals or traditions?*

▶ *Indentify when and what is the next incidence – a school holiday, a festival such as Christmas, Passover or Eid? Sit down with your family and draw up plans.*

▶ *Call a family discussion – review this chapter for how to do it. Discuss what you all want to do. Write down who wants to see whom, where, when and for how long.*

▶ *Consider competing demands, time and money. Together, come up with a plan that suits all of you in some way even if some of you don't get exactly what you want.*

▶ *Discuss what would hinder and what would help putting this plan into action. Review this chapter for coming to a consensus.*

▶ *Ideas-storm the issues of chores and responsibility with adults and children. Draw up a chore chart (review this chapter for how to do that), and assign children a measure of control.*

▶ *Ideas-storm eating arrangements in your family. How often do you all eat together? Consider what helps and hinders you doing so. Ideas-storm what you could change to make it possible for you to share meals more often.*

Part three
Working together

7

Managing sharing children

In this chapter you will learn:
- *how to share a child between two families*
- *about the difficulties in managing shared contact*
- *how to resolve conflict over shared contact*
- *how to access help with contact through Child Contact Centres*
- *how to deploy techniques to help children express feelings and keep in touch with non-resident parents.*

Having to share children with another family can be a hard task. You may welcome the time they're not with you, if there's conflict. Or you may miss them and resent having another person and another tie take them away from you. Whatever you feel about them and the time you are together, the on/off life of having children spend some nights or days with one family and some with yours can be disruptive. You may wonder whether it would be far simpler, far pleasanter and far less confrontational if they spent all their time in one place and visits to the second family – whether that's yours or the other one – did not occur.

Of course, this may be exactly the scenario in your family. The non-resident parent of your stepchildren – or of your own children – may not be around, or you or your partner may no longer see children of your own. If so, while you may feel arrangements are easier, you may discover absence can be as disruptive as presence.

How do children view a missing parent?

Some children seem to thrive when a violent or apparently
uncaring parent who cannot give affection or approval departs
from their lives. Others heave a sigh of relief when an unhappy
relationship ends and they no longer have to see parents arguing,
or be caught up in the backlash. It cannot be denied that in some
cases a stepfamily is a far safer, happier place than the original
family and a step-parent fills a gap that everyone is glad opened.

But even when someone may not have been either the partner
or the parent they should have been, many children miss them
if gone, and still need them. It may be patently true that a step-
parent is a nicer, kinder, more loyal person who will be there for
the child when their birth parent will not. The child's loyalties will
still lie with the possibly undeserving parent. And people can be
good parents, given the chance, even when they have been terrible
partners. They can become good parents once they perceive the risk
of losing a child, even if they failed in the role when they were in it
full time. Above all, the failings of a partner or parent may be more
about the losses and sadness of their own life, about not having
good role models in their own childhood, rather than about any
inherent wickedness.

> **Insight**
> Even an abusive or uncaring parent is still a parent and is
> loved. Their absence may be acutely felt and children will
> need your love, understanding and sympathy for their loss.

Why do children need contact with non-resident parents?

The real point is that this isn't about the adult's capabilities.
It's about the child's needs. Children need to have contact with
their birth parents:

▶ *It tells them who they are. You don't have to explain genetics to a child; they know, instinctively, that they are a combination of Mum and Dad. If one or both birth parents are missing, children feel rootless and cut off. They may also feel anxious and apprehensive about what surprises and booby traps may be waiting in themselves, left there by the missing parent.*

▶ *If they don't have a clear idea of why the parent isn't there, they may well try to explain it themselves. And children's fantasies about loss usually revolve around their own blameworthiness. They'll believe it was something they did or didn't do or that they were judged and found wanting. They'll believe that the parent left them, not that they left either the other parent or the relationship, and feel rejected.*

▶ *They need to feel a parent's approval and acceptance. Losing touch with a parent feels to a child like having that source of appreciation and recognition withdrawn and often results in a lack of self-esteem, self-confidence and self-worth.*

It may go against the grain and leave you gritting teeth, but managing a stepfamily often means you have to support and reinforce the other parent in their role. Don't do it for their sake – do it for the child's and your own sake. The easier the contact, the happier the child and the better the situation inside your family.

How can you cope when the non-resident parent is uncooperative?

Contact with stepchildren may not be as easy as that. You may be dealing with a parent who won't let their partner see their children, or one who makes conditions such as contact is only allowed in certain places at certain times and with or without certain people being there. Or you may be trying to manage a situation where one of the adults involved has anger management issues, is violent or has addiction or mental health problems.

Children need to see both parents but they do not need to endure bad behaviour. If there are arguments still going on between the ex-partners or involving other members of their families, these should be sorted as soon as possible, or left out of the child–adult relationship. It's very easy for a step-parent to get drawn in. They may feel upset about the way they feel their partner is treated or maligned. They may feel angry at the effect it has on themselves, their relationship, their family and the stepchildren. The worst tactic is to jump in, side by side, sticking up for their partner or carrying the fight themselves. Continuing the dispute is not what is needed. Nobody wins, least of all the children. What you need is for the quarrel to end.

Separated parents may continue to argue. Continuing hostility may, supposedly, be about such things as:

- *contact*
- *money and maintenance*
- *parenting styles.*

In fact, continuing hostility may really be based on unfinished business from the relationship and its ending. People are often left after a break-up feeling they didn't have their say about the ending of the relationship – their ex didn't hear how sad and angry, or sorry and guilty, they felt and they never heard an explanation or apology or proper goodbye. This leaves a sense of not having really parted, of still being trapped in a tug of war that plays out over the last link – the children.

The best tactic for a step-parent is to support their partner in looking for closure. What needs to happen is for the ex-partners to close that part of other lives and to move on from being partners to being co-parents. It often requires both to face up to and address what they are really rowing about – the buried and painful emotions of hurt, rejection, perhaps humiliation. And it needs to be done without spite. Since that's a hard act, help is usually needed.

Would specialist help be beneficial?

Ex-partners should settle their difficulties with:

- ▶ *a counsellor*
- ▶ *a mediator*
- ▶ *a solicitor who is a member of Resolution (an association that encourages negotiation and agreement rather than confrontation).*

Even if the other half won't agree or attend, it's an excellent idea to seek such help. Going over the situation with an objective professional often has good results. It allows one side to see the argument calmly and carefully, and can lead to them changing their approach. Sometimes, getting off the roundabout of arguing and answering back can move the situation from one of confrontation to one that leads to negotiation. This doesn't mean your side gives in – it means your side stops letting all of you lose.

It also gives the opportunity of exploring the possibility of professional help, from a doctor or social worker or one of the many charities that work in this field, if there are issues associated with mental health, violence or addiction.

Parents may need to settle certain basic agreements:

- ▶ *No arguments in front of the children.*
- ▶ *No belittling or insulting each other to the children or when and where the children can hear (or anyone else can hear and pass on to the children).*
- ▶ *No using the children to get back at the other by, for instance, changing arrangements or sending messages through them.*
- ▶ *Recognizing and acknowledging the importance to children of contact.*
- ▶ *Communicating in a positive manner and striving to make it work.*

The two concerns – what is at the root of arguments, and how to manage continuing shared childcare – should be kept separate. Once the real argument is settled, parents find the quarrels they had over money, access and parenting styles often retreat in importance. But if there are still things to settle, getting the personal stuff out of the way may leave them able to manage it.

Insight

Asking for help doesn't mean you are incompetent or incapable, nor does it mean you give up control. What it can mean is that you get the opportunity to hear and be heard and to come to an agreement.

Essential points to consider

▶ *Some children thrive when a violent or uncaring parent leaves or an argumentative relationship ends. But even when the stepfamily is a better place to be, they may still miss the non-resident parent and the original family.*

▶ *Children need contact with both parents for their sense of self-worth and identity.*

▶ *Continuing hostility between parents harms children. Adults need to settle their differences and cooperate for the sake of their children.*

Child Contact Centres

What if parents simply can't bear the idea of coming face to face? What if there are real concerns about the child's safety with a parent or someone else in the family? Or what if one parent finds the idea of letting a child be with the other parent, or other people who know them, unacceptable? In such a situation, a Child Contact Centre could be the answer.

A Child Contact Centre is a place where children whose parents live apart can spend time with them and other agreed family members.

Child Contact Centres are run by the National Association of Child Contact Centres and all of them are accredited and the staff and volunteers are fully trained. The idea is that families are either referred by a social worker, solicitor, mediator, CAFCASS (Children And Family Court Advisory and Support Service) or court order. Or, at some centres, you can refer yourself. You apply by filling out a form which names the people who will be seeing the child, and then make arrangements for a visit. Child Contact Centres can offer three levels of support for separated families.

SUPPORTED CHILD CONTACT

Children can be taken to the centre, which is warm and friendly and will have toys and areas where children can play and facilities for adults to have refreshment. The parent dropping off the children stays with them until the other parent arrives. They can handover while seeing each other, but if this is not acceptable, neither need actually be face to face at any time. After handover, children can spend as long as agreed with the other parent and any relatives that have been named on the referral form. While there, parents agree to certain rules, for the safety of the child and to ensure the visit is fun and safe:

▶ *No arguing in front of children, no abusive or aggressive behaviour.*
▶ *Only the people named to be there.*
▶ *Children cannot simply be left – one parent has to hand over to the other, even if they don't see each other face to face.*
▶ *No drink, drugs or smoking and no one under the influence to be allowed into the centre.*
▶ *The parent leaving a child must give a phone number where they can be reached.*

SUPERVISED CHILD CONTACT

When there are concerns about the risk to the child, or when parent and child have not seen each other for some time and may need help re-establishing a relationship, contact can be supervised. The child and adult are under observation at all times by a supervisor – a highly trained professional – with the support of another colleague. The visit will have a time limit, and reports will be kept to help the supervisor keep the child safe and support parents in managing the visit in the best interests of the child.

Insight

Children really do need to see both their parents and to have regular contact. If you have any concerns about their safety, a Child Contact Centre will help your child get what they need – to see the other parent – while giving you what you need, which is the confidence they are safe.

HANDOVERS

Most Child Contact Centres will function as drop-off point, where parents can go and play with their children while waiting for the other parent to collect a child for a planned visit, either for the day or longer. This is useful if for some reason one or other of the parents doesn't want the other parent to visit their home. As with supported or supervised visits, parents do not have to see each other face to face.

From the postbag

I have a really difficult dilemma. I want our child to go on seeing his father and grandparents, but I've had arguments in the past with them because they all smoke like chimneys. Also, when my son does anything his grandparents don't like, they shout at him and smack him – and being a normally boisterous and curious little boy they seem to do it a lot. I've explained we don't smack and I'd like them to not smoke when he's with them but they say in their house they'll do as they please. Is there anything I can do?

You could insist that meetings in future be at your local Child Contact Centre. All centres operate a no-smoking or smacking policy. If either object, point out you are not obstructing contact and are happy for them to see your son as often as agreed... but in circumstances you have decided are safe for him. If they change their policy in the future, so may you. Good luck!

What support can grandparents and other people offer?

Step-parents and grandparents can feel immensely helpless when the aftermath of a family break-up rumbles on. As spectators, they can often see the harm that is occurring more than the people unwittingly inflicting it. One or both ex-partners may be actively and willingly attacking and intentionally damaging the other but neither will really want to harm their children. They may not realize that any harm to a parent hurts a child, even if that child has no contact with or rejects and scorns the parent. It may be satisfying to hear children echo your own words of criticism or anger against the people who upset you, but in the long run it leaves them confused, anxious and traumatized.

When your own partner is under pressure or their children are hurting, or when you yourself are in the firing line, it's very tempting and very easy to be drawn in and to become part of the war. However, step-parents and grandparents in this situation need to hold firm. A step-parent's role in this may well be to stand back and not be involved at all, except to be supportive. They can help by encouraging their partner to talk rather than fight, to look for solutions rather than problems and to model for the children that you can be calm, firm and helpful and not have to take sides. If step-parents become directly involved, it's best to do it in a mediator role, calming things down, suggesting that people communicate and agree and leading everyone to the sort of help and guidance that can get them talking and stop them fighting.

Support strategy 1: giving in fantasy

We often believe that if a child wants something we don't agree with, or feels differently to us, and we accept and take their feelings on board, or even listen to them, this will lead to problems. We fear they will see it as a weakness and take advantage. Or by admitting to their point of view we give credence to it, while if you rebuff it you brush it away.

None of this is true. Children will feel what they feel whether you listen to them or not. What they may not be able to do if those feelings are denied is to deal with them. A child who misses their other parent and wishes their original family was back together may be being unrealistic, but the emotions are genuine. Insisting that isn't how they feel or telling them that the missing parent is a waste of time doesn't make the longing go away. Unable to discuss it out loud, the feelings come out in other ways – in depression, naughtiness or self-harm. It's very tempting as adults to want to reassure – to try to carry on as if everything is fine. By insisting it is so, we hope to carry through what we want by asserting it is. But insisting that you or they are, or should be, happy doesn't make it so simply because you say so. Children aren't stupid – they know when you aren't being real. All that this does is make them doubt their own instincts, senses and intelligence or distrust you.

> **Insight**
> Children aren't stupid and will often overhear conversations you think are private. Trying to keep things from them will often lead to anger and distrust.

When children want something impossible or difficult or simply uncomfortable for you, one strategy that often helps is 'giving in fantasy'. Giving in fantasy is a technique that listens, acknowledges and sympathizes. It allows an adult to hear and recognize a child's distress and wishes, even if you can't do anything about it. By letting them voice their emotions and making it clear you hear and sympathize, you can make a difference. Using this technique means the following:

- *Acknowledging the emotion – 'You miss your dad. That must make you feel sad.'*
- *Being sympathetic – 'I'm sad you feel so bad about it.'*
- *Stating the difficulties, but without any blame – 'He finds it hard to come and see you because everyone's still so angry.'*
- *Giving in to fantasy – 'If I could, I'd change things so you could see him as often as you'd like.'*
- *Since this is fantasy, you could go to town on it – 'I'd build a house next door – a mansion, a palace. We'd have connecting doors so you could go and be with him whenever you wanted.'*
- *Offering a realistic option – 'But maybe I could do something. What do you think would help?'*

The child may want more contact – not just face to face, but in texts and calls and emails. They may also want to have photos of their birth parent and original family easily available and on show. Above all, the child needs to hear you say that you hear, understand, allow and accept their feelings, however different they may be to yours and however difficult you may find it to hear them. Just knowing this makes an immense difference to them. And while you may find it painful to have to accept they have a different view to you – still loving, perhaps forgiving and certainly needing another adult as a parent – it won't hurt you as much as having to bow to your personal agenda will hurt them.

Essential points to consider

- *If contact visits are a problem, parents can use Child Contact Centres to give their children the safe, secure and regular contact they need.*
- *Step-parents and other relatives may feel helpless when they see conflict between ex-partners but should avoid joining in.*

(Contd)

Support strategy 2: making a family history box

Children need contact with their birth parents and the relatives belonging to both of those parents. But the reality is that sometimes this isn't going to happen. The other parent may have died or have lost contact or contact will occur sporadically and hedged around with hurt and complications. Deal with this by first reminding yourself why they need that contact:

▶ *Knowing your parents tells you who you are – where you come from and what appearance and behaviour patterns you may inherit. When children don't have contact with a parent and hear little about them it creates mystery and anxiety. They may worry or be scared about the legacy left to them, or construct fantasies about a missing Prince or Princess that makes it hard for them to relate to their stepfamily. If they hear bad things about them, they may assume that is how they are doomed to turn out. Or, indeed, they may deliberately copy aggressive or destructive behaviour as the only way they have of being close to the parent they do not see.*
▶ *Contact with a loving parent gives a child self-esteem and self-worth. When contact is difficult or non-existent, children tend to assume it's because they are somehow lacking and undeserving or did something wrong.*

Insight
Being loved and valued helps children learn how to love and value, and to accept love and value from others.

If children in your care have no contact, or little and conflicted contact, redress the balance with a family history box. This is a way of letting a child keep contact with and keep close to the other half of their genetic heritage – an aspect of themselves that is important. They will make that connection one way or another but a history box helps them turn it into something helpful.

A family history box is a way of gathering together their memories of the missing parent and the lost family. In it put photographs of the parent and objects that belonged to or remind the child of them. There may be favourite music, letters and cards, gifts, books – anything that brings them to life. You shouldn't shy away from sad memories and you can be honest about what has happened, but the key is to make it positive and put aside criticism and negative associations. Let the child choose where to keep the box – in their own room or in a room you all use. Let them refer to it and bring it out, and talk over the contents. If they don't, make a point every so often of getting the box down and sift through it with them.

Case study: Peter, Heather and Simon

Peter's father left when he was two and had very little contact, even though Peter's grandparents on that side did keep in touch. When he was nine, a school project on family trees prompted him to do his own, and he became confused and distressed when it became clear that his 'real' father was missing from his life. He went through a period of shouting at Simon, who up to then he'd got on with very well and called 'Dad', and refusing to do anything he asked him to do. Then Heather dredged out a packet of photographs of his father. She also found letters and postcards he had sent when they had been dating and in the early days of their marriage. Simon came back one day with a beautifully painted wooden box and suggested that Peter spread out on the kitchen table all the things he had from or about his father. He asked Peter to go through them and tell him all about them, and to get Heather to fill in as many stories and memories as she could. He then suggested Peter could keep them all in the box and bring them out whenever he wanted. When he told his two sets of grandparents about the box, both responded with photos and other memorabilia. Peter's behaviour improved and his anger faded away.

THINGS TO REMEMBER

▶ *Some children may be relieved if an uncaring or confrontational parent has left and been replaced by a more caring step-parent. Others will need contact with the missing parent, however 'bad' they may have been in adults' eyes.*

▶ *However painful, enraging or confusing it may be for the adults, parents and step-parents should support a child in keeping contact with their non-resident parent as long as this can be done in a safe way.*

▶ *Parents need to perform the difficult trick of finishing and seeking closure on the partner relationship with the ex-partner while still retaining the co-parent role. Instead of encouraging or colluding with continuing hostility, a step-parent can best help their new family by supporting their partner in doing this. There is specialist professional help, such as counsellors and mediators, to assist in this.*

▶ *When contact with an ex-partner is really difficult or problematic, there is specialist help to be had from Child Contact Centres, social workers, solicitors, mediation or CAFCASS.*

▶ *Use techniques such as 'giving in fantasy' and making a family history box to help children express their feelings about the situation and keep in touch with their whole family.*

IDEAS TO TRY

▶ If contact is an issue, ideas-storm with another adult the problems as you see them.

▶ Invite children to ideas-storm the issues as they see them.

▶ Is there a disparity – do you find contact with the other parent problematic while the children do not? Or do you support it while the children resist it?

▶ Ideas-storm to identify what could be different.

▶ If there are any issues you or your children struggle with, use the Taking it further section to find professional help and access it.

▶ Give something 'in fantasy' to the children in your family, and help them make a family history box.

8

You can't tell me what to do!

In this chapter you will learn:

- *how to deal with 'You can't tell me what to do!'*
- *how to balance children's and adults' different points of view*
- *about the gains and losses in a stepfamily*
- *how to model the behaviour you want.*

Become part of a stepfamily and you'll quickly realize, if you haven't already, that children have minds of their own. You and your family may be the exception. The children may get along famously with their step-relatives, and happily relate to both their birth parents. They may shuttle between both families with little trouble. However, more often there will be tension.

Sooner or later virtually every step-parent will hear the words 'You can't tell me what to do, you're not my Mum/Dad!' Children in stepfamilies can direct an enormous amount of anger and disdain at step-parents, often, it seems, unfairly. They also frequently play one parent off against the other, refuse to see or speak to a non-resident parent or take out their anger on the parent with whom they mostly live. To understand why, and to cope, you need to understand how they see the situation.

Parents often assume their wishes and needs will be the same as their children's. It can come as a shock as they grow and develop to discover exactly how much and how often you diverge. Step-parents often struggle with this even more, because you may come into the relationship with some expectations and assumptions that are rapidly and often rudely shattered. But it's not just their view of when to do homework or chores and what time to be in bed that is different to yours. Children in stepfamilies may well be significantly 'out of step' with what you and their parents see as the reasons you formed, and the benefits they may get from, this family.

Different perspectives

OF THE BREAK-UP

Adults and children in a stepfamily have a very different view of what is going on. For a start, it is the adults who make all the decisions – to end one relationship, and to begin another. It is the adults who are in charge of leaving one family unit and forming a new one. The adults concerned may feel powerless and out of control and that what is going on may simply be fate or 'something that just happens'. Indeed, the original separation or the new stepfamily could have come about because of the decision of another adult. But, however much adults may consider they are in the grip of forces beyond their control, this is nothing compared with how the children are likely to feel. Children have no say and know it.

They do, however, often feel they have responsibility. Children will feel guilt over a break-up, convinced it happened because they did or didn't do something – were too naughty, or not good enough. Once parents have separated they will often assume the burden of looking after one or both parents, and indeed see it as their job to bring them back together again. A new adult will be seen as a threat to this task, as an interloper. A new family may be seen as proof of their failure, either to remake their parents' relationship or to be a good enough carer.

OF THE OTHER PARENT

Who makes the choice to break and make a family is not the least of the differences in the way adults and children perceive stepfamilies.

Another major difference is the place separated parents occupy in the lives of their ex and of their children. For an adult breaking up with a partner, it is the end of a relationship that occupied part of their life. They might have felt their partner was central to their lives and happiness and the cornerstone of their family. But, even if he or she was a childhood friend, they will remember a time before they knew them. A partner may be important in your life, but he or she is not critical.

If you're the child, your parent seems to be a fixture. They were there, after all, before you were. As far back as you can remember, they were around – a permanent part of your life and the building block on which everything else is based. With a parent gone, the child's entire world-view shifts and becomes insecure and frightening. They may not be able to see how they can manage, because they have never managed without the person before.

> **Insight**
> Partners can be divorced, separated from, or replaced. A parent is for life.

OF THE NEW FAMILY

On top of 'losing' the former family, when one or both of their parents start new relationships this can feel even more upsetting instead of seeming helpful. When a new family comes along, children and adults have this essential difference. For the adults at the centre of a new family it is a new start – for the step-parent it may be your first taste of a committed partnership or family life. It is the launch of something exciting, hopeful and joyful. It is a beginning of an adventure, a whole new life, and – for the parent – a second chance. Most adults will feel hopeful, glad, optimistic, excited. They will be looking forward, wanting to sweep away the sadness that may have dragged them down in what went before, and to put behind them a past that seems full of mistakes, false starts and failures. For the step-parent, it is the blank sheet.

For the children it is often a calamity. Some children may not be quite as negative or sad about the ending of their old family as others, and some may not be as hostile towards the new family either. If there have been continued arguments and prolonged misery, especially if verbal, emotional or even physical violence was threatened or present, children as well as adults may be relieved at having their birth parents call an end to it. They may find more support and kindness from the step-parent than their own, or be delighted in their parent's happiness. But even if on one level they rejoice at the new regime, children still feel the new relationship is the final nail in the coffin of the old family and many of their hopes. Even beyond reason, for months if not years, children will cling to the fantasy that their 'own', 'real' family may come back together again, that it will come back in a better shape, with the arguments resolved and the people concerned happy and getting on. When a new person takes the place of the missing parent, those hopes may be dashed. If the step-parent and parent then announce they plan to make their relationship permanent, either by marrying or getting a home together, children may have a profound sense of loss. This will be a loss of their dreams, their hopes and expectations, however unrealistic, and it can lead to depression or moodiness, or the acting out of bad feelings in bad behaviour. Children may get caught up in the excitement of the new direction, especially new homes or weddings, but at the same time show feelings they themselves may not realize they have in arguments with the adults, spats among themselves or rebellion.

The consequences of different perspectives

The fact that people in the same family will see the same event in such a different light is at the heart of most stepfamily difficulties. Adults may be at a loss to see why their children are being so contrary and badly behaved. With minds focused on the upside of it all, it feels quite a wrench, and an irritating one at that, to have children pulling in the opposite direction. You may find yourself quick to be angry and cast blame for what you see as bloody-mindedness. It might seem to you to be so simple; the original relationship didn't work out, and this new one will. The person no longer in your life wasn't up to scratch, and the new one will be.

There were rows and sadness before and now you have the chance to make it better. Who wouldn't want to try to make an effort?

> ## Insight
> A new partner is a beginning – of a new love, a new life, a new family. A step-parent is an ending, of the original family, of the life before and the world as it was.

Sadly, children often feel they have no incentive to make this family work. Children may not be able to understand why a parent is so set on doing something that seems so manifestly cruel or unfair. Their parent has been discarded and another person has usurped their position. Even if it was the other parent who left and made that choice, children often feel safer in blaming the one who remains. Even if what they actually find in the new family suits them, they still may resist. Gaining a new baby, a younger brother or sister to boss around, an older one to look up to or a same-age sibling to become a good friend may be fun. However, it still spells a change to their original family and one they might view with suspicion and resentment. It's easy to recognize that everyone loses out and has something to mourn when a family breaks up. It's less easy to see that when, for you, much of what happens in the establishment of a stepfamily will be a gain, it may yet again be seen by the children as loss.

Case study: Lisa and Colin

Lisa was delighted when her new partner Colin moved in and was sure her two daughters would welcome their new family. They'd understood she and their father weren't going to get back together – in fact, he'd recently announced his engagement to an old friend. And they seemed to have welcomed Colin for the weekends and holidays he'd shared with them. She was taken aback to find them suddenly wage a campaign against him, being rude or offhand and contradicting everything he suggested or said. As the house became more and more tense and unpleasant she pleaded with them to stop as it was putting her relationship at risk, and was speechless when one of them finally said 'Well, duh Mum, so?'

In other words – yes, that's the whole point. It wasn't until she and Colin saw a counsellor for help and used communication techniques to listen to as well as speak with the girls and to acknowledge their feelings that the tide turned and they began to come round.

'You can't tell me what to do' – why it's said and how to react

This is why children in a stepfamily often hit out, verbally and even physically. Saying or implying 'You can't tell me what to do…' may be a specific attack against the new adult and what their presence means. Children may feel that one way to keep the link with a missing parent, or to try to maintain the link between their two parents using themselves as a bridge, would be to refuse any emotional tie with the new adult. Even if – in fact, especially if – they do like the incomer, getting on with them feels like disloyalty. And disloyalty may result, they fear, in an even worse breakdown in relationship between themselves and their other parent.

But 'You can't tell me what to do…' may be nothing to do with the step-parent themselves. It is usually more a reassertion of love and commitment to the parent they no longer live with and the original family they no longer have than an attack on the new family or new step-parent. It doesn't have to be a realistic stance. Indeed, the less ideal the old situation, the more stubbornly a child may cling to it and work against what they now have. The issue may not be what they actually had but what they wished they had – and that can summon up great reserves of mulish inflexibility.

'You can't tell me what to do…' is usually a general complaint. It actually says, 'My family has broken up, a new situation is being foisted upon me and I protest!' It isn't personal. It isn't even, much of the time, a reaction against the new circumstances – which may indeed in many ways be better than the old one. It's simply a way of registering pain and loss, and needs to be accepted as such.

The way to deal with 'You can't tell me what to do...' is twofold. First, acknowledge the pain and loss underneath the statement. Say, 'It must be sad seeing your family break up. I can see it's upsetting you.' Simply acknowledging the emotions underneath the behaviour often make them more manageable. Since bad behaviour is always a way of getting your needs and emotions recognized, knowing they have been heard can lessen or stop the behaviour.

Second, make it clear that when it comes to keeping rules or being polite or any other transaction in this family, it doesn't happen because of a parent–child relationship but because of a household relationship. This is where House Rules come into their own.

Essential points to consider

▶ *'You can't tell me what to do!' is more a cry of pain than a challenge.*

▶ *Children may feel they have no incentive to make a stepfamily work. It wasn't their choice nor what they would have wanted.*

▶ *Refusing to cooperate with a step-parent may be seen by a child as a way of showing loyalty and solidarity with the other parent.*

Why it's important to have House Rules in your family

By setting House Rules, everyone learns that an adult doesn't have to be a parent to merit being listened to and being polite to. Nor, indeed, does a child have to be related to the adult for them to be caring and respectful of their needs and feelings. If you live together, you owe each other this courtesy, regardless of how you feel about the situation. And keeping to House Rules to make the wheels go round at least gives you the space and time to attend to the reasons why you may feel angry, let down or upset about the situation.

If you haven't already done so, make time to ideas-storm, draw up and agree on a set of House Rules as discussed in Chapter 3. Once you have done so, agree a contract between all of you, as outlined in Chapter 4, keep to it and review it as needed. Don't forget, House Rules are something you need to keep to as much as children do. If you want children to behave well, there are three things you need to do:

1 *Model what you want – it's* not *a case of 'Do as I say, not as I do,' but 'I'll do to you what I'd like from you.'*
2 *Recognize that bad behaviour is about bad feelings.*
3 *Listen, acknowledge and understand the reason behind their behaviour. This will help the behaviour to go away far more effectively than reacting to it, punishing it or complaining about it.*

Insight

It's really important for adults to keep the rules as much as children do. You can't expect them to fall into line unless you are willing to do so as well.

Why it's important to help children be positive about the non-resident parent

Children may react to a new family by targeting a step-parent but they may also take out their feelings on the non-resident parent or indeed the parent caring for them. How should you deal with this?

It can be seen as reassuring by the adults looking after a child if s/he refuses to speak to or see the missing parent. They may feel this is a vote of confidence and an endorsement of the new stepfamily. Sometimes children enthusiastically support the new adult, to the extent of wanting to take on a new name or calling the step-parent Mum or Dad. If there is still anger or conflict between ex-partners, the child's choosing of sides can be greeted with relief and seen as their approval. It may not, however, be as positive a move as you think.

Children may feel they have good reason not to see or speak to a missing parent. If they have been let down and left feeling unvalued by that parent, they may need to make a stand and win back self-confidence and self-worth by saying enough is enough. They may need to have their feelings about the way their parent has behaved to them listened to and heard. They may need your support in putting their own point of view forward but it does have to be their, not your, agenda. If they are angry or upset, or sad and bereft, it is their feelings that need to be explained, not yours.

How not to draw children in to adult battles

Children really need the adults looking after them to be able to be grown-up and fight their own battles. If you have an issue with another adult, say so yourself to them and sort it out between you. Don't let children get drawn into the situation and do it for you. Children often will attack one parent because they want to please the other. It may feel very frightening to have had one parent leave. The unsettling experience of having a new adult arrive may make them feel they have to do anything to make sure the other doesn't go too.

Children do need contact with both parents and do need to feel loved and accepted by them. Instead of feeling vindicated when they take action against a parent, it is better to support them in making and keeping good relations. You may need to ask them to talk over why they don't want to see the other person, but try not to take some explanations at face value. They may be trying to cut off a parent who they see as withdrawing from them, in the belief that if they say no first, the separation will hurt less. Or they may be doing it to get back at the parent, to give them a taste of their own medicine. Or, as already mentioned, they may be doing it to follow your lead. Anger and pain are good reasons to talk, not good reasons to refuse to talk. Help the child examine and explore the situation. You may ask them to consider and express:

▶ *Their feelings. You may need to ideas-storm all sorts of words to describe feelings (anger, hurt, guilt, rejection, jealousy) to get an accurate picture for them and for you.*
▶ *What they want. You may need to give them permission to ideas-storm all sorts of unrealistic fantasies to end up with a working solution.*
▶ *How you might help them achieve it. They may need your support to change things themselves, or for you to take some action yourself.*

Why children play adults off against each other

Children in stepfamilies may resort to playing one parent against another, a step-parent against a parent. It's very easy for adults to find themselves competing and soon challenging each other in the most hostile way because of this. Why do they do it and how can you avoid it?

Because children often feel guilty over their parents' separation, they may ask for proof to make sure you do still love them. These demands may take the form of requests for money or items, or privileges such as late nights or access to certain films or TV programmes. Just as virtually every child will have a 'my friend' who's allowed to do or have all the things they want, stepchildren will often use the 'Dad/Mum lets me…' card.

They may make the same demands with the same tactics because they do feel anxious and vulnerable. An adult has left or been left. Does this mean they too may be abandoned? A lot of bad behaviour is 'acting out' these anxieties.

Stepchildren often feel as if they have a gap in their lives – a gap left by the missing parent. In a society in which consumer goods and food are sold as ways of filling the gaps in our lives, children can very easily assume things would make them feel better, and ask for them, to fill the hole. Since, of course, no matter how many gizmos or fizzy drinks they have the feeling of emptiness remains, it can become repetitive and damaging.

> **Insight**
> Demands for consumer goods are actually demands for attention and proof of love. Give those, not another gadget.

How to draw and keep to boundaries

Some children chase consumer items out of simple acquisitiveness. They realize they're onto a good thing with two families competing for their loyalty and play it for all it's worth. However, the game can turn sour and while at first they may enjoy the ability to make one or both families jump to their tune, they are soon likely to find it frightening and depressing. Always getting what you want means you have no boundaries. Children actually benefit enormously from having adults looking after them who can say no, and can restrict them. Having adults compete in allowing those boundaries to stretch can make them feel increasingly vulnerable and uncertain.

Parents and step-parents may give in to the demands out of guilt and a desire to make it better for the child. Giving in to demands feels as if it makes up for the loss of their original family, and eases in the introduction of a new family. Adults may feel it will make the point that they listen to and love the child – they are there for them and deliver what is wanted.

Or, the adults concerned may do it out of their own need to be best and loved best. Particularly when you have emerged from a relationship break-up, particularly when you are embarking on a stepfamily, the desire to be needed and wanted and approved of can make it hard to be the grown-up and put your own needs aside.

And indeed, let's be honest, sometimes adults allow themselves to be played off each other – or even instigate it – because they know it will cause problems with the other family. The wish to get even and score points can overcome the understanding that everyone, most of all the children, will suffer from this.

> ## Essential points to consider
> ▶ *Having House Rules means you can sidestep 'You can't tell me…'.*
> ▶ *Children often play parent against parent and parent against step-parent. By understanding why they do this, you can challenge and resist it.*

What should you do when children try to play adults off against each other?

You can:

- ▶ *Understand it. Recognize the need behind the behaviour and be sympathetic.*
- ▶ *Challenge it. Point out to the child that you can see what is happening and ask what they thought it would achieve so you can discuss the real needs and how they can be fulfilled.*
- ▶ *Resist it. Step back and either make the rules and agreements you know are right and keep to them, or recall them and discuss them again with the child.*
- ▶ *Discuss it. Raise the issue with the other family and agree ground rules and responses.*

In the long run, nobody benefits from a popularity contest. If you win, the children lose; and if the children lose, so do you. What all of you need is for adults to be truly adult – to be able to stand back from the conflict, the confusion and pain and to act in the best interests of the child (which is in the adults' best interests as well). This may mean recognizing how much cooperation is necessary between parents and step-parents. It may mean recognizing when and how your own wishes and needs differ from those of the children, and what efforts need to be made to compromise so everyone gets what they need.

Insight

Helping children get what they really need may mean asking for help so you can set aside your own arguments with other adults in the situation and agree on how to do the best for the children.

From the postbag

My ex seems to find no problem treating our daughter to make-up and new dresses but great difficulty in paying me maintenance on time. And she just keeps on asking him for things and assuming he'll come up with it no matter how many times I ask her to curb her shopping habits. She puts me on the spot too, asking for more and more pocket money and when I say no, she either goes to her stepfather who stumps up or says I'm mean and she wants to go and live with her Dad. Help!

You've all got into a spiral of buying popularity. She asks because what she's really saying is 'Do you love me and do you value me?' He, and you and your partner, pay up because you want to say 'Yes I do!' The best way of saying it in future is in words not goods: 'I love you. I don't have any spare cash. If I did I'd give it all to you. But what I have has to pay the gas bill and tonight's meal.' Point out to both your partner and your daughter's dad what is going on and say what she really needs is unlimited love and attention, not money. Good luck!

THINGS TO REMEMBER

▶ *Children have minds of their own. Parents and step-parents can easily make the mistake of assuming their own needs and wishes will be the same as the children's, or that they necessarily know what is best for the child. Parents and step-parents need to listen and hear what children really feel and want.*

▶ *'You can't tell me what to do...' is more a statement of loss and pain than of defiance. Parents and step-parents need to dive under the words to reach the real emotion to find solutions to stepfamily conflict.*

▶ *Acknowledging the child's sense of loss is the best way to build mutual understanding and cooperation.*

IDEAS TO TRY

▶ Discuss with your partner, or another adult, your perspective of the break-up of the original family, the other parent and the new family.

▶ Discuss with your children, listening to their perspective of the break-up of the original family, the other parent and the new family.

▶ Note the differences! How might that be affecting conflict and disagreement in your family?

▶ If you haven't already done so, ideas-storm and draw up a set of House or Family Rules – review Chapter 3 to help you.

▶ Consider if the children have used 'You can't tell me what to do,' or played adults off against each other. Using this chapter, ideas-storm how you might respond in future.

9

Managing long-distance parenting

In this chapter you will learn:
- *how to manage long-distance parenting*
- *how children can use today's technology to stay in touch with non-resident parents*
- *about online and mobile phone safety.*

All the evidence suggests that stepfamilies can be as happy for adults and as beneficial for children as first-time families. It's not the fact that you are in a family with children from a previous relationship that causes the problems. What makes trouble is failing to manage or deal with the special circumstances that arise because of it. And one of the particular issues to look out for is when parents live some distance apart. Managing long-distance parenting can be complicated and calls for exceptional tact, attentiveness and effort.

Long-distance parenting

Long-distance parenting is something that is on the increase. We live in a mobile society where people move from their birth place and have a high chance of living some distance from friends and family. When one relationship breaks up, each ex-partner may well stay in the same town and make new relationships with people in their familiar community. But either or both are just as likely to move 50, 100 or 1,000 kilometres away. Breaking up or forming a stepfamily is often the impetus to a fresh start, and that can mean seizing opportunities to break out and do something new, and live somewhere different.

This may be more than acceptable for the adults concerned, who may be relieved at not having to bump into their ex, or their ex-partner's new partner in the local supermarket or café. It can also get over the tricky business of having to divide up friends, some staying loyal to one and some to the other. It also helps with the feeling that this is a beginning, the beginning of a new family, and not the leftover of a previous one.

From the postbag

My new wife and I would really like to emigrate to Australia. The problem is my two sons who are being really unfair about the whole thing. It's a tremendous chance for me – I could have the chance of running my own business which I can't afford here. You would have thought they'd jump at the chance to have me over there so they can come and visit – sea and surf and all the things boys like. How can I make them see sense?

Of course it's a wonderful opportunity for you. But if you move half a planet away how often, realistically, will your children be able to come and visit? Can your funds run to every school holiday, or is it more likely to be once a year or even less? That's a wrench for children who have gone from living with their father to being visitors in his life. And it's not just the distance – it's the fact that you're putting your needs above theirs in such a dramatic way. That's understandable – you have a right to live your own life. But you have to see it from their point of view as well. If you do go ahead, get a computer with webcam so you can talk regularly. But you may have to accept you'll become less of a factor in their lives and that this will be grief and a loss to them. Good luck!

Insight
The best outcomes for children are when they live within walking or cycling distance from the non-resident parent.

As far as children are concerned, of course, being some distance away from a parent can be disastrous. When children live close by to a non-resident parent they can be in charge of access by being able to pop over when they choose and have frequent and informal contact, controlled by themselves. The non-resident parent is able to drop by and collect them, or say hi, read them a story, look at homework or share a game when both have an odd moment.

Living some distance puts a range of stresses and strains on everyone. Children can feel rejected and abandoned. It doesn't matter whether adults have good, rational reasons for living far away. As far as the child is concerned, it means the parent has withdrawn and that hurts.

SPECIAL FESTIVALS

Living at a distance means contact is necessarily limited, to a few weekends rather than every weekend or to holidays. In cases where a parent has moved countries, it can mean children may only be able to see one of their parents very occasionally and with much planning, if at all. Special events such as birthdays may become particularly fraught. Children who might otherwise have enjoyed the day may be unable to concentrate on the fun because they're worrying or thinking about the missing parent. Special festivals such as Christmas, Hanukkah or Eid may be logistical nightmares, putting everyone under pressure. The effort of planning, negotiating and facilitating meetings and travel at a distance, as well as the expense, can breed resentment and exasperation in parents and particularly step-parents, who may feel they or their own family is suffering unfairly. Children can pick up this atmosphere and feel guilty and at fault.

Next time the situation comes around they may appear disinterested in seeing the non-resident parent and accept any suggestions to defer it.

LONG VISITS

Living at a distance means contact can rarely be spontaneous and informal. Instead of being able to ring up and fix a quick visit or treat, and to see each other for short periods, visits often have to be for some period to make them worthwhile. This may mean that children are prevented from attending certain events with family and friends, and they may either grieve or resent having to miss these. Long visits can also feel awkward and difficult. In a 'normal' situation children come and go, see friends, do their own thing and chill out as well as having time with parents. Thrown into visiting a parent and stepfamily, with a clock ticking and the knowledge that they may not see each other again for some time, everyone concerned may assume they have to spend every minute together, which in turn makes them feel pressured and tense.

LOSING SUPPORT SYSTEMS

Living at a distance can often mean one parent is losing out on the support system offered by old friends and relatives. When children leave their old home, this can result in them losing touch with people they need to be there to provide continuance and stability, such as aunts and uncles, grandparents, neighbours and childhood friends. When the non-resident parent moves, it can mean they lose out on the network that might have supported continuing contact.

It's a reality that women tend to be the ones to manage emotional stuff in any family. Both girls and boys lean on mothers, rather than fathers, for advice and discussion, and frequently mothers encourage and make possible emotional ties and everyday contact between fathers and their children. If the mother is less inclined to make such efforts and a stepmother feels she has no incentive to do so either, it can be hard for contact to continue smoothly, especially if the barrier of distance is making it all the harder.

How can you manage long-distance families?

A good start is to accept the following:

▶ *A parent may have part-time contact, and live away from their children, but they are still a full-time parent and close to those children. As far as children are concerned, the distance is no barrier to their need or their love.*

▶ *Distance may throw up challenges but they need to be overcome, not used as excuses. It's a test of both emotional and financial resources but that's the reality of stepfamilies.*

▶ *You need to look for solutions, not problems.*

You need:

▶ *Agreement. Both families should accept the need for parents and children to stay in touch.*

▶ *Maturity. It may be necessary for adults who don't want to see each other to communicate for contact to happen. You have to be the grown-ups, and if you have a problem with this, seek counselling or mediation to allow you to set aside unfinished business and baggage from the past for the sake of the children if not yourself.*

▶ *Planning. Face-to-face contact over a distance doesn't happen 'just like that'. You need to plan ahead, sometimes months in advance, to take advantage of cheap travel and to make sure everyone's schedules match and that each family gets a fair share of important family events.*

▶ *Understanding. You may need to recognize that resistance and objections on anyone's part may be about emotional needs and anxieties.*

It's important also for other types of contact to continue even when face-to-face contact does not. Stepfamilies have never had it so good as we live in a time when technology can really bring people together over a gap. If you haven't already, make sure children in stepfamilies, whatever their age, have access to the following:

▶ *Their own mobile phone with unlimited calls and texts to both parents' numbers. Children living apart from a parent need to be able to ring or text them whenever they feel like it, and to be able to receive calls and texts too. This is as important when they are with the non-resident parent as it is when they are apart from them. To feel secure and at home with someone they only see infrequently, children need to be able to check in with their full-time home whenever they want. Agree that calls and texts to either parent are unlimited and will be paid for by parents – calls and texts elsewhere will be subject to discussion and they have to contribute to those bills!*

▶ *Their own email address and a device they can use to send and receive mails as often as they want. If they have a mobile with a camera, they could also download and send frequent pictures as attachments. You could also consider access to instant messaging and social network sites on the internet, so they can chat to the parent at agreed times, and a computer with a webcam and software to enable live (and free) video calls over the internet. You could also have a scanner/printer so any drawings and photos can be scanned and mailed as attachments, and anything mailed back can be printed as hard copy too.*

▶ *An address book and a supply of cards, postcards and envelopes. Encourage them to send photos, drawings, clippings they think will interest or amuse each other. Using the internet speeds up and makes day-to-day contact simple, but there is a special joy in something you can stick on the fridge or bedroom wall.*

Insight

Make use of any and every opportunity to let children be in touch with non-resident parents, and resident parents when they are on contact visits. More communication means less conflict.

Giving the children some control

It's really important that children have some control over contact. Stepping back and allowing them the opportunity to have the freedom to be in touch when they choose, how they choose and with a degree of privacy can help them find stepfamily life reassuring and supportive. Far from pushing them away or loosening the ties they have with you, it strengthens both their commitment to you and to their other parent – the two are not incompatible. Distance obviously makes this more of a challenge but it can be overcome if you use the tools available.

Some parents will have special concerns about using mobiles and the internet to facilitate contact. This may be because they feel children could use such access inappropriately. The fear may be that children would either use the internet to look at sites or chat to friends that have been deemed inappropriate, or that they may run up bills on mobile phones, or be at risk of phone and cyber bullying. Some parents feel mobile phones are a health risk. Another perceived risk is that the other parent may use unlimited or unsupervised contact to upset, confuse or sway a child to their point of view. If you have genuine concerns about this, then bring your fears out into the open. Discuss the matter with your partner and do some research. Reasonable mobile phone use appears to have little effect on health and the best way to keep children safe is to discuss issues with them.

Rules for safe internet and mobile use

To make it easier for you to be confident in letting children have access to modern technology, make some common-sense rules with them. Talk through the issues with children and make these the family rules:

▶ *If you're communicating with anyone you don't already know in the real world, don't tell them anything that could let them contact you offline. Keep your home address, school name, and telephone number to yourself. Use an online name that doesn't reveal your real name, age or where you come from. Be careful to whom you reveal your age.*

- ▶ *Be choosy about handing out your mobile number. Only give it to friends and ask them not to pass it on without your say so.*
- ▶ *Never say yes to a face-to-face meeting with another user without a parent or step-parent knowing and agreeing. If a meeting is arranged, it has to be in a public place and with an adult along.*
- ▶ *Don't get into 'flame wars' – angry and abusive exchanges. Never respond to messages or chat that are dirty, hostile, threatening, or make you feel uncomfortable. Tell an adult if you see any messages like that.*
- ▶ *Don't forget that in cyberspace, nobody can see you. That 12-year-old girl or boy who likes the same things you do could in reality be a 40-year-old man out to exploit you.*
- ▶ *Remember that not everything you read online is true. If it's 'too good to be true', it probably is. Don't accept any offers that involve your going to a meeting or having someone visit your house, or that involve you responding with information about yourself.*
- ▶ *Computer use is a family activity. If parents want to get to know your online friends, it's for the same reasons they'd like to know your other friends – to keep you safe and happy.*

Insight

The technology is safe – it's unsafe use that can make it hazardous. Learn the problems and the solutions yourself and talk over rules with your children to make sure all of you are confident about safe use.

You might like to write out this contract, talk it through with your kids and ask that both of you sign it:

- *I will not give out personal information such as my address, telephone number, my parents' or step-parents' work address or telephone number, or the name and location of my school without my parents' or step-parents' permission.*
- *I will tell my parents or step-parents right away if I come across any information that makes me feel uncomfortable.*
- *I won't say yes to a face-to-face meeting with someone I know online without first checking with my parents or step-parents. If my parents or step-parents agree to the meeting, it will be in a public place and a parent or step-parent will come along.*
- *I will never send my picture or anything else without first checking with my parents or step-parents.*
- *I will not respond to any messages that are mean or in any way make me feel uncomfortable. It is not my fault if I get a message like that. If I do, I will tell my parents or step-parents right away so that they can contact the service provider. I won't use my computer or mobile phone to send nasty messages to anyone else.*
- *I will talk with my parents or step-parents so that we can set up rules for going online. We will decide on the time of day that I can be online, the length of time I can be online and sites I can visit. I will not access other areas or break these rules without their permission.*
- *I will not give out my internet password to anyone (even my best friends). My parents or step-parents will need a very good reason and we will discuss this if they ask for it.*
- *I will check with my parents or step-parents before downloading anything or installing software or doing anything that could possibly cause any damage to our computer or give access to a virus or worm.*
- *I will not clear history to hide what sites I have visited after being on the internet and will be prepared to discuss with my parents or step-parents the sites I have been to.*
- *I will help my parents understand how to have fun and learn things online and teach them about the internet, computers and other technology, if they need it.*

Your responsibility

Parents have a responsibility to keep up with their children in these areas. To make sure you have some knowledge and confidence with the technology your children are using, parents should:

▶ *Get to know your computer, learn how to access the internet and familiarize yourself with the services your child uses. If you don't know how to use a chat room, get your child to show you.*
▶ *Report anything in chat rooms or in messages that is inappropriately sexual or threatening by forwarding a copy of the message to the service provider and asking for their assistance. Keep a copy on your computer. If your child is the subject of mobile text bullying, keep the messages and take it up with the school or the police.*
▶ *Don't fall for internet scams and hoaxes. Visit <u>www.snopes.com</u> regularly to see the latest and catch up on the old ones. If you want your child to keep safe, you need to learn how to do so as well.*
▶ *Make computer use a family activity. Keep computers in public areas – kitchens, living rooms, landings or hallways – so children know that while you should and do respect their privacy, you can and will at any time wander by and see what they are doing.*

Making the visited home familiar

When staying at a distance from their full-time home, children, even teenagers, may really welcome some familiarity. They may love taking home clothes, souvenirs, presents from their visit but equally they may want and need to leave items to be there, waiting for them, when they next come. It gives them a stake and a feeling of belonging. Having extra clothes and items in the visited home can also help deal with the inevitable forgotten item – socks or a toothbrush or nightclothes. Even if children only visit irregularly and infrequently, both families need to cooperate on making sure the right things travel with them, that some things can stay at the home they visit, and that there will be duplicate items if needs be.

Insight

Children need to feel a parent's home is their home too, even if it is far away and visits are sporadic.

Case study: Vijay and Mina

Vijay lived with his partner Mina and her daughter, and his son visited every other weekend, sleeping in the spare room. When the boy started visits he slept badly and would often wake Vijay in the middle of the night, demanding a drink. Every time he came he would spend the first half hour walking round the house, checking that things he remembered were still there. After six months, Mina suggested they decorate the spare room with Vijay's son, the way he would like it to be. Vijay was reluctant – he said they needed the room to be available for other people too, but Mina's daughter made a strong case for the idea. So the next weekend that he was with them, they spent the first evening drawing up plans and went the next day to a DIY store to get paint and material for curtains, and a chest in which he could leave toys and other belongings. Mina and Vijay also bought some extra clothes and suggested to Vijay's ex that some items should be left behind to be waiting for him when he next came. They started to refer to the room as his bedroom, not the spare room, and when he next arrived his first action was to dash up to his own room, now decked out to his design. From then on, there were no more midnight demands and the boy slept well in his own bedroom.

SHOULD VISITS BE ALL FUN AND GAMES?

When children visit from a distance, it can be tempting to fill all the time with fun, treats and events. This has several downsides:

▶ *It can mean children go home full of what they did, hyped up and often asking for more, to the immense irritation and distress of the other family.*

- *If they have stepsiblings who stayed behind, it can cause conflict within that family.*
- *It may cause distress if the family caring full-time for the children feels that money might have been better spent on day-to-day items rather than fun and games.*

But the most important reason is that constant treats don't benefit the child, or the relationship with the parent being visited. By only doing special things, you are underlining the fact that this is not a 'normal' situation or a 'normal' family. Children may enjoy what is happening but they often ask for more and more because it doesn't actually satisfy them. They feel empty and discontented, and think if the treats were more unusual and more expensive they'd feel all right. In fact, what they really need is to share the sort of time parents and children have when they live together. You all need 'chill out' time – time when you merely are in each other's company, not doing anything especially. Instead of going out, you can stay in and chat, play games, watch a DVD together, make a meal together. Children should also be able to contact their friends and other family, as they would normally.

Parents often try to pile on the treats in order to:

- *make up for what they feel kids have lost by being in this situation*
- *assuage their own guilt*
- *show they love the child*
- *win the child's loyalty*
- *get back at the other parent and their new partner.*

In all cases, the person who suffers from this is the child, and it doesn't actually make the person handing out the treats feel any better. If you feel this sort of behaviour is going on, think it through and discuss the situation with your partner. You may need to suggest getting together with the other family, possibly with the support and guidance of a mediator, to sort out and settle matters.

Flexible arrangements

One size doesn't fit all. One child in a family may have different
needs or wishes than others. One child may be at the age of
being able to stay overnight with a non-resident parent, another
may not. One child may have decided he or she wants to see a
non-resident parent more often than another. Even more than
when children and their other family live nearby, the fact that
one size does not fit all is vital to consider when families live
some distance apart.

It is tempting to assume that if time, effort and money are
being expended on sending one child to see their other family
that any siblings should go along too. Or, indeed, if one child
is going through a 'Don't want to go, shan't go' phase, that this
covers all of them. There may well be extra cost and work involved
in letting children visit at the rate each wants and needs, rather
than trying to shoehorn all of them into what amounts to an
ill-fitting compromise. Parents and step-parents may need to get
together and talk it through to recognize that no one should take

this personally and that it is important to go at the rate the child is ready to accept.

> **Insight**
>
> Keep up to date. An arrangement that works well one month may be entirely unsuited a month or so later and almost certainly will be inappropriate a year or so down the line.

In the same way, parents and step-parents may need to keep on their toes and be sensitive and open to the way children change and develop. Small children, for instance, may find it very hard to be apart from parents for more than a night – very small children can only manage a day. Older children may benefit enormously from overnights and longer. Teenagers, who have reached the age when their peer group are more important than parents, may resent being taken away from events they see as vital or from friendships that are fluid and need constant management. So, whatever agreements you reach now may need to be revisited regularly, and if you've had a system in place for some time, remember to revise it.

How much information do non-resident parents need?

Non-resident parents need to be kept up to date on what is happening in their child's life – just as parents and step-parents who have full-time care need to know what might have happened while a child was on a visit. Official reports such as school or health checks need to be sent to both addresses, but parents should also pass on important information between each other. That doesn't only include things such as test results or health checks – it also means briefings about friends, favourite films, programmes, food and drink, clothes – anything the child is interested in and which a parent should know about. Of course, parents can often be out of date – how often, as a child, did you hear a parent of yours confidently tell someone about your tastes and sigh because they had it so wrong? But if a non-resident parent at least has something to go on, they can open the conversation and be told how out of date they are. For the sake of the child, parents and step-parents need to update each other as frequently as possible.

GRANDPARENTS AND OTHER RELATIVES

We've looked at the issue as it relates to parents but it's equally true of other family connections – we'll look at that in more detail in Chapter 12.

THINGS TO REMEMBER

▶ *In our mobile society, there is a high chance of children living a long way from the non-resident parent. Special attention and communication between the adults involved is needed if there is to be successful and as regular contact as possible between the child and the distant parent.*

▶ *Separated parents need to communicate and work together to make contact arrangements function smoothly. All adults involved have to be grown-up and put aside their own reluctance to have anything to do with each other, and need to have an understanding of the sort of resistance, objection and anxiety the children may have about the situation.*

▶ *Children need some sense of control over contact, so the sooner they can arrange it themselves or are asked what they want, when and how, the better.*

▶ *As well as visits, children benefit from frequent communication via cards or letters, mobile phone calls and texts and email or instant messaging. Parents and step-parents need to keep up and familiarize themselves with new technology.*

▶ *One size does not fit all. Children in a family may be at different stages and want different levels and types of contact. Needs can also change, so being sensitive to these variations and being flexible enough to accommodate them is the aim.*

IDEAS TO TRY

▶ *If the other parent lives some distance away, review what this means for contact with them and children. Does it affect face-to-face contact? Other forms of contact? How often are children and parents in touch?*

▶ *Has distance meant anyone in the situation has lost support systems? How has that affected the situation? Ideas-storm how problems might be minimized.*

▶ *Review how your children use means other than face-to-face contact to be in touch, e.g. mobiles, computers, snail mail etc. Are you in agreement over use? Ideas-storm how you and the children can support each other in this.*

▶ *Draw up, between you and the children, agreements and a contract for the use of technology, at home, with friends, in public and at school.*

▶ *Discuss and draw up, between you and the children, agreements and a contract for safe internet and mobile use, using the suggested format in this chapter.*

▶ *Consider whether your contact arrangements are up to date and flexible and that you have discussed this with other adults and children involved. One size does not fit all, and circumstances and children change. Does your arrangement suit everyone at the moment? How will you keep up to speed with change and effect it when necessary?*

▶ *How do the separated parents involved keep each other informed about the children's changing interests, abilities and other necessary information? Review how you do so and discuss it with the children involved too.*

10

Schools and the stepfamily

In this chapter you will learn:
- *the importance of schools and parents working together*
- *how to involve your ex and your partner in a child's education*
- *why children in a stepfamily may truant and what to do about it*
- *how to help the school help you.*

School as a child's support network

School plays a really important role in children's lives. It can be a haven, somewhere to go which stays the same when all else is changing. It can be the place where their own support networks, both peers and trusted teachers, sustain them. The people around them at school can help them feel centre stage – often vital when the adults in their lives may be caught up in themselves. But it can also be the place where uncertainty and lack of self-worth can make family change even more difficult.

The break-up of one family and the establishment of a new one can often mean a child moving from one school to another, either because the new family moves or because for various reasons it's felt desirable. If the new stepfamily contains several children who are stepsiblings, adults may feel it would help if they all went to the same school. The new school may be felt to be better, just as the new family may be felt to be a step in the right direction – and indeed children may have had unfortunate experiences in the old school, as they struggled with family break-up and the establishment of the new family. But even good change is change and means children are uprooted even further, not only losing their old family but leaving behind people who knew them and might have helped them.

Step-parents and non-resident parents may feel helpless about how choices are made about school moves and subjects to be studied, but children need all the adults caring for them to be involved and also need to have a say themselves. Indeed, a step-parent's role may not be to contribute to the decisions but to support those involved to have their say and be heard and to listen to all the views.

A child's desire to be with friends in a familiar place may be set aside as a less important reason to choose one school than nearness to home or academic excellence. But keeping that support network may actually be the most important aspect possible for their wellbeing. Also, proximity to the non-resident parent's home may be worthwhile factoring in and actually more important than being close to the day-to-day household. Being near a non-resident parent may mean they can collect children and have breakfast or tea with them before or after school, and make it easy for informal, spontaneous contact.

Insight

Never underestimate the importance to a child of their own support network – friends of their own age and adults who are their contacts, not yours.

The dangers of keeping school and home separate

Children often like to keep school and home separate. They tend to see the two as very different spheres. After all, home is a place where you can eat, watch TV, get angry, speak up and even occasionally be boisterous more or less as you like. School is a place with formal rules and timetables, where you have to keep to rigid mealtimes, may be punished for losing your temper or making a noise. Home is a place where you might expect to be hugged and accepted for who you are. School is somewhere you have to compete and excel, and have to keep a 'stiff upper lip'. The predictability of school may be a relief if home life is unsettled and unstable. It's a place that does not alter, with old friends and support when so much is shifting about them.

Children may behave very differently at school than they do at home. Some will try to hold it together at home, not wanting to put extra burdens on a parent who may be struggling with new conditions. School may then become the one place they can act out their anger. Others may use home as the place to 'kick off' while retaining a normal appearance at school. Whatever their actual behaviour in school, teachers may be oblivious to the changes in a child's life. Unless you explain, the child may keep quiet about it. Which means children may be attracting punishment for behaviour that is the natural and understandable reaction to distress and may not be receiving support.

You may have a fight on your hands with the child when you want to tell the school what is going on. You may accept that it helps for the school to know so they can understand the circumstances surrounding a child's behaviour. Children, however, may say they don't want to let school know about family change or problems. It's often tempting to give way on this. Young people may feel unwilling to let you know if they are having problems in school. They may feel you have too much to cope with already, or can't help them anyway, or feel the two separate worlds should be kept apart. I'm all for respecting a child's choice and wishes, but sometimes we have to take responsibility for stepping in. The fact is that schools really do need to know what is going on in order to make sense of what children do or say or feel while in their charge.

*My son seems to be having a bad time at school recently.
He's been on report for fighting and they are threatening
him with exclusion. His father has cancelled the last three
visits at the last moment and I'm sure it has everything
to do with that. I think the school needs to know what is
happening in his life and how much it hurts and makes him
angry but he totally refuses to let me go and speak with his
teacher. He says it will just mean he's picked out and it's
none of their business. What should I do?*

You son has the right to be listened to and consulted, and to
have some control over the choices in his life. That, after all,
is what some of this is about – his anger and pain at having
no control over contact with his father. But equally, he
needs to know that his feelings of shame and anxiety about
anyone at the school knowing about his circumstances are
entirely unfounded. If they knew, they may well offer some
help in the form of anger management or counselling – and
he deserves and needs both. I'm sure they'd also make some
allowances and be supportive. You're the adult; he may say
he doesn't want you to go but he can't stop you. Discuss
this with him, laying out the options and your perception
of how helpful it would be. In the end, it's your call and it
sounds as if communicating with the school is preferable to
leaving them in the dark. Good luck!

Why do stepfamily children truant?

It can only make things worse if adjusting to a new or still
awkward situation at home is intensified by bullying or harsh
treatment at school. Children often prefer not to have details of

their home life made open to their school. They feel it risks having them picked out and made visible and vulnerable. This is fine when their lives in both spheres are on an even keel. It's often not helpful during family change. Their need for privacy, boundaries and a say in their own lives often leads them to keep quiet about trouble at school rather than bring it home to you, or risk you going to the school. The problem is that young people often do not see the connection between unhappiness at home and difficulties in school. They may not recognize that they are reacting to what is going on in their home life by being moody or failing at their studies, and that the school knowing what is going on might help.

Insight

It's important to listen to and respect children's wishes. It's also important to be the adult and to sometimes take important decisions because you know you're right.

A child may also become a truant or school refuser in the midst of family change. Parents, step-parents and the school may search desperately for reasons why they might be refusing to attend, and focus on some of the usual reasons:

- *bullying by other children*
- *treatment by teachers that shuts them out or scares them*
- *fear of being shown up in class having dropped behind in studies*
- *the fear of punishment for not keeping up with work, or for non-attendance.*

The sad reality, which adults in a stepfamily may not want to accept, may be that the child is afraid of what might happen if they leave home rather than what is waiting for them at school. With so much changing around them, they may be scared that if they turn their back to go to school, they could come home to yet more surprises. It could be that the following are the reasons for refusing to go to school:

- *Their family is transforming, they are losing touch with people that matter to them and they don't know what else may happen next.*

- *They feel they should be available to care for a parent or sibling.*
- *A parent or sibling may be drowning their grief or uncertainty in drink or drugs and the child may be worried about what will happen while they are away.*

The school may be the one to make a call to you if the child is being seen as badly behaved in class. Or, you might go to them, especially if the bad behaviour is coming out at home too. Parents may feel able to approach the school even when such behaviour is only experienced at home because they don't know where else to go. If the behaviour is happening at school as well as at home, the feeling may be 'Well, it's not all our fault – they can't do a thing with him either!'

Why the school needs to know what is happening

Talking to the school may be of immense help to parents and to the child. The point is that schools are often in the dark about what is going on in a child's life. Unless you actually tell them, how are they to know what might be affecting a pupil's feelings or behaviour?

You may not want to go to the doctor and ask for a referral for specialized counselling or child behavioural support. Talking with a teacher, who after all we expect to be 'an expert' in children, feels safer. Sometimes, what seems to be 'bad behaviour' in children is nothing of the sort. Small children who run around screaming, grab things off the shelves when you take them shopping, draw on the walls at home or ask 'Why?' every two seconds are not naughty. They are perfectly, normally curious. A teenager who argues back isn't being defiant or rebellious but working through a normal stage of development – the journey towards standing on their own two feet. This would have happened anyway – it just may seem hard to cope with at a time when so much else is happening. Something that appears to have started around the time the family broke up or the stepfamily formed may be the normal developmental behaviour of a toddler, child or teenager. But it may also be a reaction – an understandable, common, natural reaction – to the situation.

A trusted teacher may help you work towards an understanding of what is going on. You, and they, will want to explore:

▶ *what might be the cause of the behaviour*
▶ *what might help*
▶ *where support may be found.*

Insight

The vital questions to ask will be: 'What changed around the time this behaviour started?' or 'Has this happened before – when, and what was happening then?' The answers may help you and the school to unpack what might be the trouble and to find a solution or support.

Talking to the child and saying 'It sounds as if/it feels like/I would imagine you are feeling angry/sad/upset/confused. Can you tell me what you feel?' can give them the opportunity to explore their emotions. Sometimes children (and adults too) can't put their feelings into words. They don't know what emotion is setting them off – it's all too overwhelming. Issues around school can be the impetus to talk this through.

Essential points to consider

▶ *School can be a haven to children experiencing family change.*
▶ *If a new stepfamily means a new school, children can lose valuable support networks.*
▶ *Children like to keep school and family separate. This can cause problems if it means the school is not aware of the cause of bad behaviour.*
▶ *School and parents need to communicate and work together to support children.*

How to support children in their schooling

Children benefit from having both their parents, and any new step-parents, show an interest in their schooling, even when they do not live together. It's really vital that both parents receive notice of parent–teacher meetings and that you have some agreement between you, and the school, about how you are going to manage this. Not only can you ask the school to make sure information is sent to both parents, you can also ask for special help if work or family commitments make it difficult for both of you to attend parent–teacher meetings. Instead of both parents going to the meetings together, you could ask for one of you to have a one-to-one with members of staff at other times.

Ask to see both your child's main tutor or teacher and a head or deputy head and tell them that the child now has two homes. Explain that both parents are remaining in contact and will be supporting the child's learning and give the names and contact details of those adults who have responsibility, who may pick up or drop off the child and may be involved in making decisions or giving permission for various situations.

Some stepfamilies may feel it appropriate for step-parents to talk to teachers, too – if they are intimately involved in the day-to-day life of the child and their schooling, it does seem fair. But both the parents' and the child's feelings need to be taken into account – this is something for new partners to discuss, for children to have input on and then parents to agree together.

OVERCOMING SCHOOL ANXIETY

Young people cannot contribute to and gain from their education unless they feel protected from ridicule and bullying, from other children and from teachers. They need to feel safe and confident, both at home and at school. The problem is that adults often feel uncomfortable when in contact with our children's school, especially after family change. You may shy away from going through the school gates or asking to speak to a teacher – especially a head or deputy head – because it feels as if you have travelled back 20 or so years to being a pupil yourself once again. If all you can remember from your school days is being small and insignificant, not being listened to, being humiliated, being powerless… it's hardly surprising you may not want to risk feeling like that again. You too can start feeling angry, defiant, defensive – not the best beginning for a reasoned, supportive and helpful chat.

It may be because you are still hamstrung by the culture of silence that exists in many schools – don't tell, grass or sneak. Or it may be because you feel the teaching staff won't support, listen to or believe either you or your children. You may feel it shows you up as an incompetent parent – as 'a failure'. You may feel the school won't listen or will deny there is a problem – and you may be right. While many schools are making great strides in acknowledging and tackling all the issues that worry children in the middle of family change, some still are not. Some schools realize the difficulties parents face and do their best to send out messages that welcome you in and make it clear you can speak to them. Others are less aware, so it's up to you to recognize that while you may feel 12 years old again, you are an adult in control of yourself and your own life and able to be in control of a situation.

Case study: Kerry and Mike

Kerry's son Sam was put in detention three weeks running for twice not having his sports kit and not bringing back a letter that had to be signed. The reason he'd been unprepared was that Sam's father had had to change arrangements for when Sam stayed over and he'd not had his kit with him on the following morning. The letter had been lost sometime over the weekend, in the scramble. Mike was furious and felt it was really unfair, and threatened to go to the school and have it out with them. Kerry realized this would only make things worse but felt unable to deal with the school herself. Both Kerry and Mike had bad memories of their own school lives and poor expectations of a helpful response. Fortunately, one of Sam's teachers felt he hadn't been given enough chance to explain himself and questioned him. She rang and discussed the situation with Kerry, and suggested in future that if Sam had similar problems again he should say. More importantly, she said that since Sam was not the only child in such a situation, the school was about to revise procedures for sending letters out, in order to take account of separated parents and stepfamilies.

Insight

Most schools recognize that working in partnership with parents is the best way to support children.

Communication with the school

Children can pick up on whether you have anxieties about school and have poor expectations from their school or schooling. Being involved in your child's school tells them that you value it as a place to be and a place to learn, and that learning is important. Most teachers encourage and welcome your involvement and encourage parents to take part by attending parent–teacher meetings and open evenings. The big issue for separated parents is who should attend and who should receive communications from the school.

Some schools still send notices back through children. This can be especially hard on stepfamilies on two counts. If a child goes to school from one home and travels on to another for a stay at the end of that day, a letter that is intended for the resident parent may be handed to the other – or, more often, get forgotten and lost at the bottom of a school bag. Equally problematic is when a letter is given to one parent, usually the parent the child lives with during the week, effectively cutting off the other parent from involvement in a vital aspect of their child's life – an aspect, moreover, that both parents (and indeed the step-parent) need jointly to be involved in. Even when schools do send vital communications by post, they often neglect to confirm whether parents live apart, and if so which addresses they should be sending notices to.

When schools do not routinely ask if parents live together, it can seem awkward and embarrassing to specify that you live apart. You may fear it singles out your child unfairly. However, it is certainly preferable for the school to understand the circumstances surrounding a child's home life. If a child who is usually on the ball about having their games kit or the proper books turns up at school without them, teachers are more likely to be lenient and understanding if they know it's hard to keep track when you may arrive at school from one home and leave to go to another.

It's important to recognize you're not alone in struggling with a lack of confidence in speaking to teachers. It's a common difficulty and will be shared by many other parents of children at the school. It might help you, and other parents, to take a checklist to the next meeting you have with the school. You can use this to check on what your child's school is doing, to inform them of your situation, and to ask for changes if they haven't taken your situation on board.

Essential points to consider

▶ *Children benefit from having both parents and step-parents involved in their schooling.*

▶ *Parents may need to confront and deal with their own anxieties about school to enable them to be in partnership with the school over their children's wellbeing.*

▶ *Parents and step-parents may need to discuss strategies and challenge procedures to make sure both families are kept informed of their child's progress and needs by the school.*

How to make sure the school is on board

Ask the school:

▶ *How do you take children's different family circumstances into account? Do pupil records show whether parents live together or whether children live with adults who are not related to them? Do they show whether children have more than one regular address? Are the records you keep on children kept up to date and are they changed if the child's circumstances change? Do you make sure all members of staff who deal with a child know about what is happening to them?*

▶ *What do you do about parents living at separate addresses? Do you keep the parent who doesn't live with the children on a daily basis informed about reports, school events and trips? Do letters sent home assume both parents live there? Does the school use text messages and the internet to keep both parents informed?*

▶ *Does the school accept that family change is normal? What are teachers' attitudes towards family change? What do you teach about families and family lives? How might a child's out-of-school life and family circumstance come up in the classroom? Do the teachers and the learning materials indicate that families come in all shapes and sizes?*

▶ *How do you know if pupils are having difficulties in their family lives? How do you think such difficulties may affect pupils, parents and the school? If children have problems or get into trouble, are their family circumstances or how they may be feeling about this taken into account?*

▶ *How do you help children who are new to the area? How do you deal with a child who arrives during the school year?*

▶ *Can you do more to support pupils with family problems? Does the school have a formal policy to offer support, or does it only happen if a particular member of staff takes a lead?*

▶ *What sort of extra, outside help can you recommend? How good are your links with outside help?*

Of course, it's not only formal interaction with the school that might make a difference to the child. Social events such as sports days or school plays are also important. Would your child welcome all the adults caring for him or her to attend such events? Or would they only want their original parents there – allowing a step-parent to step in if one parent cannot attend? Or would they not want to have a particular person around? The situation can be a minefield and the only way you are going to sort it out is:

▶ *to talk it through with the child, respecting and hearing their views*

▶ to discuss it with all the adults concerned – parents and step-parents – and agree to do whatever the child wants and needs.

Insight
Children really do want parents and sometimes step-parents to attend school events, even if they say they don't care. Make sure the adults they want to be there do attend.

Getting support from other parents

All parents know how useful and reassuring it is to be in contact with other parents of children at your child's school. Stepfamilies can find this difficult to manage – sometimes because they live at some distance from the child's school or because the other parent is the one who has such contact or because they feel different and stigmatized. It helps the child and yourself if you make efforts to break such isolation and to have contact with other parents. You may have to discuss this with the other family or the school itself, but it's worth taking the initiative to do so. If the child is able to see their friends when on visits, that's an opportunity for non-resident parents to get to know the parents of school friends.

THINGS TO REMEMBER

▶ *School can be one of the most important features in a child's life – a constant place to be when everything else around them has changed or is changing.*

▶ *Choosing a school when so many factors can be involved – nearness to the non-resident parent, where stepsiblings go, etc. – can be difficult and confusing. All the adults involved, and the child, need to have a say in this.*

▶ *School-refusing is not always about a flight from problems at school – bullying, unsympathetic teachers or fears of not fitting in. Some children from families undergoing or having undergone family change refuse school because they fear that if they leave their recently destabilized home, further unwelcome changes will happen in their absence.*

▶ *A parent and school partnership is the basis of a child being happy at school. Talk to the school and keep them informed fully about developments in the child's family and ask them what measures they are taking to support all the children in their care.*

▶ *If your child's behaviour becomes overwhelming, you can ask a trusted teacher for support or request that your doctor refers your child for specialist counselling.*

▶ *Non-resident parents should strengthen their own support networks and make contact with other parents at the child's school.*

IDEAS TO TRY

▶ *Consider how you feel supported, included and understood by the children's school. How do they, or how might they, help or hinder your family?*

▶ *Ideas-storm with the children how they view their own peer group support system.*

▶ *Ideas-storm with the children how they feel supported or let down by their school.*

▶ *Review how the child's school handles separated families. Using information in this chapter, clarify their system for taking children's circumstances into account and keeping parents who live separately informed and involved.*

▶ *With the children, ideas-storm how much information the school should have about your family circumstances. If you have different views, discuss what they might be, why and how this may affect the situation.*

▶ *Consider how much support you feel you have from other parents. With another adult, ideas-storm how you might change this if necessary.*

11

Fighting the myths

In this chapter you will learn:
- *how stepfamily myths can cause problems for you*
- *how to separate the person from their behaviour*
- *why love is not enough.*

Mention stepfamilies and everyone thinks they know all about them. Stepfamilies either mean wicked stepmothers or psychotic stepfathers, or saintly men or women 'taking on' other people's children. Stepfamilies, possibly more than any other family arrangement, suffer from the fact that the myths obscure the real issues.

Are stepfamilies like the image we get from fairy stories?

There are so many negative myths about stepfamilies and it's easy to see where some of them begin. Fairy or children's stories are full of stepfamilies, and seldom in a positive light. Most of us have heard about Cinderella and her Wicked Stepmother. Hansel and Gretel, in most tellings of the tale, are abandoned in the forest by their father at the urging of his second wife. And the Wicked Queen who targets Snow White is also a stepmother. In some tales, horrible stepsiblings also appear such as the Ugly Sisters in Cinderella. Both Shakespeare and Dickens feature second marriages and evil stepfathers such as Claudius in *Hamlet* and Murdstone in

David Copperfield. Furthermore, modern media tend to end up showing stepfamilies as disaster zones – *Domestic Disturbance* and *The Stepfather* feature stepdads as murderers, *Your, Mine and Ours* shows them as chaotic. *Love Actually* is one of the few films that show a step-parent can be as loving and caring as a parent, given a chance and making some effort.

> ### Insight
> Stepfamilies get such a bad press in stories and in the media. You may need to tackle the myths head-on to deal with them.

Can positive myths be as unhelpful as negative ones?

Negative myths can mean children approach stepfamilies with anxiety and pessimism, expecting there to be difficulties. They may remember the fairy tales or they may hear remarks by friends, relatives and neighbours all tainted by the expectation that stepfamilies are a bad place to be. This can affect their behaviour, as they react to what they expect to happen rather than to what is actually happening. Similarly, step-parents can go into the situation expecting the worst. They might resent the 'bad press' they may feel they have attracted simply by being a step-parent, before they as a person have had the opportunity to show what they can do and who they really are. But they may still allow the bad press to colour their own expectations, anticipating both apprehension and resistance on the part of the children and other relatives, and problems in the general situation.

But positive myths can actually be almost as destructive. Some people expect stepfamilies to be an instant solution, or assume that a step-parent is saintly or superhuman, willing to love and accept the children of another man or woman. It may be hard to admit there are problems or to ask for help if everyone assumes you can cope or that no problems should exist.

From the postbag

I've been seeing my fiancé for almost a year and my kids both get on with him really well. We're getting married in two months' time and while they were excited and happy about it up to now, all of a sudden they've gone into a flat panic. I tried to find out what was wrong and what changed their minds and it seems their nan and some friends have been filling their heads with stories about wicked stepfathers and awful stepfamilies. How can I get them back to seeing it as a plus?

Make a joke of the situation. Gather together all the wicked stepfamily stories you and they can find. Have a night together when you read/view them and then ask the children what they think. Are they true? What reality do they have? Why? And do they think your fiancé, who they like, is going to change overnight and why would that be? Confronting and exploring myths is the best way to deflate them. And then they become a family joke – like the family I know where the kids call their stepmum 'WSM': Wicked Step Mum. Good luck!

What are the myths and how do you counter them?

'ALL STEPMOTHERS, STEPFATHERS AND STEPSIBLINGS ARE WICKED'

People can do wicked things and sometimes they can get stuck in hurtful or cruel patterns. Being part of a stepfamily can be difficult, complex, often confused and certainly overwhelming. All the issues that led to your being in the stepfamily and all the ones that surface when you are there can give rise to very bad feelings, and it's bad feelings that lead to bad behaviour. So, stepmothers, stepfathers and stepsiblings, as well as mothers, fathers and children who live apart from their original family, can sometimes act imperfectly. Rather than writing them off or assuming they're like that simply because of what they are, it pays to communicate. They're usually like that because of what they're feeling about the situation, and talking about it often makes a difference. Anyone in a stepfamily needs to understand what is going on and why the situation makes it so hard. Once you can separate the behaviour from the person and accept that it's the behaviour that needs tackling not the individual, you and they may be able to find a point of contact and then move on. Ask yourself what you or other people may feel about the situation and what they can do about such feelings. If you can recognize they may be feeling angry or abandoned or frightened or rejected and behaving badly because of it, you could open the lines of communication. Say: 'It sounds like/feels like/ I imagine you might be feeling upset/angry/etc. Can we talk about it?' You too may be doing things that hurt other people. Asking yourself the same questions and following through on what they tell you could help.

Insight

People usually behave badly because they are hurting or because they don't realize the effect of what they do. It pays to communicate.

'ALL STEPMOTHERS AND STEPFATHERS ARE SAINTS'

The converse myth to the one above is the belief that any man or woman who 'takes on' another person's child is somehow a saint, showing superhuman patience, selflessness or kindness. It certainly takes a certain amount of generosity of spirit to be a good step-parent, but it needs to be said that all step-parents will at some time also struggle with feelings of jealousy, resentment and anger. And being a step-parent isn't all altruism. A step-parent is in the relationship because they love their partner.

Their primary focus is to be a partner, not a parent – the children tend to be an afterthought and a necessary add-on, not the reason they took on the relationship. And, of course, being a step-parent in itself may also bring benefits. Adults unable to have children of their own, adults separated and out of contact with children they love, may find redemption in the relationship they have with their stepchildren. Just as with the wicked step-parent myth, you need to recognize that people and relationships are all individual. No one is either a saint or a sinner and it helps to be able to consider why people act the way they do in order to ask for help or offer it.

'SECOND RELATIONSHIPS ARE EASIER THAN FIRST ONES'

Samuel Johnson said that second marriage was 'The triumph of hope over experience'. You might expect that the experience you had in your earlier relationships would stand you in good stead and make this family more straightforward to manage. It doesn't work like that. A first relationship may be a blank sheet or could have been blighted with baggage from the past and your childhood. A second one includes all the issues that affected the first, with extra ones. Just moving on doesn't leave the original problems behind. Unless the concerns that made the previous partnership come apart are addressed, you are at risk of repeating the same pattern in your new family. But on top of that, the unfinished business surrounding the ending of the last partnership can affect a new one. The continuing contact with ex-partners and the presence of children can put particular strains on any second relationship, and can make things not only complex and complicated but tense and hard. You are more likely to divorce in a second marriage – two in five first marriages end but one in two second marriages do so.

You can make a better go of a second relationship and be one of those who succeed. But to do so you need to recognize the myth and accept that insight, understanding and some work will be needed. Second relationships are successful if the issues that sunk the first are addressed. The feelings of all those involved have to be considered and expressed, and everyone needs to understand that the best tack is to communicate and cooperate, if not for themselves then for the sake of the children.

'CHILDREN WILL ACCEPT THE NEW SITUATION QUICKLY'

Children are human beings. They are no less intelligent, insightful or aware than adults. They may lack experience and access to information but they often make up for that by being able to pick up all sorts of things from adults who don't realize they can hear and understand very well. Children may adapt to a new situation quickly but that's not the same as accepting it. Often their way of coping is to shut down – to stop trying to tell those around them how upset or even desperate they are about what has happened, if they realize they aren't being listened to or heard. After all, they may feel they have absolutely no way of changing what is going on. In which case, they may think there's no point in saying it makes them miserable and that they wish it were different, since saying so only makes the situation worse. Quiet children are not always good, obedient, content children. They are more often unhappy children who have learnt the hard way that trying to speak out doesn't get them heard. And badly behaved children aren't acting up simply for the fun of it. Bad behaviour is invariably a way of expressing feelings that aren't being expressed in any other way. Don't expect children to fall into line at once. Give them time, respect what they say and accept some bad behaviour as a way of them showing you their feelings. It does take time.

'PART-TIME STEPFAMILIES GET ALONG BETTER THAN FULL-TIME ONES'

Being a part-time stepfamily may give you some breathing space. If you see children at particular times and not at others, at least it gives you time to recoup and regroup before the next visit, and sending them off for contact visits gives you some time to yourselves. There may not be open conflict and you may feel that means everyone is happy with the situation. But most people's experience is actually that being in a part-time family is far harder than being in a full-time one.

For a start, just because children do not live with you every day doesn't mean you don't consider them all the time. Their physical presence may be intermittent, but your emotional commitment to them is constant. Non-resident parents often feel left out of important decisions and may feel their children are growing up without them. Part-time living means almost daily management, as you negotiate or plan or worry about when you'll see them next. Part-time families mean so much more planning – the financial arrangements, travel and handovers, clothes and items that need to be in one place or the other, childcare cover for holidays, food for when they are there... it goes on. Part-time contact also means far more complication over who sees whom – children may not see grandparents as much as everyone would choose – and what happens when children are not there. If there are children living full time in one family they may resent having other kids dropping in and out of their lives and taking up time, attention and space. Or, indeed, they may miss them fiercely when they are at the other family. Part-time children may resent full-time children having continuing access to a parent they only see sometimes.

If yours is a part-time family, it may be necessary to acknowledge the full-time impact it has on all of you. Lack of conflict may be more about everyone's need to brush anger or hurt or resentment under the carpet so as not to spoil the little time you have with each other than because it isn't there. Separated families need daily connection and if this can't be done face to face it should be done by text, phone or email. If nobody argues, make sure it's because everyone is getting on rather than because everyone is scared of rocking the boat. Have a family round-table discussion (see Chapter 1) and make it possible for children and adults to express their feelings so you can clear the air and resolve problems. Above all, don't expect everything to be simple or easy. It rarely is in stepfamilies.

Insight
However infrequently children see the people who are important to them, a part-time family is 100 per cent part of their life.

'IF PARTNERS LOVE EACH OTHER ENOUGH, PROBLEMS WILL DISAPPEAR'

Relationships need to be founded on love. But love is never enough and even good, solid, loving relationships can founder on the rocks of unresolved stepfamily issues, just as they can be sunk by any argument that isn't properly handled. Problems never disappear simply by being ignored. If it's assumed that problems will go away on their own, if partners persist in behaving in the same way, the chances are that the problems will actually get worse.

> **Insight**
> Love is a good beginning but any problems in a stepfamily need patience, understanding and effort to solve.

'RELATING TO STEPCHILDREN IS THE SAME AS TO NATURAL CHILDREN'

Stepchildren are not your own. They are as good, as delightful, as loving and lovable... but they are not your own. A stepchild can become someone you love as fiercely, as naturally, as unconditionally as a child who is yours by birth. But the journey to that position is different. With a birth child there can be a gut-deep connection, something that develops during the nine months in the womb and overwhelms both parents when the child is born. The feelings both parents can have for a newborn child can be described as falling in love – a love that is abiding and overpowering. Not all birth parents find that their experiences are as quick or as definitive as this. Some birth parents take longer to develop the bond with their children, and have to be patient and persistent in building the relationship.

Step-parents very rarely 'fall in love' with their stepchildren. Some do. But most find themselves in a similar situation to the parent who has not had the fortune to be hit by this wave of instinctive emotion. Problems arise if and when they, and everyone around them, assumes they should feel as strongly for a stepchild as they might for one of their own. Step-parents who don't meet this emotional 'standard' often assume there must be something wrong with them – they are unnatural – or that there is something wrong with the children – they deserve hostility and are wicked. The truth is that we have instincts working against us. In the natural world, we may be driven, like lions, to remove any offspring who are not related to us. Being human, we can think our way around such primitive drives. But we need to understand and forgive ourselves for not having the same feelings immediately for stepchildren as we think we should. Step-parents should act the same way towards their stepchildren as they would to their own, but it takes time for the feelings to grow. They will, given time. But you need to give it time.

THINGS TO REMEMBER

▶ *The popular myths about stepfamilies – the Wicked Stepmother on the one hand or the Saint taking care of other people's children on the other – do not represent real stepfamilies, which are places where real people try their best to succeed and flourish somewhere in between.*

▶ *Sometimes apparently positive myths can be almost as destructive and misleading as the bad ones. They can lead to false assumptions, such as that a stepfamily is an instant solution or that a step-parent must necessarily be saintly and superhuman to take on the role.*

▶ *Love does not conquer all and love and good intentions alone may not be enough to secure a good relationship in the face of the stress and pressure of stepfamily issues. Love is always a good foundation and a beginning, but a successful stepfamily will need patience, understanding and effort from all concerned.*

IDEAS TO TRY

▶ *While all together in a relaxed mood, challenge the family to come up with as many stories, films, TV programmes and books based on the theme of stepfamilies or with stepfamily characters. Give a prize for the most-named and the most unusual or obscure!*

▶ *Note and discuss how positive or negative is the portrayal of stepfamilies in stories, films, TV programmes and books.*

▶ *Ideas-storm the myths, expectations, assumptions and beliefs about stepfamilies, step-parents, stepchildren and stepsiblings.*

▶ *Discuss how these may have affected beliefs, emotions, attitudes and behaviour.*

12

Grandparents and other family members

In this chapter you will learn:
- *about the importance of relatives*
- *how to maintain links between children and the non-resident parent and their family*
- *how to keep support networks.*

Very few families live, out of choice, in a vacuum, cut off from parents, siblings, uncles and aunts. As far as children are concerned, cousins can be playmates and friends while uncles, aunts and particularly grandparents are often adults who offer gifts, treats, fun and games and vital emotional support.

In stepfamilies these relatives often take on a vital protective role. They give the parents and step-parents some backup and security. But more importantly they often hold out to children the one stable point in a universe that has changed. Children who may have felt their sense of certainty and security had become uncertain as their family altered can at least be reassured that this part of their supportive network remains the same.

> **Insight**
> Grandparents may be boring and old-fashioned and visits to them never vary – but that becomes an absolute virtue when everything else important in your life has changed all too much.

Are family connections important?

Grandparents often become central in a child's life when one parent has been left on their own, stepping in to provide increasing levels of childcare or respite. Children often lean on grandparents or aunts and uncles when they want someone to talk to who they feel they can trust but who is outside the immediate family. If one parent has died or contact has become erratic, their relatives become a real anchor point in somehow keeping the link between a child and their missing parent. Grandparents and aunts and uncles often help maintain the connection between a child and a birth parent when parents have separated and they may otherwise lose touch.

This is why it can be devastating to children if the bonds they have with grandparents and other family members begin to fray and come apart as their family alters. When a relationship comes to an end, battle lines are often drawn. Many family members feel their place is defending their own relation against an ex-partner. Even if the ex-partner themself wants no conflict, it can be triggered by family members who feel they are doing the right thing. If there is tension, it can be made far more hostile by relatives wanting to stand up for what they see as 'their side'. Hostility doesn't always follow genetics, however. In some families, members may turn on their own, accusing them of being the cause or to blame for the break-up and siding with the other partner. This can particularly occur if separation happened because of an affair or some other upsetting behaviour.

When a new relationship comes along and a stepfamily is created, disputes may flare up again or new ones emerge. A step-parent may move in to find the new partner's relatives resent their presence because the ex was particularly liked. The two new partners may find the family expressing anger with both of them. Or, relatives of the ex who has moved out react angrily to someone taking their family member's place, and often refuse to see the parent and children with the new step-parent and any children they may also have.

Case study: Lara, Barnaby, Kitty and Cameron

Lara married widower Barnaby and came to live with him and his two children, Kitty and Cameron. Barnaby's sister-in-law was upset about the marriage, even though her sister had been dead for five years, and she and Lara quarrelled. Lara refused to have her or her family in the house and said she wouldn't join in Christmas celebrations if they were there. The row soon spread to all their family until Kitty and Cameron's grandparents became involved. Barnaby didn't particularly get on with them so he was quite happy to break off relations but Kitty and Cameron were distraught. However, Barnaby was keen to placate Lara so their views went unheard. Barnaby and Lara saw a counsellor when the relationship between her and Cameron reached a low point but one of the remedies suggested – looking at the losses the children had sustained, listening to their views and remaking the family links they missed – was something Lara was not prepared to do.

Who keeps children in touch with non-resident parents and their relatives?

The relatives involved may argue with the new couple and refuse to see them and, in doing so, lose touch with the children. Alternatively, every time they do interact, it becomes so unpleasant that the couple or the children eventually feel they can't take it again and cry off any further visits. Or visits and meetings simply fade away. This particularly happens with relatives from the side of the family that no longer has the children with them full time – usually, the father's side. Contact with children is often mediated and arranged by mothers, or at least by the women involved, rather than by men. If it's the woman with whom there is a quarrel – as many parents of separated men see it – then there is no one looking out for, taking responsibility for and facilitating the continuing relationship between grandparent and grandchild. Even when there is no overwhelming hostility, awkwardness and hesitation may have the same affect. Contact, which the children may feel is important but the adults haven't realized is so fundamental, can be lost. This may happen particularly when relatives live some distance from where children are living. When the parents were together, they or the grandparent might have felt it easy to organize regular contact. Once the parent no longer lives there and has their own difficulty with contact, visits may lapse. The resident parent may not bother, and the grandparent, aunt or uncle may feel awkward about chasing it.

Relatives who want to cut off ties with an adult with whom they feel upset may forget that however hurt or rejected the adult may be, the children caught in the cross-fire feel that and more. The reasons for the quarrel go straight over their heads. All they know is that Auntie so-and-so or Grandpa obviously doesn't love them or want to know them anymore.

Insight

Whatever your feelings about or quarrels with family members, allow children to have contact and their own relationships with them.

Children feel to blame if grandparents lose touch

As far as children are concerned, a grandparent is a grandparent. They see very little difference between a Dad's Mum or a Mum's Dad. In many families, however, there may already be a distinction. Women tend to have closer ties to their parents than men do with theirs, and may already have enabled children to have a closer tie with Nan and Gramps than Grandma and Grandpa. But to children, who have made little distinction, it can be horribly unsettling to suddenly lose people who matter and not to know or understand why. All human beings search for meanings in situations and children always have a tendency to blame themselves when something goes wrong. Instead of looking to the difficulties in communication between the adults, children may conclude that it's because they are unlovable, unworthy or bad that Gran and Grandad no longer stay in touch.

Step-parents become scapegoats when families fight

Sometimes the anger washing about over the ending of a family can become focused on the new partner. They may be seen as being the cause, if not of the break-up then at least of parents not getting back together again – even if that was never on the cards. But even when there is neither a break-up to lay at their feet or a chance of reconciliation – such as after a death – relatives may simply blame the new person for not being the missing person. Their grief and anger has to go somewhere, and the new member of the family seems to be the best target.

This can be especially tough on a step-parent who comes into a family after an ex has left in bitterness and ill will. For the sake of the children, the step-parent should be nice about the ex in front of the children and ease their seeing each other. They should do the same for that person's relatives, even if these people seem to be stirring up arguments and bad mouthing them. The step-parent may feel they have no rights at all and be an utter irrelevancy and wish to have done with the relatives, for some peace and quiet. But for the children, keeping contact may be really important. Quite apart from the emotional fallout of losing touch with relatives, they provide a support network that parent and step-parent as well as children may need.

STEP-PARENTS MAY FACE HOSTILITY

When a family comes together, new arrivals may find themselves excluded and made to feel like trespassers by some relatives. They may make it clear that blood ties are more important than any other form of link. Arguments often erupt between incoming adults and other relatives because of the way each sees the other's place in the family. Grandparents of the resident parent often feel they have more rights with the children than the incoming new adult, especially if they have had a caring role during or after a break-up. They may deeply resent the way a step-parent assumes a certain caring role with the children. Arguments can be even more bitter if it's their own family member that the new adult is seen to be supplanting. When a parent dies, their family may take greater offence over anything a new partner does than when it's after a divorce or separation. A new relationship may be seen as finally sweeping away all the memories and the last lingering presence of the loved one who is gone. The relatives' grief may turn to rage, and be discharged on the incoming adult as if it was their fault the other parent is dead. When this happens and the family of a dead parent withdraws or becomes hostile, it can be especially hurtful for the children left behind. They have lost a Mum or Dad. Now they may have to stand by as the family of that parent becomes distant and unapproachable. It's not only a loss in itself – it's a further loss of the last remaining links with the parent they miss and mourn.

STEP-PARENTS MAY FACE INDIFFERENCE

It may not be hostility that a new partner has to face but indifference. Grandparents and other relatives may reluctantly acknowledge that this new person has a relationship with the adult, but not want to accept they have any link with the children concerned, and thus with them. They may be very polite, but distant. Invitations issued to family events will subtly exclude the step-parent – not by specifying they won't be welcome but simply by 'forgetting' to include them.

This lack of connection is particularly likely to be extended to new children, especially when these are weekend visitors. Birthdays and festivals are often the times when such gaps are most obvious, as some relatives treat one set of children differently from others. Their own family will be treated with specially chosen presents. Other children will receive nothing, or offhand gifts noticeably inferior or bought at the last minute. The excuse may be 'I didn't know what to get' – a reminder to all concerned that the child is seen as a stranger.

Insight
You may need to make it clear that children in your family are *of your family* and should be treated the same as any other child related to you.

Maintaining links can be difficult

It isn't always easy to maintain the links between children and grandchildren in a stepfamily. If grandparents are the parents of the resident parent, visits may go on as before. But step-parent and resident parent may find it hard to be in touch with the grandparents from the other side of the family. It can also be difficult for the non-resident parent to keep up the connection with their own family when they only see their child for a short time. Sometimes, the resident parent can be incensed when an ex has kids for access visits and takes them to see, and may even leave them with, other relatives. This may be seen as reneging on their own responsibilities or selfishness or laziness, when in fact it can be an essential opportunity for grandparent and child to spend uninterrupted time together, something the child values and benefits from.

Essential points to consider

▶ *Grandparents can be essential to children in a stepfamily as the one point in their lives that does not change.*

▶ *Grandparents can be especially important if they have offered childcare and support after a family break-up.*

▶ *Grandparents and other relatives can lose touch if their son or daughter is the non-resident parent and the parent with full-time care does not keep the link – a link they may not value but which the children may want and need.*

How to keep support networks

So what can be done to keep the support network both adults and children so greatly need? Grandparents, aunts and uncles, brothers and sisters and even adult children all play a role that is not simply that of being spectators. Their feelings are important and their actions highly significant to all concerned. You might have sorted out how you, your new partner, your children and previous partners are going to manage this new stepfamily. If other members of your family aren't in agreement or on board, you may find their attitudes, beliefs and behaviour can put a spoke in your hopes for a smooth ride.

▶ *Step-parents and parents need to recognize the importance of other family members to the children involved, whether those children live with the couple full time or part time.*

▶ *Even if you have limited contact with the children, you need to make space for them to see and spend one-to-one time with other relatives of theirs, whether they are relatives of yours or not.*

▶ *There needs to be communication between the step-parent and their partner, between parents who no longer live together and between family members. Adults need to listen to children and to each other, and to take on board the anger and hurt and guilt all may be feeling and find a way round them.*

▶ *Family members need to understand and support the way you are managing your stepfamily. This doesn't mean they have to say or do exactly the same things you say or do. But you need to be confident that the children are not going to be confused or stirred up by anything they hear. It's up to all the adults involved in a family break-up and in new families to be grown-up and do what's best for the children. And what is best for them is communication and friendship, not distance and hostility.*

▶ *Some children may be relieved at a good excuse to avoid a tedious or unpleasant relative. However boring or difficult you may feel they are, family are family and can be important. But talk it through with them so you don't insist on visits that are actually unwelcome or distressing.*

▶ *Even if relatives live some distance away, make the effort to include them in keeping in touch with the child. If face-to-face visits are difficult, use the advice in Chapter 9 to invest in making it easy by text, mobile phone, internet, webcam and messaging as much as you would for the other parent.*

Of course, many grandparents and other relatives are able to recognize the roots of any resentment and anger and put them aside for the sake of the children.

How to ask for help from relatives

Grandparents and other relatives need to recognize their worth and importance, and adults in a stepfamily may find it useful to appeal to them by stating and underlining the importance they have to all the children in a family. Recognizing how much the pride in a child's achievements may help and support children can encourage grandparents and other relatives to be there for stepchildren as well as 'their own'. Parents and step-parents also need to acknowledge how hard it may be and how long it may take to build up the bonds between those relations and a stepchild or step-parent. But given time and patience, it will come.

New couples may find it useful to invite relatives when they decide to set up home together, to explain what is going on, to ask for support and invite discussion. Even if this was not done at first, it is never too late. Introduce the step-parent as someone who wants to do their best and who'd appreciate support and invite the family to back them, if only for the children's sake.

Relatives may particularly need to hear what might be considered supportive and what might be considered interference – a distinction that both sides may worry about. Some relatives may be seen to be offering too much help and they may need to be able to hear a positive request on the lines of 'What I'd really appreciate from you is…' to sort this out. But equally, some may be holding back too much out of a fear of being seen to be barging in, and they also may need to hear a specific request outlining what would be felt as helpful.

THINGS TO REMEMBER

▶ *Stepfamilies do not exist in a vacuum. Wider family connections – grandparents, ex in-laws, cousins, nephews and all – are vitally important. Children and adults benefit from the support an extended family can give.*

▶ *It can be very unsettling for children to suddenly lose people who matter to them. The anger or distress this can cause them is often focused, unfairly, on the incoming step-parent and any children they might bring with them. They can be seen as 'trespassers' and become ready-made scapegoats.*

▶ *Making long-distance grandparenting easy is as important as making long-distance parenting easy. Use all the strategies outlined in Chapter 9 to keep the link between children and other relatives.*

▶ *Maintaining or keeping existing links and generating new ones as a good support network are central needs for a successful stepfamily.*

IDEAS TO TRY

▶ *Review what contact you have with your relatives. Are you happy about the amount of contact? How supportive do you feel they are?*

▶ *Review what contact your children have with their relatives. Does this include people you do not consider relatives to you, i.e. people related to their other parent? How supportive do you and your children feel they are? Are there differences of opinion between you and the children on this?*

▶ *Ideas-storm with adults and children about what contact each would like. Is it different to what happens at present?*

▶ *Ideas-storm with adults and children about what helps and hinders contact and what changes you could make.*

Part four
Moving on

13

New babies for both parents

In this chapter you will learn:
- *the effect a new baby has on a stepfamily*
- *to understand the emotional reactions of everyone concerned to the newcomer*
- *about the shifting dynamics in a family with a new child.*

Stepfamilies can form at any time in an individual's or a family's life. You may be 21 or 71, one of you could be child-free or a parent too and the children can be babies, toddlers, teenagers or have children and partners of their own. In some stepfamilies there may be no question of further children joining you. You've been there, done that and got the tiny T-shirts, and your shared view may be that another child is not an option. Or one or both of you may no longer be able to have children due to age or medical intervention.

But in many stepfamilies 'mine' and 'yours' are soon joined by 'ours' as a new baby of the new couple arrives. Babies can make or break stepfamilies. They can form a bridge between a step-parent and stepchildren, and provide a link between stepsiblings. Or, they can trigger feelings of rejection, jealousy, fury and hurt. How do you make sure your new child brings your family together rather than pushing it apart?

Insight

Once a new baby arrives, children who feel a step-parent is an outsider and nothing to do with them may gradually develop a bond with the new brother or sister and, through them, the step-parent.

How you may feel about a new baby on the way

Parents-to-be in a stepfamily may feel uncomplicated excitement at the prospect – a baby of your own, a baby with your new partner. But many feel anxious. If this is not your first child, you may worry about having a child some time after your previous children. Will you feel out of touch and out of step as an older parent of a baby? Will you remember how to manage babies, after having become used to older children? Will other parents be supportive or excluding? All are common fears and issues. Try to:

▶ *Talk your anxieties over with your partner and with friends and relatives.*
▶ *Trust in old skills coming back – they will.*
▶ *Look for other stepfamily parents among your friends and acquaintances. Don't forget how many stepfamilies there are out there, and how many who, like you, may be having another child. Support and help each other!*

Whether you're the birth parent or step-parent in an existing stepfamily, you may worry about the first family being pushed out of the limelight and getting less attention than the new baby. You may feel guilty about this but not be sure how to manage it. And if you're a member of the other family, you may be watching the pregnancy unfold, apprehensive that the children you look after could lose attention and not be sure how to react. In all cases:

▶ *Talk to all the adults concerned about your fears.*
▶ *Agree how you are going to manage your feelings and behaviour.*
▶ *Agree to keep in touch and support each other in order to support the children.*

If this is the first child for one of you, you may be anxious that while your partner knows the ropes you do not. You may worry

that you'll be shown up and not be as competent as they are.
You should:

- *Accept that looking after babies is a skill you learn, not an art you're born knowing.*
- *Be prepared to ask – your partner, your friends and professionals such as midwives, health visitors and parenting advisors.*
- *Read, learn and practise. The more you handle your own baby, the more capable you will be.*
- *Learn from your stepchildren – they may have plenty to teach you.*

Your fears and anxieties are normal and natural – that's the most important thing to understand. There's nothing wrong with you for having them. Suffering in silence, however, can lead to misunderstandings and complications. Speak out, get some support and this will be a welcome addition to your family and to you.

What are your reasons for having a child?

It often helps to consider why you are having a child. You may both feel that a baby of your own would cement this relationship and that having a shared child will prove your love for each other. Many couples feel a family isn't real, isn't truly committed, unless there are children of your own to hold you together. If one of you doesn't have children from a previous relationship, or has little contact with them, and feels being a step-parent isn't enough, they may want to be a parent to their own. All are common and genuine reasons for deciding to have a child and what you choose to do has to be your decision. Nobody else has the right to judge or criticize. Your children, however, may want to raise the issue and some of the reasons which work for you may be experienced by them as a slight. It helps for you to have thought it through beforehand and to have considered how they may see it.

When to tell the children that a new baby is on the way

You need to tell existing children that a baby is on the way as soon as you know, even if this means breaking the news before you're sure the pregnancy will go to term. If the worst happens and you do have a miscarriage, while you may wish to keep this from friends or extended family, children will realize something has happened. You may keep the pregnancy and miscarriage a secret but you can't protect them from your feelings about it – they will be affected by your emotional reaction. For you to manage the fallout and for them to cope, they have to know what is going on.

They also deserve to be the first to know about a new baby on the way, not to pick up the hints and whispered conversations or knowing looks between you or hear it from someone else. They'll feel excluded and unwanted if they do.

The next people to tell are all the grandparents, stepgrandparents and ex-partners. All of them will be affected by the new situation and need to feel part of it rather than left out. All may have various reactions ranging from unalloyed joy to jealousy, competitiveness, sadness and longing. All may react in ways that impinge on you and on existing children. The earlier they know and the more they feel included, the less potential for responses that harm you or the children.

The effect of the new baby on the stepfamily

Stepfamilies are often large families. One or both partners may have an existing family involving children, and to this you may need to add children of former partners. You may feel your ex-partner's new children or stepchildren have nothing to do with you, especially if you have little contact. They will, however, affect any children of your family. Those who visit and keep in contact will have to come to terms with living with step- and half-siblings in both the homes that are theirs. And children who have no contact may still have to process the fact that a parent they no longer see, or see infrequently and irregularly, has other children in their life apart from them.

Some parents choose to have large families and have very positive feelings about them. Some children thrive being surrounded by siblings, and step- and half-siblings, of varying ages and sexes. However, it can be more of a challenge when having a large family was not your choice or aim – the size came as a side effect of forming a stepfamily. Parents and step-parents may then find the situation overwhelming and may feel out of control. Children may find it even more alienating – they may feel lost in a crowd and that their privacy and territory has been invaded and compromised. They may feel that their parents not only have less time for them but also love them less.

Insight

When new babies arrive, it's always important to make time for and give gifts to existing children so they don't feel left out. This is doubly so in stepfamilies!

Some parents-to-be find the new baby and their new status far more life-changing than they anticipated. You may expect that second or third children will have less of an impact on your lifestyle and the dynamic between partners. Once you've had your first child you're already a parent and a family, after all. But a new baby in a stepfamily has to be seen as someone who may have an even more profound effect on the individuals and the group interaction than a first child in a first-time family may have had. After all, when a baby arrives to two childless parents, they only have themselves to consider. When a second child arrives, you do have to recognize the potential for sibling rivalry and how a child who was both the eldest and the baby of the family may feel about the newcomer. A third baby makes the second child a middle child rather than the baby, and that needs managing. But a new baby in a stepfamily throws up many more changes to the family process.

WILL EXISTING CHILDREN FEEL LEFT OUT?

A new baby in a stepfamily can be enormously divisive. Existing children can feel cast aside and pushed out. Whether they live with the baby or see him or her on visits, children may fear they're no longer good enough, that they've been replaced and no longer wanted. Older children may feel called upon and expected to be grown-up and responsible at a time when perhaps they needed more coddling and care, especially if their help is required or requested to feed, change and look after the new child. Younger children may feel their position as baby of the family has been commandeered and stolen from them. Whatever their age, existing children may be right in thinking adult concern and attention has been diverted from them and concentrated on the baby, and feel bitter about it. Children in a family may not all have the same reaction to a baby among them. In some families, different siblings may have different feelings and reactions to a newcomer, and this can drive a wedge not only between them and their own parent and the step-parent, but also between themselves.

NEW BABIES CAN ACT AS A BRIDGE

But a baby can often bring stepfamilies together, by providing a bridge between step-parents and children. Children have no material link to a step-parent. Their own mother or father may love this person and indeed have a legal tie to them in the form of marriage, but step-relatives have no such legal connection and sometimes very few emotional ones beyond dislike or suspicion. A baby, however, is a bond, sharing as it does a blood tie with both the step-parent and children of a step-parent's partner. The baby is a half-brother or sister, and even where there is anger and hostility between adult and child, a baby may be accepted as having no part in the quarrel. The baby may be seen by them as 'theirs' where the step-parent may have been seen as nothing of the sort. But because the baby has a bond with them, so now by extension does the step-parent.

Babies are also fun and fascinating and are talking points. In playing with, taking care of and talking to the baby, children can have something to share with an adult with whom they might otherwise feel they have nothing in common. They may have felt embarrassed about family change, and mortified at the graphic proof that a parent is having sex, but on the whole, children and teenagers of both sexes find a baby in the family is something to boast about and show off to their friends.

Essential points to consider

▶ *If a new baby is on the way, existing children need to be the first to know and as soon as possible.*

▶ *New babies can alienate children in a stepfamily as they may fear the newcomer will get all the love and attention available.*

▶ *However, new babies can also form a bridge between child and step-parent, being related to both.*

Insight

Warring stepchildren may find a new baby brings them together in one thing – resentment of the newcomer. 'The enemy of my enemy is my friend' is a truth universally acknowledged and it often works to the advantage of stepfamilies. Initial dislike which develops into mutual antipathy can soon become teamwork.

How the new family shape can affect children

As well as levering in another member of the family, with all the potential for making people feel sidelined and rejected, a new baby shifts the shape of the family. Boys may suddenly have a sister; girls, a brother. Youngest children are no longer the babies of the family. Eldest children have even more children claiming to need more attention than them, or over whom they have some sort of authority. A group that had sorted themselves out into being a twosome or threesome and might have managed new alliances and patterns has to regroup. This new configuration may help children see themselves in a new light, no longer the youngest or the eldest of two or an only child or the piggy-in-the-middle, but a whole new person with a whole new family. Someone struggling with accepting the changes that have happened may feel this is the straw that breaks their back – or, may discover a new image of themselves and a new place in the family that gives them self-confidence and self-worth. A new member of the family can shift the dynamics of the relationship with the step-parent, moving it from suspicion, hostility or insecurity, to acceptance.

Case study: John and Jane, Adele and Sam

When John and Jane told her daughter Adele she was pregnant, Adele was furious. At ten, she was used to being the only child – never having to fight for space, always listened to and the centre of both her mother's and her new stepfather's attention. She felt rejected and marginalized and repeatedly asked if the baby had to come, if she would have to give up her room, if it meant she might have to go and live with her father. She refused to join in any of the preparations, although both John and Jane tried to involve her. John especially wouldn't give up on her, and made great efforts to help her feel included. When Sam was born, he took Adele to see mother and baby against Adele's sulky objections and bought her a new game for her games console, and made sure all the relatives who came with gifts for the baby brought something for Adele too. While John was really careful about who could hold the baby, he handed her over to Adele saying 'Here, I know you can be trusted.' Within a week, Adele was showing off 'my baby brother'. One of the things she was most taken with was the fact that she might have lost being an only child but now she was an older child – top of the family tree, with a brother to look up to her and boss around. She may have to share, but she also had an ally in the making, just as her mother had with her Uncle Nick, who she knew her mother adored.

What should you do to pull your stepfamily together with a new baby?

The more you see the potential for difficulties, the better prepared you will be to manage them. Talk through with your partner and the children how they feel, what they like about the situation, what they dislike and what they'd want to be different.

Involve everyone. Ask for help from children in choosing names and later clothes, in decorating bedrooms and later in feeding and playing with the baby. But make it a request and a choice – give them time to come round if they need it and don't make them skivvies for the newcomer.

Reassure children that your loving feelings and appreciation for them have not changed. Make time to spend with them away from the baby.

Support the step-parent in enjoying their own child, but in continuing to build a strong and loving bond with their stepchildren too. New parents may be so overwhelmed with having their own child they may not realize they are excluding other children in their family and need help to be even-handed.

Support the new parent in asking for and accepting help when it's needed. Sometimes new parents with partners who have been there before feel jealous that their partner has already had the experience. Or they may feel incompetent by comparison and reluctant to show inexperience by asking for help.

Draw a family tree. Original family trees may look fairly neat – children on the bottom gradually opening out on top to take in grandparents, aunts and uncles. Stepfamily family trees can be chaotic and rambling, with extra adults and children all over the place. Putting it down on paper has two vital consequences. One is that it helps you to see the chaos, and to recognize and understand why managing this family should be so overwhelming and difficult.

If you're feeling incompetent and foolish, seeing it can help you accept that anyone in the same situation would find it hard. The other is that it gives you some control and order, in being able to see the size and the shape of the situation.

Once you can see the shape of your family, you could try an exercise to help you and your partner understand what may be going on. Only do this if you are sure you can talk through and thus manage what may be hurtful or thought-provoking revelations. You may consider doing it with the help of a counsellor or mediator. Using your own coloured pen, each of you draws a line on the family tree around yourself and the people you think are 'yours'. You may find one of you excludes children, or other adults, that the other includes. For instance, a parent may draw a line around their own children as well as their partner and their shared baby, while the step-parent may exclude all or some of their stepchildren. This is not meant to be a blame-setting exercise but one that allows you to see what could be underlying any difficulties. Once you are aware that some children but not others may be felt to be 'beyond the pale', you can work together to extend that boundary to make your family inclusive.

Insight

A new child in the family redraws the family dynamic. A child used to being an only child, the sole boy or girl, one of two, or the youngest of three, will suddenly have to rethink their place. Talk it through to make it an acknowledged and positive change.

THINGS TO REMEMBER

▶ *Existing children need to know about a pregnancy as soon as possible, followed by the wider family and anyone else this event will impinge on. The earlier everyone knows, the more they feel included and the less possibility of negative responses.*

▶ *The arrival of a baby in a stepfamily can produce more complications and needs more consideration than one coming into a first-time relationship.*

▶ *The birth will shift the dynamic of the stepfamily as the status and alliances of existing children are altered. Birth order, a child's position in a family, can have a considerable effect on their feelings and relationships.*

▶ *The new baby can provide a bridge between stepchildren and step-parent, who now have some tangible link to them. This can move the step-parent from being a suspicious 'trespasser' to a real member of the family.*

▶ *Having a new baby within a stepfamily – adding an 'ours' to 'mine' and 'yours' – can provide a link between stepsiblings. However, it can also trigger feelings of rejection, jealousy and hurt.*

IDEAS TO TRY

▶ *Ideas-storm with your children how their place in the family changed when your stepfamily began. When the shape changed how did it affect them? From being an adult supporter to being a child again? Going from being an only to having stepsiblings? From oldest or youngest to piggy in the middle? How did/does that feel? If it's difficult, ideas-storm what would make a positive difference.*

▶ *Consider how a new baby affects children already there. Using suggestions in this chapter, what can you do to manage it positively?*

▶ *Consider how a new baby affects you; do you have new parent nerves or are you feeling 'Here we go again'? How can you and your partner manage any differences?*

▶ *Using suggestions in this chapter, what can adults and existing children do to make the arrival of a new baby a positive experience?*

14

Building cooperation and
avoiding conflict

In this chapter you will learn:
- *about discipline issues*
- *how to build cooperation*
- *why children misbehave*
- *what it means when children 'act out'*
- *how to use 'I' statements*
- *about positives, trust, timers and other techniques.*

All families have conflicts. Children argue among themselves, adults have rows and parents and their children often clash. It can be over differences of opinion but more often it's about what parents often classify as 'discipline issues'. As a parent, an adult often feels he or she knows best how a child should behave and what they should be doing. As a child, the young person often either feels they should have a say too, or doesn't really care whether they have a voice or not; all that matters is that they do or don't do whatever it is that is occupying their attention at the time!

In stepfamilies, arguments and disagreements take on a different tone and significance. Step-parents worry about children being rude, defiant and disobedient. Parents worry about what happens when they leave their children with their partners and whether they will be aggressive or uncooperative. Step-parents often say their stepchildren only seem to show that side of themselves when their parent isn't there. New partners may despair about how stepsiblings behave when they meet, or how they get on if they live together full time or part time. And every adult in the equation often tears out their hair about how they will persuade or make their children 'behave well'. Discipline (in the sense that it is usually used in this country: using punishment to make children do as you say) becomes a hot topic.

> **Insight**
> That you argue is not the problem – it's how you argue that is the point. Conflict can be healthy if it ends in resolution and if nobody sets out to hurt or say anything unforgivable.

Why ending arguments is so important

Life in a stepfamily doesn't have to be unpleasant or argumentative. That you disagree isn't the issue, because nobody can expect to always be in line with those around them. How you express disagreements and how you resolve them is the important thing. If you want to build cooperation and avoid conflict instead of cracking down on children, you are better off looking for tips and strategies on listening, discussing, looking for solutions and making agreements.

In many families, the only time adults really talk to children is to tell them off. This is possibly even more acute in stepfamilies when the atmosphere is strained and critical. It is certainly often the only point of contact between parent, step-parent and non-resident parent. Frequently the other parent is called on when a child is considered to be naughty or behaving badly, not when parents want to praise or celebrate successes. Sometimes this is because the parent or step-parent genuinely wants help from the other parent. He or she may feel unable to tackle the situation themselves, or may feel that asking the child to behave differently might be inappropriate coming from them. Sometimes, the reason for the call is to pass the parcel – not just of responsibility, but of blame. It's a way of saying 'Look what you have landed me with. If I'm having a miserable time with your child, it's your fault and I'm going to make you feel guilty about it.' Sometimes it's a genuine desire to give the birth parent a taste of what it's like with them gone. More often, it's to make the other parent the bogeyperson and leave the step-parent and their partner feeling it's not their fault that the child behaves like this.

Why do children misbehave?

The problem when feelings are running high and people are angry and upset is that everyone feels out of control, and therefore tends to concentrate on how to assert control. And the obvious people that parents and step-parents may wish to practise control on are the children – hence the importance of the issue of discipline. But does laying down rules or handing out punishment always work? The reality is that on the whole, and especially with children in stepfamilies, children misbehave for reasons. And if you want to build cooperation and avoid conflict, the first important strategy is to understand why a child may be misbehaving.

WHAT IS BAD BEHAVIOUR REALLY ABOUT?

Children often find it hard to understand or explain their feelings. So, they tend to 'act them out'. So called 'bad behaviour' is often the only way they can express their emotions and reactions. While rules and boundaries are important, it's often more effective to consider the various needs being expressed when the idea of discipline comes up. Adults wish to be seen as in control, to be acknowledged as doing the right thing.

Children, on the other hand, often need to have their different response to the new family at least acknowledged. If children 'defy' you, it's better to dive under the behaviour to understand what's going on than get into a head-to-head fight. All behaviour is a way of getting what you need. Bad behaviour is actually a way of trying to show bad feelings. When we as parents or step-parents can understand what our children need and why they do what they do, we can help them help us.

Useful questions to ask yourself

What's the need? It is probably for comfort, security, reassurance, approval.

What might a child be feeling if their needs aren't being met? They may be feeling scared, angry, jealous, rejected.

What might they be saying? 'I hate you!' 'I wish the baby wasn't here!' 'I want to live with my Dad!'

What might their behaviour be? Crying, slamming doors, refusing to sleep, fighting.

WHY CHILDREN FIGHT TO GET CONTROL

One thing children lose when families break up and when they reform is control. It wasn't their choice for their parents to separate nor their choice for a parent and step-parent to get together. What is happening around them can make them feel utterly powerless. This can lead to their trying to gain some control and exercise some choice in their lives, often with drastic and sometimes confusing effect.

When someone says 'discipline' most of us think about punishment. It's about keeping our children in line and doing the right thing. But the original meaning of the word is 'to teach'. Discipline is something we do to help children learn. And the best way to get children to behave in ways that please us is to help them understand what they actually want and need, and to see how they can get those needs met in ways that don't upset other people. Respond to the underlying need rather than the 'bad behaviour' and the child's reason for behaving that way melts away.

Conflict tends to be about people feeling out of control.
Make it your business to give everyone in your family a voice
and you'll see the conflict diminish.

Getting our own needs met

To do this we may need to get our own needs met. When concentrating
on the children and how they behave, we may be ignoring the fact that
we too can be feeling angry, left out and rejected. We may be showing
this through shouting, being depressed and not listening to them.
The best way of 'disciplining' children is often to set out to help, not
punish them. After all, half the time if you punish a child for acting
up in a separated family, what you are actually doing is punishing
them for being sad at what has happened to them and trying to let
you know about it. Where's the justice in that?

It may not seem like it sometimes, but children want to please
their parents, and the adults they live with, and win their approval.
When they feel we have understood what they need, and can
understand us in turn, they have the incentive to change. If you can
tell them clearly what you want and why, and respect and listen to
them, you'll get a better result than simply coming down hard on
them. Whenever you find yourself feeling fraught, the best strategy
is to say the following to the other person:

▶ *'When... (describe the situation)'*
▶ *'I feel... (describe your emotions)'*
▶ *'because... (explain why the situation makes you feel this way).'*
▶ *'What I would like is... (give a clear and direct description of
   what you'd prefer).'*

Or:

▶ *What are we going to do about this? (Enlist the other person
   in coming up with a solution.)*

How to cut down on the shouting

Using the previous technique cuts down on the shouting. Having to remember it allows you to focus and count to ten. That means you pick and choose your fights and only say something when it matters. More importantly, it helps you identify what is really going on. Sometimes it's not because of anything the child has done in the here and now, but because of old angers. Think about things as you use the technique:

- ▶ *'When you...'* – *You have to identify exactly what the child is doing or what is happening to make you lose your rag. That helps you and the other person see precisely what you're really objecting to.*
- ▶ *'I feel...'* – *This helps you pin down the real and precise emotion. Anger? Or fear? Or sadness?*
- ▶ *'because...'* – *Now you really get to the point. Because the child is winding you up? Or because it reminds you of something from your own immediate or distant past? Or because you've had a bad day and the child takes the brunt of it? So is the real emotion about the child, the here and now or something else?*
- ▶ *'What I would like is...'* – *This helps all of you find a solution instead of continuing to go round and round in futile conflict.*

Why they show their feelings in actions

The acting out that so often leads to debates about discipline takes place because children and young people may find it hard to tell you how they feel about the changes and losses they have suffered. Instead, they are likely to show their feelings by what they do. They often believe the change or loss is somehow their fault, which can add to their confusion and make it harder for them to talk about their feelings. Children may show distress by:

- ▶ *acting younger than their age*
- ▶ *wetting the bed*
- ▶ *throwing tantrums*
- ▶ *forgetting skills they've learned*
- ▶ *becoming clingy and fretful*
- ▶ *refusing food, being picky or eating too much*
- ▶ *having difficulty sleeping or in waking up.*

Teenagers may:

- ▶ *refuse to talk*
- ▶ *be angry*
- ▶ *experiment with drugs, drink, early sex.*

How to put a name to feelings

All of us have feelings. At times we feel happy, sad, angry, rejected, confused and much more. However, many of us have picked up from parents and other influences the idea that some feelings are 'bad' – not things we should be feeling. Feeling angry is often seen to be unacceptable; so is being jealous. When we have these feelings we feel guilty: 'I shouldn't be feeling this. I must be a bad person to feel like this.' Sometimes, we blame others: 'You make me feel angry. It's all your fault. You're the bad person!'

In reality, all feelings are natural and having them is normal. Feelings are just feelings – we can't help them and there's no shame in having them. What we can help is what we do about them.

Insight

Taking out anger on someone in an unhelpful way doesn't make us feel better, or deal with the feeling either.

But often, we can't deal with the emotion we are feeling because we don't actually know what it really is. Children particularly can find it hard to put into words what they are actually experiencing. Using the following technique can help you and anyone else to isolate, understand and put a name to the feelings.

Get a pack of post-it notes or slips of paper and write out these words listed below, and any other words you can come up with, to describe feelings. Stick them on a wall or spread them out on a table. Then mull them over, talk them through to pinpoint the word that best describes what you are feeling. You or the other person may be angry. Or, you might be feeling abandoned or worried or embarrassed. Once you know what it is, you can discuss why the feelings are there and what you might do about it. Simply acknowledging the real emotion and realizing you don't have to feel guilty for having it can help and often makes the feeling diminish or lose its power.

abandoned	frightened	panicky
alarmed	fuming	peaceful
angry	glad	pleased
anxious	gloomy	quiet
bored	hacked off	rejected
bothered	happy	relieved
calm	humiliated	resentful
cared for	ignored	sad
cheerful	in despair	scared
cheesed off	in high spirits	sensitive
cold	jealous	shamed
confused	jittery	shown up
content	jumpy	sick and tired
cross	left out	snappy
dejected	loved	stressed
depressed	loving	tense
disgusted	low	thrilled
down in the dumps	miserable	troubled
dumped	neglected	uneasy
edgy	nervous	unwanted
embarrassed	nervy	upset
envious	on edge	uptight
fed up	out of sorts	warm
forgotten	p***ed off	worried

Sometimes simply recognizing and accepting the feelings and needs is enough. At other times, we may need to help our children sort out what they are going to do. Moving on may mean having to accept there is nothing that can be done to change a situation, but we can always change how we ourselves act or feel about it. First, we may need to let the first flush of emotions die down. What often blocks any advance in a stepfamily is the anger that is flying around.

Dealing with anger

Just as with any other strong emotion, anger is a natural feeling to have and neither right nor wrong. But how we use our anger – or let it use us – and how it comes out can make it hurtful and scary and entirely destructive. Anger in itself can have an important function. Just as pain tells you not to lean on a hot stove, so anger tells you that what is happening is not acceptable and that something needs to change. There are other feelings underneath anger – fear, sadness, worry, frustration – and working out what these are will help us to identify what is really upsetting us and what we'd like to be different.

Feeling angry can be:

- *an early warning signal that important needs aren't being met*
- *a push towards making some changes*
- *a way of helping other people understand how we feel and what we need to happen.*

Both adults and children in a stepfamily situation may often find themselves feeling angry, and find it difficult to deal with the strong emotions.

Feeling angry and not expressing it:

- *makes us feel powerless and helpless*
- *means our needs don't get met*

- *makes us ill – depression, headaches, stomach ache, back ache*
- *leaks out as resentment, souring and damaging relationships*
- *builds up and then explodes in dirty anger.*

IS SOME ANGER MORE DESTRUCTIVE THAN OTHERS?

'Dirty anger' is a helpful concept to understand. Anger is normal, is something you'd expect to feel in certain situations and can be helpful. Letting anger spill out in uncontrolled and hurtful actions or words is what harms the person who is angry and everyone around them. This is 'dirty anger'.

Dirty anger is:

- *blaming, insulting, hitting or bad mouthing*
- *'kicking the cat' – dumping bad feelings where they don't belong*
- *raking over past grievances.*

Dirty anger does us and our children no good at all. It makes them defensive, harms our relationship with them and their self-esteem, leaves us ashamed and guilty and doesn't get the result we want. In stepfamilies, dirty anger often results in adults blaming either one particular child or several children as 'the problem', or becoming convinced that another adult is setting them up. Stepchildren often get drawn into dirty anger, blaming and shouting at the parent with whom they live instead of the parent they're really angry with, the one who has left. Equally they can start blaming the step-parent, who may have nothing to do with the original source of pain but is felt to be more expendable and thus a better target than either parents.

Insight

Learn to spot dirty anger and to deal with it. Anger is a natural emotion and it's ok to feel it. It's what you do about it that matters.

Dealing with temper tantrums

The problem is that criticism and fault-finding doesn't help anyone. Pointing the finger at an ex, whatever their faults, only hurts children further, and often leads to them behaving even more badly. Letting children sound off at adults involved may, initially, allow some steam to be let off but more often results in circular arguments and deadlock. How can anger be expressed in a way that gets needs met and doesn't damage anyone?

Sometimes, children in difficult stepfamily situations seem to push you too far. When children are in the grip of strong feelings they are not able to think straight or listen to reason. What they may need is to get the feelings out, safely, to calm down enough to sort out the problem.

In the face of a temper tantrum:

▶ *Don't take it personally.*
▶ *Listen to the tune not the words. Dive under the words to help them work out what it is they need.*
▶ *When the storm is over, acknowledge the painful and strong feelings they have been experiencing. Help them work out how they were feeling, what they needed, what they can do to express angry feelings and get what they need without hurting others.*

Communicating by using 'I' statements

One vital technique to use when building communication is an 'I' statement. 'I' statements are all about being able to say what 'I want' and what 'I need'. They help the person speaking, and the person being spoken to, be clear about what is really going on.

When we use an 'I' statement, we can:

- *be aware of our own feelings about what we want*
- *stand up and be counted about our feelings and needs*
- *help other people understand what we are saying*
- *be clear, honest and direct*
- *make our point without blaming, criticizing or judging other people.*

When we're upset we sometimes blame the other person for what has happened: 'Look what you made me do', 'You make me so angry!' Or we try to avoid taking responsibility for angry or critical remarks by saying they belong to someone else: 'Everyone thinks it's you're fault.'

These are 'you' statements and they seldom give the other person a chance to understand what we're upset about, how we feel or why, or give them an opportunity to make any changes. 'You' statements are a way of not being overwhelmed by anger or despair. Instead of 'owning' feelings, we hold them at arm's length: 'One feels like that, doesn't one?', 'That's how you do it, don't you?' But instead of helping, they make the other person defensive and increase hostility and conflict.

Using an 'I' statement respects the other person and their point of view. It helps you say what you feel and want but avoids making the other person feel like the problem. This makes it far easier for both of you to come up with a solution, take responsibility and act positively.

Insight

The trick is to see yourself, and the other person, as part of the solution rather than the problem.

It can take some time to get into the habit of using 'I' statements. Most of us have had a lifetime of being told it's selfish or big-headed to say 'I'. But the more you use them, the more you'll find they work and help you and the other person feel good about the exchange.

An 'I' statement:

- ▶ *describes the behaviour I'm finding difficult*
- ▶ *says the effect it has on me*
- ▶ *tells the other person how I feel about it*
- ▶ *invites them to join me in finding a solution.*

For instance, 'When I come home and find you haven't done your chores I feel really upset and angry. I feel as if you're taking me for granted and not listening to me. I'd like you to do the chores we've agreed, when we've agreed. If you're having a problem with that let's talk about it.'

Understanding what is underneath the behaviour

It's not discipline in the form of punishment or control that children mainly need when they behave badly in a stepfamily situation. What is underneath their behaviour is often a need for attention, acceptance, appreciation and some independence. They are often fighting to get these when they act up. We can help them by:

- ▶ *talking openly about the change or loss that has lead to their being in a stepfamily*
- ▶ *helping them show their feelings*
- ▶ *sharing our own feelings with them*
- ▶ *telling them it's OK to feel bad, even if other people in the family are happy about the change*
- ▶ *telling them what's going to happen and asking their opinions*
- ▶ *giving them plenty of time and attention*
- ▶ *making sure some things don't change*
- ▶ *helping them keep in touch with people, places, things that matter to them*

- *helping them remember people, places, things that matter through photos, letters, drawings, objects*
- *keeping them busy doing things they enjoy*
- *giving them love, reassurance, support*
- *cutting them some slack and accepting they will act up.*

> ## Essential points to consider
> - *Anger is one of the strongest emotions and one that is often present in stepfamilies.*
> - *Anger is normal and no more 'bad' than any other emotion. However, when people cannot express and deal with anger they often resort to 'dirty anger', letting their feelings spill out in hurtful words and actions.*
> - *Diving underneath the behaviour to understand and discuss it can help children and adults.*

Making our own choices and helping children make theirs

We need to recognize that when it comes to a stepfamily, it's the adults who choose to be there, not the children. We need to take our ability to make choices a step further – to choose to act in ways that make that choice work. And that may mean having to let go of some elements – to give your children some choice and more control of their own.

Insight

Children are far more likely to cooperate if they feel trusted and part of a team, and asked what they want rather than told what you don't want.

Giving children responsibility and choices neatly sidesteps disagreements. Instead of scratching your head about how to punish them, use another form of discipline: positive learning. Build a close relationship with them so they trust you to give them attention and understanding. Notice and acknowledge their strengths and achievements. Let them make decisions wherever possible. You'll soon notice they don't need to be disciplined in the form of punishment at all.

Being positive

One way of helping children behave in ways that please us is to be positive rather than negative. It's easy to get into the habit of saying what you *don't* want instead of what you *do*. When we're angry with children, we tend to focus on the behaviour we're not enjoying:

- ▶ *'Stop shouting!'*
- ▶ *'Don't hit your brother.'*
- ▶ *'Don't keep pulling at the trolley.'*

The problem is, all they may hear are the words describing what we don't like... and repeat them. Instead, ask for what you *want*, not what you *don't want* – it makes a difference!

- ▶ *'Please talk to each other.'*
- ▶ *'Please play nicely.'*
- ▶ *'Please push the trolley for me.'*

Trusting the child

When we tell children about our lack of trust or confidence in them, we give them the message that there's no point in trying; they can't manage it, and even if they did, we wouldn't notice:

- ▶ *'You've got a bad report from school again – playing up, as usual. You're never going to get those exams, are you?'*
- ▶ *'Put that plate down – you'll get crumbs all over the carpet again.'*
- ▶ *'You haven't fed the dog again – I can't trust you to do anything can I?'*

But if we trust our children to be able to do things, we feed their self-belief and confidence:

- ▶ *'I'm confident you can pass those exams.'*
- ▶ *'I'm sure you can eat those biscuits without scattering crumbs.'*
- ▶ *'I know you'll feed the dog while I make tea.'*

Why labels can be so unhelpful

When we call a child lazy or naughty or stupid, we label them. Labelling a child is like putting them into a box, stuck at being the bad boy or naughty girl for good. We don't tell them what it is they're doing we don't like or how to do it differently. A better technique is to be clear about what is wrong, and what we would prefer. Instead of labelling them, *describe* their behaviour:

- ▶ *Instead of 'You're lazy' say 'You left your stuff on the floor.'*
- ▶ *Instead of 'You're such a mess' say 'You haven't combed your hair'.*

Insight

It's not the child who is wrong or bad – it's the behaviour. Focus on what you'd like to be different rather than on whom you might be angry with.

Even 'good' labels set limits. Being told you're good or sweet or wonderful doesn't say what you've done to earn praise. Describing what they've done gives children a clear idea what you like, and don't like. It allows them to take a step back and view their own achievements so they can value them as well and to see exactly what it is you don't want and to change it.

Try:

- ▶ *'You tidied up your room and left it looking so clean!'*
- ▶ *'You walked the dog, without me having to ask!'*

> ▶ *'I can see you've done your homework and put your clothes in the washing machine.'*

Don't discipline, teach

Discipline is not about doing what you are told. It's about understanding your behaviour and knowing what is acceptable and not acceptable to those around you. Disciplining is a way of teaching this and the more positive we are, the more children internalize the lessons and regulate their own behaviour for the better. The more we listen to them, the less they have to resort to bad behaviour to make us listen or act out their feelings.

The importance of spending time together

If you want to build cooperation, one essential requirement is to spend time together. This may be hard if children share time with another family, if you or your partner – or both – have full or irregular work lives or if ill will in the family means people don't want to be in the same room for long. Even if it feels uncomfortable, when a family is having difficulties certain traditions and rules need to be put in place and kept up:

- ▶ *Always eat together around a table, not from your lap while watching TV.*
- ▶ *Have TV or game consoles in shared rooms not bedrooms, so children can't absent themselves and you can monitor them.*
- ▶ *Play board games together – even today's sophisticated technical child enjoys board games.*
- ▶ *Find ways of sharing your thoughts and your experiences.*

Alter work schedules, remove TVs, and buy a dining table to achieve this. If you find conversation hard, over the evening meal play Three Things. Go round the table with everyone sharing three things about their day: one thing they were proud or pleased they did, one thing they wished they had done better and one thing they've decided to do soon.

Case study: Chris and Rosie

When Chris joined Rosie and her four children he was horrified to find all of them had TVs of their own and the two eldest had laptops in their rooms, wirelessly connected to the internet. Rosie had been on her own for three years and in trying to juggle a job, a home and a family had resorted to letting the children pick and microwave their own meals and entertain themselves. As she pointed out, personal TVs cut down on the inevitable spats over the remote.

Chris said there was a much better way to manage that – strict rules over what was watched. He and Rosie talked it over and she was sceptical but let him call a family meeting. He explained he was really troubled by several things. He said he did trust them, but that unrestricted access to the internet and late night TV was not something he felt was appropriate. And he missed talking with them and spending time with them when they were all locked away in their rooms – that wasn't his idea of what a family was all about. So he was keen to hear what they would say, but he proposed a new system. Meals would only be eaten together, between six and eight o'clock, and he would cook – he was a good cook – and welcome help. Everyone could have a look at the TV listings at the beginning of the weekend and say what they wanted to watch. They could each nominate five hours of TV only, but the TV was banned from breakfast and would only be on between eight and ten o'clock at night and weekend mornings. And they could each be on the computer for half an hour a day, except for proven school use or if he or Rosie were involved. He also announced that laptops should now be in public areas only, not bedrooms. There was total uproar but Chris held firm. He also said he'd buy any board game the kids wanted for them all to play together, which they all sneered at. So Chris came home

(Contd)

the next night with Monopoly and having made a meal and eaten it with hardly anything said by the children, he and Rosie played. And one by one, the children joined in. A week later, by which time all were gathering in the kitchen each night to help prepare the meal, they all grudgingly admitted the food was an improvement, and could they try Cluedo?

Using a timer

Sometimes, before lightweight, team-building and general conversations can be held, serious discussions need to take place. If children are angry or guilty, if parents feel they have something they'd like to say, a listening and talking exercise can break the ice. It's often hard to say what is really meant, whether we're talking about the day-to-day trivia of what happened today or saying something really important about our needs or anxieties. It's often hard because we fear we'll be interrupted or the other person won't be listening. And hearing what another person is trying to tell us is just as hard – we often don't take the time or make the effort to tune in.

You can use a clock or an egg timer to start talking and listening between you. Toss a coin for who will go first. The first person sets the timer going and has one minute to talk, without interruption. They get to say exactly what they want or need to say to the other person – but it has to be an 'I' message, not an attack. The listener has to listen, with active listening – leaning forward, making eye contact, nodding and saying 'Uh huh' to show that they are paying attention, but without interruptions or comments on what they are hearing. After the set amount of time, change roles. The new speaker shouldn't use the opportunity to simply come back and argue with what they've just heard – they should say something they'd already got ready to speak about.

Using a timer can allow you to set aside special time to listen, hear and be heard. As you get practice in doing so you won't need the timer to talk to each other, although it often remains a very useful technique in a family to allow both adults and children the opportunity to say 'Hold on! Stop everything! I need to have you hear what I'm saying – and I want to listen to you too!'

Insight

Children love the opportunity to be listened to without interruption. Give them the chance and you may hear something you really need to hear.

THINGS TO REMEMBER

▶ *All families have conflicts. Children and adults row among themselves and parents and children have ongoing arguments about their day-to-day lives. In stepfamilies, the arguments and disagreements can take on a different tone and significance.*

▶ *Children usually misbehave for a reason and this is particularly so within a stepfamily. Building cooperation and minimizing conflict is best done by understanding why a child is misbehaving.*

▶ *Misbehaviour is usually due to a child 'acting out' dissatisfaction or unhappiness with a situation. It can also happen because a child is attempting to gain some degree of control over what they see is the confusion of a stepfamily with all the unwelcome changes and uncertainty it has produced.*

▶ *There are techniques (such as the 'When I...' statement, 'Name the feeling', and the 'I' statement) that can help to prevent or defuse anger and blame in situations and promote compromise and negotiation between parent and child.*

▶ *Be positive and say what you want rather than what you don't want. If you can do this in an atmosphere of created trust, where the child then feels included in what's going on, you can give the child a degree of responsibility and choice and avoid unnecessary disagreements.*

IDEAS TO TRY

▶ Make a 'feelings jar' or wall. Ideas-storm and write down all the emotions you can think of on slips of paper and put them in a jam jar, or on sticky notes and fix them to a wall. Next time there's an argument, call a time-out and ask everyone to name the emotion. It will help you address the real need. It will also slow down the situation and allow people to calm down.

▶ Look for the reasons behind or underneath 'bad behaviour'. Consider the behaviour and then ask yourself; what's the need, what might be the feeling, what might they really be saying?

▶ Learn the technique of using 'I' statements. Practise 'When…I feel…because…what I would like is…' until it becomes second nature.

▶ Next time you want to make a point, with an adult or a child, be positive. Say what you want rather than what you don't want; not 'Don't make a mess,' but instead 'Please put the packet of biscuits away.'

▶ Address behaviour rather than people. Instead of 'You're so noisy!' say 'That music is a bit loud. Please turn it down. Thank you!' Use techniques in this and previous chapters to listen to and talk with members of your family – ideas-storming, using a timer, and family discussions.

15

Money and what it often means

In this chapter you will learn:
- *how to sort out money and maintenance*
- *about separating maintenance and contact*
- *what money stands in for*
- *the emotional issues behind the finances*
- *about budgets, pocket money and allowances.*

Money can be a really hot issue in stepfamilies, particularly if there is little or no contact. Stepfamilies may struggle with the issues of child maintenance and support, budgets and allowances. Finances can be a tricky issue in any family – doubly so when children are living apart from one parent or when there are several children of different parents living or staying in a family.

Child maintenance is the money that both parents pay to support their child's day-to-day expenses and is often the catalyst for much conflict between ex-partners and new ones. The non-resident parent should expect to contribute a sum towards the everyday living costs of a child living with the parent with residence. Contact and maintenance are, and should be, entirely separate. Paying up does not give extra rights for contact nor should disagreements over the money affect what is actually the real issue, which is the child's right to see both parents. In the real world, of course, the issues frequently become entangled. How can you sort out the best result for all the people involved?

Financial support for your child

Children remain the responsibility of both their parents whether those parents live together or apart. Parents are parents for the rest of their lives and children look to them for love, support and care, whether contact is daily or only occasional. As far as both natural law and the legal system is concerned, a parent remains financially liable for their children until they are 18 years old, whatever the contact arrangement. Most parents, of course, continue contributing to and subsidizing their children well beyond this.

Money can be a source of bitterness in stepfamilies because it feels as if there is too little, spread too wide. Parents and step-parents may feel resentful about having to pay towards children's maintenance, particularly if some of their focus and much of their income is now invested in a new family. They may feel that money is being diverted unfairly away from what is or has become their primary family.

How money has significance other than mere cash

EMOTIONAL VALUE

But it is not just about the finances. Money is like food or presents; cash is one of those things that often stands in for something else. Lovers and parents set forth tasty treats and luxurious meals as a way of showing love, attention and commitment. Presents are given as a way of assuring the recipient that you care and they matter. In families that have undergone change, money may be given as a way of assuring or reassuring children that the missing parent is still on the scene. More often, money may be requested or demanded and pursued for much more than to simply pay the bills. It can be required as a form of revenge. The missing parent may be seen to have cheated in taking themselves away but at least the abandoned parent may demand a form of presence, or dish out punishment, in taking their cash. Or the motive may be sadness rather than anger and the money may be seen as a reassurance that the missing person is still committed to them.

> ## Insight
> Money tends to stand in for so much – attention, time, love, control. By all means, buy children whatever they need and some of what they want, but be aware that it is you and your time they most need, not your cash.

MONEY CAN BE USED AS CONTROL

For the parent paying maintenance, money can be seen as a way of exerting control from a distance. Some non-residential parents may be very generous with the amount they offer but with open or hidden strings. The relationship may outwardly be over, but it actually continues through the conditions imposed along with the cheques.

Money and contact may often be seen as conditional, one upon the other. The inference here is that if you don't pay you can't see. In retaliation this may be interpreted as 'If I can't see when and how I like, I won't pay.'

Managing finances between two families

If you want to manage finances split between two families, you should:

▶ *Separate emotional issues from financial ones. Are disagreements and demands over money actually about leftover anger or pain? Before you talk about money, it might be useful for ex-partners to use counselling to seek closure. Have your final say, be reassured the other has listened and heard you, and then move on.*
▶ *Separate money from any other issue. Money is necessary to pay bills and to reassure children that their parents still see*

them as their responsibility. If one parent needs to let the other know they are hurt, angry or disappointed, say it, don't use covert means such as manipulating financial or contact arrangements to pass the message.

▶ *Separate adult needs from the children's. Adults need money to care for children, but as far as children are concerned, the only priority is staying in contact. Don't jeopardize or affect one with arguments or actions over the other.*

STEP-PARENTS AND STEPFAMILY MONEY

How do step-parents fit in when it comes to money? Although the law says step-parents should not be expected to fund someone else's child, it doesn't always work that way. Realistically, a step-parent will be part of a household that contributes towards a stepchild's keep.

A step-parent does not assume financial obligations to a child who is not theirs simply by living with the child's parent, or even marrying them, and even if the child is in their care full time, a step-parent is not expected to pay anything towards the maintenance of a child who is not theirs. However, if a child eats your food and shares your home, over a period of time the step-parent assumes some responsibility for them. If the relationship breaks down, a child can pursue a claim for maintenance against the absent step-parent (although the Child Maintenance and Enforcement Commission, CMEC, excludes step-parents from their remit) and after a death could equally put in a claim for inheritance. The period is not defined in law but would be assessed in court.

The presence of a step-parent in a child's home does not affect the amount of money the other natural parent is expected to pay for maintenance. A non-resident parent will be expected to pay exactly the same amount to a child who lives alone with the other parent as to one who lives with a parent and step-parent – and whether they are married or not makes no difference. However, when calculating the amount of child maintenance owed by a non-resident parent, any children who live with them – their own from a new relationship and stepchildren – are taken into account.

Essential points to consider

▶ *Both parents have a legal as well as moral duty to maintain their children even if they no longer live with them.*
▶ *Money is more than a means to pay bills. It also has emotional significance.*
▶ *We can use money to convey value and exert control.*
▶ *The presence of a step-parent does not affect the amount of maintenance a non-resident parent should pay towards their children's care.*

Calculating maintenance

How do parents living apart decide what should be paid to the family with whom the child spends most of their time? There are two ways for maintenance to be set up between parents. The first, and in many ways the best, is as a private arrangement between them. This can be as an informal arrangement or as a formal written agreement. A parenting plan can give you a framework for working this out between you (see Taking it further). The issues that you might like to consider in discussing finances between you would be:

▶ *What amount should be paid towards day-to-day living expenses by the non-resident parent?*
▶ *How will travel for contact visits be paid for?*
▶ *How will special expenses such as school trips or large purchases such as computers, bicycles or mobile phones be paid for?*
▶ *How much pocket money will children receive and from whom?*
▶ *How will you re-negotiate and adjust financial matters if circumstances change?*

To assess expenses, you would need to take into account the non-resident parent's income, how many nights the child regularly stays with them, how many children the non-resident parent is paying maintenance for, and how many they have living with them.

From the postbag

My partner wants to buy my son a new bike for Christmas and I know he'd love it. The only thing that worries me is what his Dad would say. My ex takes any excuse to wriggle out of paying maintenance and I'm sure if my partner started buying these sorts of things for my son, he'd claim it means he doesn't have to pay since my partner was now taking responsibility for my son. What do you think?

Parents have a legal responsibility to pay for the upkeep of their children – and that means items such as bikes and computers, mobile phones and clothes as well as food and shelter. If someone else – anyone else – buys them an item such as this, that's between them and the child. It doesn't in any way affect maintenance or a parent's responsibilities. If the child's father wanted and had already planned to buy the child something as important as a bike, I would say it would be tactless for anybody else to get in between a child and his father. But if that isn't the situation, your son certainly shouldn't be deprived of a loving gift you know he will treasure from his stepdad. It would not affect the amount his father is required to pay for maintenance at all. Good luck!

Pros and cons of voluntary agreements

There are advantages as well as disadvantages when making a voluntary agreement between you. The advantages of making a voluntary agreement are:

▶ *Personal negotiation avoids conflict. Involving other people or statutory agencies can feel confrontational and keep parties at arm's length, allowing misunderstandings to occur and blow up into arguments.*
▶ *Arrangements can easily and quickly be altered to meet a changing situation.*
▶ *What is thought mutually fair and agreed is what is paid.*

The disadvantages of making a voluntary agreement are:

▶ *The couple need to communicate to arrive at a mutually acceptable result. If there is hostility or any lingering feelings of abandonment or pain it may be hard to meet face to face or to keep discussions objective.*
▶ *If an informal agreement breaks down, the parent supposed to be receiving the money may have difficulty in enforcing it.*

If a voluntary agreement breaks down, a court is only likely to confirm it if it was recorded and properly witnessed. For this reason it is always a good idea to have a solicitor's help in drawing up an agreement and to have it signed and witnessed. A family solicitor who is a member of Resolution and who will encourage agreement rather than confrontation would be the best choice to guide parents through the process.

Applying for maintenance

The other way to apply for child maintenance is to go through the government agency that calculates and collects child maintenance and enforces its payment. This was the Child Support Agency, replaced in 2008 by the Child Maintenance and Enforcement Commission (CMEC). The Commission can offer help to parents agreeing child maintenance in various ways. It can help parents calculate what maintenance should be, depending on the number of children concerned, the income of the non-resident parent, the amount of time children spend with that parent and the number of children who live with that parent. This can be done via an online tool, on the phone or face to face. Asking the Commission for help in calculating maintenance does not mean you have to ask them to collect it for you. The idea is for help to be given to parents to make their own choice about how to manage finances between them. The preference is always for parents to make their own private arrangements because the reality is that when this happens, discussion and continued payment usually goes more smoothly. However, the parent asking for maintenance has the option, at any time, to ask the CMEC to step in to enforce the payment of maintenance that they have calculated.

Insight

Because money and maintenance are such emotive issues, it can really help to have supportive, sympathetic yet professional and non-partisan help in discussing and agreeing them.

The advantages of using the CMEC are:

▶ *Parents don't have to communicate if this has become difficult.*
▶ *The CMEC will do all the hard work – calculating the amount to be paid and collecting it.*
▶ *If money is not paid, the CMEC will pursue it.*

The disadvantages of using the CMEC are:

▶ *Any conflict between parents is not resolved and may increase.*
▶ *Settlements imposed by an outside authority tend to be resisted and resented.*
▶ *Neither parent has any control over the amount awarded.*
▶ *The amount given may be slow to be changed if the situation alters.*

Emotional effects of financial difficulties in stepfamilies

Money matters in stepfamilies are not just about child maintenance and the separated parents. There can be issues between the partners, and between adults and children. Money can always be a difficult issue in any relationship and in any family. As already mentioned, money often represents things other than mere cash and has emotional meaning. Money is one of the ways in this society in which we show value. High salaries confer high status, a bonus or award is a way of giving recognition, and presents say 'I love you'. We try to say 'It's the thought that counts', but in fact the price tag is often felt to be the important thing.

The problem within stepfamilies is that there are often many competing agendas, so many opposing demands, that where money goes and who it is spent on can often be the cause for hurt feelings or angry exchanges. Money spent on what one partner feels are people outside 'their' family can be seen as a betrayal and as valuable resources stolen from their own.

When dealing with financial matters it is often absolutely essential to first sort out any emotional ramifications. If there are arguments over money, or resentment or hurt feelings around it, you need to sit down and sort out:

- ▶ *what you are really feeling*
- ▶ *what are the real issues behind your emotions*
- ▶ *what you might like to be different*
- ▶ *what you might have to settle for.*

Once the underlying emotions behind an objection are brought out and discussed, you may be able to make arrangements that are both fair and acceptable. Simply being able to voice a degree of understandable resentment or jealousy or confusion can actually make those feelings far more manageable.

Drawing up a budget

The fact that money may have to be spread around more people than it must in a first-time family means that stepfamilies, even more than first-time families, need to budget. However alien or boring or silly it may seem, particularly if you have managed for years without having to do this, it may be worthwhile drawing up a budget to give yourself a picture of how you are going to manage.

You need two columns. In one write down all the money that comes into your family every week. This may be:

▶ *income from work*
▶ *benefits and allowances*
▶ *tax credits and child benefits*
▶ *any child maintenance received*
▶ *any other regular payments.*

In the other, list all the money that has to be paid out. This may be:

▶ *rent or mortgage*
▶ *council tax and water rates*
▶ *child maintenance*
▶ *fuel*
▶ *phone*
▶ *TV and car licences*
▶ *travel*
▶ *childcare*
▶ *food and household items*
▶ *regular costs – clothes, haircuts, entertainment and Christmas or birthday gifts.*

Writing it down allows you to take stock and to manage your finances with less of a shock than suddenly realizing your stepfamily may be costing you more than you realized.

Should you involve children in setting and maintaining a budget?

One enormous benefit of writing this all down is that you can show it and talk it through with the children. Children need to understand from quite an early age that money is not inexhaustible. In a stepfamily, money may often be used by the resident and non-resident family to compensate for losses in a child's life. Because they've had such a hard time, both families may be lenient about requests or demands for certain items, hoping a new pair of trainers, a visit to a music festival, a new bike may in some way make up for the difficulties of the situation. The problem is that because it does not do that, children may find themselves in a cycle where they keep asking for things both because they know they can and because they think it will make them feel better. When it does not do so, they just ask for more. Children most certainly must not be made to feel responsible, or in any way liable, if there are financial difficulties. But it is an important learning experience for them to see that the bank of Mum and Dad has its limits.

> ### Insight
> Children can be surprisingly mature and responsible when they can see how much is coming in, and how much is already earmarked. It's the best way to deal with 'I want... I want... I want...'

Giving children pocket money, or should it be an allowance?

Having given children a glimpse into what you have to think about when balancing what comes in and what goes out, it might be a good idea to talk with children about how they too can learn to manage their own money. Some children are given pocket money – a small amount each week to spend on whatever they choose. Some are allowed to earn extra cash by doing work around the house that does not come under the heading of 'chores' – such as cleaning cars or mowing lawns. Purchases not covered by either pocket money, earnings or gifts, may be negotiated separately. In other families, children are given a steadily increasing allowance, and made responsible for certain purchases themselves.

How liberal parents are with the amount of money they give as pocket money and the amount they are prepared to spend on such things as computer games, designer clothes and entertainment may have more to do with their feelings of guilt or difficulty in drawing boundaries than the amount of money coming in. Particularly in stepfamilies, it may be important for children to have some unrestricted money of their own to spend on what they like. The feeling of control and the knowledge of having some exercise of choice will be important to all children but particularly to those who know the loss of power that can be felt in family upheaval. But equally it is really important for children to learn to live within a budget and to recognize that in the real world to have money you need to offer something in exchange, and that the family purse is not bottomless.

Essential points to consider

▶ *Maintenance can be agreed voluntarily between separated parents or collected by the government agency, the CMEC. The CMEC can help in calculating the amount of maintenance owing even if you do not choose to have them involved.*

▶ *Working out a budget can help both parent and child in managing money and arguments over money.*

▶ *Children benefit from having some control over their own finances and from understanding the family budget.*

Negotiating an allowance

Allowances can be set from quite a young age. You will need to:

▶ *Work out what is spent specifically on the child, apart from household expenses. You might include their out-of-school clothes, entertainment such as games consoles and games, cinema trips and other outings with friends, travel, school lunches etc.*

- ▶ *Agree for what items the child will be responsible. Talk this through with the child and vary it depending on their age. Agree increases in the amount and the number of responsibilities as they get older.*
- ▶ *Agree how often to pay the allowance. You might total up an annual amount and then pay it weekly or monthly (which might mean they would need to save more to allow for larger purchases out of the averaged amount) or quarterly (which would mean they would have to resist spending a large amount at once).*
- ▶ *Agree with the child's other family whether the resident parent will pay all the allowance using child maintenance, or whether one parent will pay most and the other will top up. Make a clear undertaking that only the agreed amount will be paid and that you will discuss any other requests together so as not to undermine each other.*
- ▶ *Keep the limits! Make it very clear to the child that when money is spent, you will not issue more till the next pay day. If they blow the whole clothes allowance on one item, or spend all their travel costs, it's their lookout if they grow out of clothes or have to walk to friends' houses before the next payment.*

Giving an allowance helps children learn how to set aside money that is required for things they need or want. It helps them learn how to prioritize and pace themselves. But they won't learn these essential skills if you bale them out if they make a mistake. All financial disasters are learning experiences. Far better to have to cope with a misspent allowance when they still eat and sleep under a secure roof and have clothes to wear (even if not the latest thing), than discover they can't manage to budget when they're out in the world because they've never had to learn.

Children in stepfamilies often need to flex their muscles around responsibility and control, and giving them control and responsibility for their own cash from an early age can achieve this. Perhaps most importantly, children (and adults) in stepfamilies need to understand the meanings we attach to money and how money can be manipulated to control or worry others. By making the issue a debate, stepfamilies can manage the problematic potential of money and improve the functioning of the entire stepfamily.

Let them make mistakes over money and don't rescue them. Having to go without a much-wanted treat because you blew the lot earlier is the best way to learn!

Case study: David, Sophie, India and Toby

David and Sophie decided they would give her children, 15-year-old India and 14-year-old Toby, an allowance rather than the pocket money they had been receiving. She and the children's father agreed he would give them £10 a month for anything they wanted but that she'd pay them a quarterly allowance out of the maintenance money to cover non-school clothes and all entertainment, presents and out-of-school travel. The family sat down and had a long discussion about it, and Sophie and David emphasized the importance of keeping a budget and a check on spending because there would be no leeway on this – once spent no more cash would be forthcoming until the next pay day. But they also agreed that within sensible limits they could buy what they chose without having to agree each thing with their Mum and stepdad. The children were delighted and both enjoyed having control over what they spent and when. Toby started using his bike more, to save on bus fares, and India became adept at trawling charity shops to make her clothes spending go further. With five weeks to go until next pay day, India couldn't resist showing off to a friend and blew all her remaining money on expensive make-up. She asked for a sub until next pay day, and Sophie, David and her father stuck together and said no. Even Toby, normally her best friend, said he was managing and so should she. India raged and stormed but none of them cracked. India had to pass on almost every event with her friends for the next month – they lent her money for the first week or so then all said they couldn't afford to subsidize her anymore. In the next quarter she had to be careful as she had to pay back her friends and then make the remaining money stretch. When she got over her anger she had to admit it was a lesson well learned – and she was glad of the new system, after all.

THINGS TO REMEMBER

▶ *Money can be a hot issue in all families and relationships. It can be an even more contentious issue in stepfamilies where questions of child maintenance and support can be very much at the centre of discord.*

▶ *Money often stands in for love or attention or care. Money may be used as an attempt to reassure children, demanded as a form of revenge or asked as a token of continuing commitment.*

▶ *There are two ways of agreeing child maintenance. The first is by private agreement, the second is through a government agency – the Child Maintenance and Enforcement Commission (CMEC). A private arrangement, if manageable, is the better choice but if cooperation is lost in the heat of separation, the CMEC should provide you with support and safeguards.*

▶ *Stepfamilies need to budget even more than first-time families. However alien budgeting may have seemed in a first-time family, it is an absolute necessity in a stepfamily where money is a far more complex issue as it has to be spread around more people than it was before.*

▶ *Use budgeting to involve the children as much as possible. When they have some realistic knowledge of what money means within the family, it will make negotiations about pocket money and allowances, or family lifestyle or choices, far easier and more acceptable to them.*

IDEAS TO TRY

▶ *When money is the concern, sit down and make the opportunity to think about what is really the issue: financial and practical matters or emotional ones. Use honest discussion and ideas-storming, and support from a counsellor or mediator, to clarify. Review and use the suggestions in this chapter to sort out the emotional issues.*

▶ *Having a budget really helps, whether it's to set the scene for discussions over maintenance or to manage the debate over finances within a stepfamily, or negotiate pocket money and allowances with children. Use the suggestions in this chapter to calculate yours.*

▶ *The more children understand and share in calculating and assigning family finances, the more in control they feel and the less likely they are to make unrealistic demands. When you draw up your family balance sheet, involve the kids.*

▶ *If you haven't already done so, call a family round table to negotiate children's allowances. Use the suggestions in this chapter to discuss and set. If they do already get an allowance, review it – they need to be flexible and to change as children grow up and family circumstances change.*

16

Parental responsibility and other legal issues

In this chapter you will learn:
- *about parental responsibility, contact and residence*
- *about stepfamily adoption*
- *about the importance of inheritance and making wills.*

Up until the late 1980s, children tended to be seen almost as objects belonging to their birth parents. When a relationship broke up, custody battles were fought over who 'got' the children or who might be allowed access. The Children Act of 1989 changed this. Instead of rights we began to talk about responsibilities, and instead of custody we began to see what happens after a separation in terms of contact and residence.

The whole focus has now shifted towards the child's needs and what can be done to support children to keep both Mum and Dad in their lives. At the heart of what the law now says about separated parents is the assumption that parents have equal responsibility for their children and should go on having contact and a relationship with them. The courts would far rather parents decided contact – how much time a child may have with one parent – and residency – which parent they will live with or whether they will have an equal home with both – between them. When there is disagreement, however, the courts may step in to make or confirm that decision for them.

Insight

You don't get custody. Children get contact and residence.

Who has parental responsibility and what does it mean?

The key concept with children and parents who live apart is parental responsibility. Someone who has parental responsibility can decide important issues for the child such as:

- ▶ *what school they go to*
- ▶ *what subjects they might study*
- ▶ *what religion they are brought up in*
- ▶ *whether they can have medical treatment*
- ▶ *if they can go abroad on holiday.*

Mothers always have parental responsibility. Fathers do, too, if:

- ▶ *they were married to the mother when the child was born*
- ▶ *they were registered as the father on the baby's birth certificate, if the birth was after 1 December 2003.*

Fathers not married to the mother of their child at birth can acquire it. They can:

- ▶ *marry the mother*
- ▶ *re-register the birth to put their name on the birth certificate*
- ▶ *make a parental responsibility agreement with the mother*
- ▶ *get a court order – either a parental responsibility order or a residence order (with residence comes automatic parental responsibility)*
- ▶ *become the child's guardian.*

A parental responsibility order gives you the right to make those decisions about the child. It also confers duties – to care for and support the child. Not having parental responsibility, however, doesn't mean a father doesn't have a duty of care towards a child of theirs – a father may not have parental responsibility but still be liable for child maintenance. More importantly, parental responsibility is not lost by separating or divorcing. Neither does someone gaining this status mean someone else has to lose it – a child may only have one mother and one father but can have several people with parental responsibility for them at the same time. Grandparents can ask the court to give them parental responsibility and may be awarded it, and a mother may ask them or another suitable person to take it, so safeguarding her child. But if a father has it, he will not lose it by the mother doing this. And if for some reason he did not have it before separation, he may still be able to gain it. The courts will consider an application and take into account:

▶ *how committed the father is to his child*
▶ *how attached are father and child*
▶ *the father's reasons for applying for parental responsibility.*

Simply being a child's father is not enough for the powerful rights and duties of parental responsibility to be conferred – the court will need to know the father is requesting it because he wants to be part of his child's life, not as an attack on the mother or the new stepfamily.

STEP-PARENTS AND PARENTAL RESPONSIBILITY

Step-parents may also get parental responsibility, but it is not acquired automatically by living with the parent or even through marriage. A step-parent can gain parental responsibility by:

▶ *making a parental responsibility agreement with everyone who already has it*
▶ *getting a court order for parental responsibility or residence*
▶ *adopting the child*
▶ *being appointed guardian to care for the child if the parent is seriously ill or dies.*

Everyone who has parental responsibility has to agree to this. If someone does not, the case can be taken to court and if it's agreed it would be in the best interests of the child, parental responsibility would be granted.

....
Insight

Anyone requesting parental responsibility needs to be aware that it is more than just a title – it does make you liable for the child in all sorts of ways.
....

Why is parental responsibility so important?

If you have parental responsibility you have equal say in the important issues, and the less important ones, of the child's life and upbringing, just as anyone might expect to be able to do if they lived together bringing up a family. This would mean the person with parental responsibility could have as much say as the mother in decisions such as which school a child went to, whether they took or dropped certain courses, whether they left school or went to college. A parent living apart from a child could say yes or no to the child having pierced ears or going on school trips, as they would if they shared the same house. They could also say yes or no to emergency medical treatment. This instance may be one reason to consider step-parents having parental responsibility, since someone without it cannot agree to medical help in the event of a distressing but non-life-threatening accident or illness. However, a parent can give a step-parent the right to act 'in loco parentis' or in the place of the parent in other ways, with a signed letter outlining the responsibilities, such as the right to collect your child from school or to agree to emergency medical care.

Who decides about maintenance, residence and contact?

When families change, the courts far prefer that parents sort out between them issues such as maintenance, residence and contact. It's a lot cheaper and infinitely less stressful for everyone. Parents who can't agree will usually first be asked to accept help from an officer of the Children And Family Court Advisory and Support Service (CAFCASS) to try to settle the issue. Only 10 per cent of parents now have contact arrangements ordered by the courts, and orders are only made if it is decided that it would be better for the child if an order was made. If maintenance is being collected through the CMEC (see Chapter 15), changes such as a new family do have to be reported to them. But private arrangements can be privately agreed and adjusted.

Specific issue and prohibited steps orders

In many cases, the arrival of a step-parent may shift the emotional balance within both families. But it need not fundamentally change how parents continue to support and see their children. If parents have particular issues they can't agree on, such as where a child should go to school or their religion, the court can make a specific issue order. And if one parent wants help on stopping the other parent doing something specific, such as taking a child away or letting certain people be present during visits, the court can make a prohibited steps order, forbidding it.

Essential points to consider
▶ *Courts no longer award custody of children. The assumption is that children have the right to contact with both parents and that it is best for parents to agree where a child will live and how they will be in touch with the non-resident parent.*
▶ *Parental responsibility is a key issue. Mothers always have it, as do fathers married to the mother of their child.*
▶ *An unmarried father can gain parental responsibility with the agreement of the mother or be awarded it by the courts.*
▶ *Parental responsibility gives you certain rights and also certain duties. However, not having it still means you are liable for child maintenance.*

276

Can step-parents adopt their stepchildren?

In some stepfamilies, either the parent or the step-parent or both may express the desire to make theirs a complete or 'real' family by having the step-parent adopt their stepchildren. This may seem desirable but it can only go ahead in certain circumstances. What you may not realize about adoption is that it not only makes binding family ties between the adoptive parent and adopted child but it also severs entirely all connection between that child and their former family. For that reason, when a child is adopted by a step-parent they are also adopted by their own parent; the act of adoption breaks the previous bonds and new ones have to be made.

But also for that reason, a stepfamily adoption order is only agreed when the link between the other parent and their family has or should be entirely severed. An adoption order means that a child may now legally be considered the child of their step-parent. But they are no longer the child of the other parent, and no longer the grandchild of that person's parents or a niece or nephew or cousin of that family. For all intents and purposes, including inheritance, the family bond is cut. Because the effect is so final, even when contact has been broken between non-resident parent and child, the courts may still decide the child needs to preserve some link with that parent, or other family members such as grandparents, and will not make an adoption order.

The courts will look at the situation from the child's point of view and with the child's best interests at heart. The important issues are:

- *whether everyone holding parental responsibility agrees, or the court accepts that the other parent's wishes should be overruled or are not relevant*
- *whether an adoption order would be preferable to leaving the situation as it is.*

Making a will

It is essential in any family for parents to make wills. This is doubly so when parents live apart. If the separated couple has not divorced, they remain each other's next of kin unless a will has been made saying otherwise. Even if divorced, if the resident parent dies, the non-resident parent has sole responsibility for their children, unless a will has been made saying otherwise or the step-parent has acquired parental responsibility. This, of course, may be what both parents want. But in some situations it may not be the choice of anyone – neither the resident parent, the non-resident parent, the step-parent or the child. In a will, parents can specify who they would like to be guardian for their child in the event of their death. Several guardians can be named, to oversee together the wellbeing of the child, and the parent can say with whom they would like the child to live full time. As with any legal document, it must be drawn up clearly and unambiguously, signed and witnessed.

WHO INHERITS IN A STEPFAMILY?

It's not just the care of children that needs to be thought about in a will. Inheritance is something that needs to be considered. Anyone who dies without a will is said to have died 'intestate'. If someone dies intestate, it can take many months if not years before belongings are released to the family who inherits. Meanwhile, bills need to be paid and debts may mount up. And who inherits may not be exactly who the deceased might have chosen. Depending on how much was in the estate, a spouse may find they receive it all, or a certain amount plus a 'life interest' in half the remainder and children receive the rest. A life interest means the spouse can live in a house and use income from the estate for their lifetime but cannot leave it to anyone other than the people who properly inherit it, in this case the children. If not married but living together, a partner and any children not related to the deceased receive nothing. Children related to the deceased would get the lot. If the deceased did not have children of their own, their money would go to their parents or siblings or nephews and nieces or other relatives. And if they had no relatives, the inheritance still wouldn't go to a stepfamily but to the Crown. As already mentioned, if the children had been brought up for some time by the step-parent, they may be able to make a case for inheriting some proportion but it would require a court case and expense, and would not be the full amount they may have expected or the deceased person may have wanted.

Insight

Everyone should make a will. Doing so protects the people you love and care for. This is true in any family and whatever your assets. It's doubly true in stepfamilies.

From the postbag

My partner and I have been together 20 years and I've just made a new will since one of my sons has recently had a daughter. I wondered if my partner should make a new one too but he says it's not necessary. He has a will that covers all his children and grandchildren, and since he brought up mine since they were almost toddlers he says they would be covered as well. Is this true?

No, it most certainly is not. Unless he names them or specifies them, a will that talks about 'his' children or grandchildren would only cover the children that are his by birth. If you had children between you, they would come within the definition of 'his'.

But his stepchildren or stepgrandchildren are not legally related to him, even if he is married to you. If he does intend that they benefit from his will, he must make a new one with the help of a solicitor who can guide him on the legal terms that will ensure all the children he considers his can inherit. Good luck!

HOW TO MAKE A WILL

So it cannot be too highly stressed that making a will is important. You can draw one up yourself and as long as it is direct and clear, signed and witnessed, it would stand up in court. But it's best to ask for the help of a solicitor in making a will because there are various pitfalls you can fall into if you don't understand the law.

Anyone wishing to include people in a will needs to name and specify who they are. Leaving money to 'my children' or 'my grandchildren' would result in only children who are directly related or adopted inheriting. If you have stepchildren or stepgrandchildren, they would not be recognized as qualifying as 'my children' or 'my grandchildren' unless you named them. Setting out exactly what you want to give and exactly who you want to give it to is the only way to be certain your wishes will be honoured.

People often opt out off making a will, for various reasons:

- ▶ *It's so morbid even thinking about it.*
- ▶ *It's tempting fate – if you make a will you may soon need it.*
- ▶ *It's too time consuming.*
- ▶ *It's too expensive.*

Thinking, talking about or going ahead and making a will can have no effect on your life expectancy. If the worst is going to happen, it will go ahead and happen whether you have a will or not. The only difference is that it might cost your intended heirs untold misery and effort if one is not made. Wills are easy and quick to have drawn up and do not cost that much from a solicitor.

THINGS TO REMEMBER

▶ We no longer think in terms of custody or access, or allow parents to fight over who 'gets' the children. The focus now is on the child's needs and what can be done to support a child in having contact with both their parents.

▶ The key issues associated with parents and children who live apart are: residence, contact and parental responsibility. Mothers, and fathers married to the mother of their child, have this automatically. Other adults can acquire it. Parental responsibility confers rights and duties; it not only gives care and control but also an obligation to support.

▶ Fathers who do not have parental responsibility still have an obligation to pay maintenance for their children. Contact and maintenance are separate issues.

▶ A step-parent does not acquire parental responsibility for a partner's children by living with them or through marriage.

▶ Adoption of a child by a step-parent is not an easy process and is now only granted in exceptional circumstances. This is because adoption severs all connection between the child and the entire original family. When a child is adopted by a step-parent, they are also adopted by their own parent. Adoption by a step-parent is only agreed when links between the child and their other parent have been, or should be, entirely severed.

▶ Since stepchildren have no legal link with a step-parent, or any other step-relative, couples in a stepfamily need to consider the making of wills. If they do not, children may find the step-parent and parent's wishes are not reflected after their death.

IDEAS TO TRY

▶ *Familiarize yourself with the terms and concepts now used to describe the responsibility and agreements in separated families. We no longer talk in terms of 'custody' but about contact and residence. This isn't simply a change in language – it's a change in focus and attitude. Children have the right to a relationship with both parents as far as is possible.*

▶ *Review parental responsibility in your family. Who has it and who might need it?*

▶ *Consider what you would want to happen for the children if you died. Thinking about it isn't going to make it happen. But not thinking about it and acting on those deliberations may mean untold misery if something does happen to you and you haven't made provisions.*

▶ *Make a will or review the one you have. Because stepfamilies are complicated, it's best to do this with the support and advice of a solicitor.*

17

Names and their significance

In this chapter you will learn:
- *about names and their significance*
- *the legal issues and practicalities of changing names*
- *how to decide what stepchildren call their step-parents.*

Names and titles are important and significant to all of us.
Your personal name is something you learn at an early age
and know is yours – is 'you'. In many families, personal names
are passed down through generations, placing you as part of a
continuing tradition, sharing a name with a grandparent or aunt
or uncle or even a parent. In others, names are specially chosen for
particular reasons by parents – a memory or a link to something
or someone important to them. Personal names can often be
shortened or otherwise played around with to make them very
individual.

Family names are just as important. Sharing a family name
tells you who you are, who you belong to and with. In most
cultures, when women marry they take the family name of the
man they join, and their shared children have that name too.
This says loud and clear that these people belong together and
group with each other. Titles are of consequence, too. We like
having a job description that gives us some status, and to most
people being Mum or Dad is a job title they wear with pride.

Insight

Names say who you are and who you belong to. If you're in a stepfamily, you may need to consider the names you use carefully.

Should stepchildren change their names?

This is why names can be an especial cause for grief and anger in stepfamilies. It can be embarrassing, difficult and painful for children to have to negotiate the tricky question of what family name to use, especially if their mother has married a new partner and changed her name. The adults in a stepfamily may feel it's important that everyone in a household shares the same family name, to make it clear they are a unit together, whether the adults are married or not. In some cases, it may be seen as a break from a past the adults would rather leave behind.

It's easy to see why a household taking on the same family name may seem desirable. It can be complicated in a family that might have children who have the name of the man in the house, children who have the name of a father who no longer lives with them, and maybe even children from different fathers, each with their own father's family name. You could have four children in a school who all live with each other at times, but you wouldn't know exactly where they live from their names. John and Joe Smith may share a father, Jimmy, but not a home; Jake Jones and Jenny Owen may live with Jimmy, his wife Jane and their son John but Jimmy isn't either's father although they and John have the same mother.

Children may feel torn. The confusion outsiders may feel about their family and the way this singles them out could lead to their wanting to change names to be the same as the other people in their main household. Equally, they may stubbornly cling to the same name as a father who no longer lives with them, to retain the link they have with him, even when contact is sporadic or lost.

How do the adults change names?

If adults in a family would like to change their family (or indeed, their personal) name, it can actually be very simple. The court does not have to be involved for a name to be changed. Anyone can call themselves anything they want, as long as there is no intent to defraud or commit any offence – you cannot give yourself a title by adding 'Sir' or 'Lady' or call yourself by the name of some famous person with the intention of having people assume you are them. But if all you are seeking to do is change your name to lose a personal or family name you no longer want or gain one you do want, all you need to do is start using the new name and tell everyone it is the name you would like to be known by from now on.

You would tell anyone who needs to get in touch with you or has any dealings with you that your name is now different. That means not only telling your friends but also informing any organizations so they can change their records to show your new name. Among others these would be your employer, bank and credit card companies, GP and dentist, the Passport Agency, the DVLA, your mortgage company or landlord, your local authority and a child's school.

Some authorities and organizations will simply accept a letter from you explaining that you have changed your name. Others may ask for more proof. If you have changed your name because you have married, you simply show your marriage certificate. If not, you may need to provide one of the following:

▶ *A change-of-name statement. In this, you state the old name, the new name and have someone witness and sign it. Some solicitors can provide, or you can download from the internet, a statement like this for a small sum.*
▶ *A statutory declaration. This is a change-of-name statement that has been witnessed by a magistrate or solicitor. It may cost a bit more than a simple change-of-name statement but it still not very expensive.*

▶ *Deed poll. This is the most expensive option. It is a formal document that needs two witnesses. You can 'enrol' the deed poll, which means it is published in a weekly government publication and the information is kept safe in the Central Office of the Supreme Court. You would need to pay to have the document drawn up by a solicitor and another fee to have it enrolled. But you can choose to simply have it drawn up, signed and witnessed and then you keep it to show anyone who needs to see formal proof.*

Can you change children's names?

When the name change you are thinking about is for a child under the age of 18, the situation can be more complicated. The adults may feel they have entirely justifiable reasons to change. You may point to children feeling singled out when they have a different name to the parent they live with and any other children in the household. Having the same name may also be felt as an important step in bringing the family together and making it feel like a unit. Children themselves may give similar reasons for wanting to change. And, indeed, strictly speaking you can change a child's family name in exactly the same way and with as little fuss as an adult's.

But a non-resident parent can object, can take it to court and the court is likely to uphold the request for the family name to remain as it was. If this happens, there would be a court order – a prohibited steps order (see Chapter 16) – to prevent the name being changed. The reason for this is that an adult has every right to sever the link they had with the adult with whom they no longer want to share a name. Partners, in other words, can divorce. A parent is a parent for life, however, and children often desperately need that tie, to remain not only in contact with their parent but also with their own past, and thus themselves. It's bad enough losing a parent, the family as it was and a sense of family being something stable and secure. Losing your name on top of that can be a step too far, even when the child feels they would like this to happen.

Insight

Take advice before changing names, not only to be sure about the legality of what you want to do but also about the emotional consequences.

Why children may want to change their name

Children may opt for a name change in the middle of or as a result of the upheaval of family change. They may, indeed, want to express a sense of belonging to the new family, especially when contact with their other birth parent may no longer be possible. But, equally, their underlying motive may be one of anger, hurt and loss – a way of striking back at a parent who is no longer there and saying 'Keep your rotten name – you don't want me so I don't want it!' Sometimes children make this move when they feel the parent is withdrawing and use it as a way of taking control, of getting their rejection in first so it may not hurt as much when they are abandoned. Sadly, the result sometimes is that the non-resident parent feels they are no longer needed or wanted and the withdrawal becomes complete, when it need not have been so.

If relations have really broken down, or there has been no contact for an extended period, changing a child's name is something you can discuss. But it is worth considering what a change might actually mean. Can the child continue feeling connected to the people he or she lives with without a change in name? And if the name did change, would that prevent any question of connecting with their origins forever? There can be no hard and fast rules on this – what would be best for you and your child is something you need to work out. But above all it is the child's best interests (and their interests over the long term, not just on the first day of school when they may be asked why they have a different name to their mother) that matters. Courts are most reluctant to let parents change children's names when new families form. If it goes to court, they are likely to uphold a child's or non-resident parent's insistence on keeping the birth name. If the father has parental responsibility, his consent is essential. Even if he does not have parental responsibility, if he is in frequent contact his wishes will be taken into consideration. If the courts do uphold a request for a child's name to be changed you cannot change a birth certificate to match – that will continue to show the original surname.

Instead of a full change, substituting one name for another, you may like to discuss the following:

▶ *Adults can take a double-barrelled family name of both names with children keeping their birth names. That way, the adults can celebrate their partnership while the parent still has the same name as the child.*

▶ *Both adults and children can take both names. This way, both adults and children can celebrate the new family and the child still retains a link to their past. Non-resident parents may prefer this addition rather than their name being removed.*

▶ *Accept that in today's society, a variety of family names is no longer unusual.*

Essential points to consider

▶ *First names and surnames are an important indicator of personal identity and family connection.*

▶ *An adult can change their name relatively easily and with minimal expense as long as there is no illegal intent.*

▶ *If you want to change a child's name and the non-resident parent objects, the court will almost certainly uphold the request to keep the name intact as a link.*

What should stepchildren call their step-parents?

The titles we call ourselves as family members are as important as our personal or surnames. In some families, it feels really important for a stepmother or stepfather to be called Dad or Mum by their stepchildren. This may be particularly so if they share a house full time, but some weekend step-parents feel it important too. Some may insist on this because they think it shows disrespect for an adult to be called by their personal name by a child. 'Stepmum' or 'Stepdad' wouldn't exactly feel natural, comfortable or acceptable in this society. Usually, the options are first names or Mum or Dad.

A title such as this can be seen as an important indicator of how well you are doing. If you're doing a good job as a step-parent, you might expect to be rewarded – to be given a smiley face or a gold star or a badge in the shape of the name Mum or Dad. If they won't address you by that name, it feels as if they are saying they don't feel you are doing it right. They are rejecting you and telling you they don't and won't accept you as a part of their family.

Insight

Being called Mum or Dad by a stepchild isn't the same as being awarded a prize. You can have the name without the feeling, just as much as you can have the feeling without the name.

CAN A PARENT BE REPLACED?

A stepfamily can be just as much a family as a first-time family. In it, children can be cared for, loved and appreciated as much by a step-parent as they might have been in a family with two parents who gave birth to them. In some case, more so. However, a stepfamily *is* a stepfamily. It does not contain two parents for all or some of the children there, instead it contains one parent and one step-parent. Children have two parents – the ones they are born with. One parent may have gone missing; they may have left, never to be in touch again. Or have died. Or be out there and sporadically in touch. Or in touch once a month and some holidays. Or around every other weekend. Or every weekend and two nights a week and on the phone every day. It doesn't matter how often they are in touch. These are their parents and they cannot be replaced as parents – as Mum and Dad. Children know this, and often feel under stress and under pressure when it comes to looking at names in their new family. It's bad enough losing the everyday face-to-face contact with a parent. Having their title given to someone else simply rubs salt in the wound. Being expected or even told to call someone else Dad or Mum only underlines that their lives have changed, and something precious to them is missing, and that nobody seems to care or notice or realize how important this is to them.

Keeping the name Dad or Mum special and reserved for the birth parent retains a link with them when all other links may be fraying. And it takes nothing away from any new and often close relationship that children can forge between themselves and a new adult. The fact is that the thing itself isn't the same as the name. Either deciding or being told to call someone a parent doesn't mean they accept you are a Dad or Mum. Indeed, when children jump quickly into calling someone 'Dad' or 'Mum', far from being a genuine display of affection it can be an attempt to create or strengthen bonds they desperately need but may not yet feel.

A DAD BY ANY OTHER NAME...

A step-parent can be a really important figure to a stepchild without needing the name of Dad or Mum as a badge. Children don't see it as cheeky to call an adult by a personal name. Indeed, it could be argued that it does children good to know the adults looking after them do have proper names of their own. If you're only ever referred to as Dad or Mum, it's as if that's who you are; not an individual in your own right with frailties and needs and wishes of your own, but a figurehead and institution. Mum/Dad is often seen as someone who doesn't hurt, who knows everything, who never needs sleep, time off or a life of any sort of their own beyond being Mum or Dad. Calling a step-parent by their name may not result in their also calling their own parents by their name but at least it alerts them to the fact they have one. As a step-parent you are a Significant Other, and being recognized as such is worth a lot.

Children often like making their own names for the adults who care for them and mean something to them. It may be a shortened – or lengthened – version of your own personal name or a nickname. Or, a child can have two dads – a Dad and a Daddy – or two mums – a Mum and a Mummy.

If names become an issue in your family, talk it over with your children and listen with care not only to what they say but also to the feelings behind the words. Wanting to belong, to the people they live with and the people they originate from, is such a basic need and right for children. It's up to us to help them keep the links. Don't grasp at titles or names because you feel you need to in order to explain yourselves to others. What you do that works between the children and other adults concerned is all that matters.

From the postbag

I live with my Mum and her man, Steve. I really like Steve – he's always there for me. My Dad lives in France and I only see him in school holidays. But he's my Dad and I love him. I know my Mum would like me to call Steve Dad, but I don't want to. I don't want to hurt his feelings but it doesn't feel right. How can I stop her putting the pressure on, trying to make me do it?

Tell her what you've told me – that Steve is important to you but he's not your Dad. That doesn't make him any less significant to you but it's a different sort of relationship than father and son. Ask if you could come up with a nickname or a shortening of his name that is unique to you and would show you feel really special about him. My stepson calls me Suz which is his special name for the Significant Other in his life and I've always felt it's as valued a name as Mum would be. Good luck!

Insight
Nicknames or personal names can be just as much a sign of affection and bonding as calling you Mum or Dad.

THINGS TO REMEMBER

▶ *Names are important and significant to everyone. They can assume even more importance in a stepfamily where they can easily become the cause of grief and anger.*

▶ *Changing an adult's name is relatively simple. When the name change is for a child, the wishes of a non-resident parent and the best interests of the child must be taken into account.*

▶ *Some children would welcome a change of family name and see it as a sign of belonging to and being included in the new family. Others might resist any change strongly, seeing their name as being the only reminder they have of a past and a link that has been taken from them.*

▶ *Insisting on or expecting a child to call a step-parent 'Dad' or 'Mum' can be a difficult issue for a child still longing for the past. Equally, the use of a Christian name or a very informal name might be seen as almost rude and disrespectful by an adult. Families may need to discuss and confront conflicting and complicated questions when deciding who is to be called what in a stepfamily.*

▶ *Being called 'Dad' or 'Mum' is not a badge that tells everyone – and the wearer – that they are doing a good job. One child may call a step-parent by such a name through gritted teeth, with resentment and anger. Another may call the step-parent by their first name, with affection and respect.*

▶ *If you are finding names becoming a real issue in the family, talk it over with the children. Listen carefully to what they say and be sensitive to the feelings behind the words.*

IDEAS TO TRY

▶ *Think about the names in your family – personal names, family names, nicknames and titles such as Mum, Gran or Auntie. Have a family discussion to identify them all.*

▶ *Is everyone happy about what they do use or are expected to use, and with what they are called?*

▶ *If you have an issue with names, ideas-storm to sort out who wants what and why, or who would prefer not to use certain names or terms.*

▶ *Take advice or use counselling or mediation support if there are difficulties involved. Review the issues discussed in this chapter but recognize that an adult's need to have their role acknowledged may have to take second place to a child's need to retain a tie with a parent.*

18

Looking after yourselves

In this chapter you will learn:

- *how parents and step-parents can look after themselves*
- *how to 'fill your cup' by caring for your own wellbeing*
- *the importance of making the couple relationship work.*

Being a parent or a step-parent is a complex and tiring job.
It's always a challenge but that challenge can be constructive or
destructive. It can be as fascinating, energizing and joyful as it
is stressful and hard. What often makes the difference between
struggling or managing is the attitude you bring to the situation.
And whether you have a positive or a negative attitude frequently
depends on whether you are prepared to look after yourselves as
individuals and as a couple as well as look after everyone else.
A strong relationship is the bedrock of a functioning stepfamily,
so to be selfish occasionally and concentrate on the wellbeing of
yourself and each other can often be essential.

If children are to get what they want and need from a family, it's
vital that parents and step-parents look after their own needs too.
Parents often spend all their time looking after everyone else in the
family and leave themselves to last. Instead of being generous and
helpful, however, this can become counter-productive.

Insight

It can be difficult and painful to give other people what they
need if you feel nobody looks after you.

Filling your emotional cup

Trying to fulfil people's needs for emotional support and attention is like trying to share a cup of tea or coffee. The state of your cup entirely depends on whether your own needs are being met or not.

WHEN YOU HAVE UNMET NEEDS

If you feel tired and resentful and ignored, that means your own needs for care and attention are going unfulfilled. When asked for help by someone else, it's as if your cup is empty and when someone asks for a sip, you have to say 'I'm sorry – there's nothing for me so there's nothing for you, either.' You may feel angry or guilty or maybe even sourly triumphant that you can't offer anything to the other person, because nobody is offering anything to you.

WHEN SOME OF YOUR NEEDS ARE BEING MET

If some of your needs are being met, it's as if your cup is half full. You may be able to say 'Well, you can have some...' but you'd have to add '...but there's not much for you and if I give you a sip there won't be any left for me.' Again, you may feel angry or guilty or frustrated that you can do no more.

WHEN YOUR NEEDS ARE MET AND YOU CAN OFFER HELP TO OTHERS

But if your cup is full, you can say 'Have as much as you want!' You won't feel giving something to the other person robs you. Instead, you have lots to spare and feel ready and willing to be generous and to pass it on.

It's easy to be overwhelmed by competing needs in a stepfamily, and for everyone's cup to get emptied very quickly and sometimes never to be filled up. If you're running on empty, you have nothing to give to yourself and nothing for the other important people in your life. This can leave you feeling worthless and useless, and all of you feeling rejected, resentful and angry.

Stepfamilies can strain the relationship between new partners, particularly when pulled this way and that by the varying demands and expectations of children, stepchildren, ex-partners, grandparents and stepgrandparents. To not only survive but also thrive, a couple needs to make particular efforts to build their relationship and make it strong as well as to make time to enjoy themselves, together and separately.

> **Insight**
> It isn't selfish to look after yourself. You can't look after other people if you feel unsupported or frustrated.

The importance of looking after yourself

Treating yourself and looking after yourself isn't being selfish. It's being aware that you're important too and deserve to be cared for just as much as anyone else. The better you feel, the better you can help other people feel too. You owe it to:

- *yourself*
- *your family*
- *the others in your life*

to do things – even small things – to make yourself feel good. Every little treat helps to fill your cup so you've got something to give out.

Take some time to work out what makes you feel looked after, cared for, rested and refreshed. It might be:

- *having a bath*
- *listening to music*
- *reading a newspaper, magazine or book*
- *gardening*

- *taking a walk*
- *being on your computer*
- *going to the gym or for a run*
- *going shopping with a friend*
- *planning a holiday*
- *phoning or texting a friend*
- *watching a favourite TV programme*
- *meeting a friend for coffee or a beer*
- *having a meal alone with your partner.*

MAKING TIME FOR YOURSELF

Work out what helps you and set aside certain times in the day and week to fill your cup. You may tell the family that:

- *the first 20 minutes after you get home from work are yours to get clean and chill out with a favourite music track*
- *the last hour in the evening is adult time – kids to their rooms or else*
- *bathtime is not to be disturbed, on pain of death*
- *one night a month is adult night in – kids to relatives or friends while you have a meal and DVD of your choice*
- *one night a month is adult night out – a meal, a film, or just a drink on your own*
- *you'll negotiate TV programmes throughout the week, but these are your must-watch programmes.*

How do you make your personal relationship work?

From the postbag

I never seem to have any time for myself – or ourselves. Our children are there all the time and are so demanding. Don't get me wrong, I love them and love being with them.

(Contd)

It's just that we've only been together for four years – it's a second marriage – and it feels as if I'm either working at my job or working at home, keeping the family happy. My husband is a rock but I know he'd like us to have some time for ourselves. I just feel so guilty when we sneak away for a private moment and I can't remember the last time we went out together without the children.

If the only reason you take care of yourself is for your children, you owe it to them to have some time off. But you also deserve it for yourselves. Don't feel guilty; there's nothing in the job description that says you have to be at your children's beck and call all day, every day to be doing a good job of being a parent. Get your diary out and schedule some private time, much as you would arrange a business meeting or a date. It's often the only way you can make sure you get what you both deserve. Depending on their ages, get a babysitter or arrange for them to manage on their own or all be out with friends or relatives at least twice a month. And twice a month arrange it so you can have a meal and an evening on your own. They'll benefit from it – and so will you. Good luck!

Insight
Relationships need to be fed and watered and otherwise encouraged to grow and stay strong.

Many parents find their couple relationship coming apart at the seams because family life takes over. It can be wonderful, fun and heart-warming to spend most of your focus and time on bringing up your family but, as many couples sadly find out, if you only run your relationship through your children, when they grow up and no longer need you the essential bridge between you can be gone and your relationship no longer functions. First-time families have the advantage of beginning as two people on their own, so can remember what it was like to be together minus children. With stepfamilies, children were there first, before this relationship came into being. When times are rough, with pressure on all sides, if you don't have a good connection and understanding between you, it may be difficult to stand side by side against the world. So it's vital for you to take steps to strengthen your private, personal rapport. You should:

▶ *Talk. Intimacy is what brings people together, and you can only be intimate with someone you really know. Share your thoughts, your opinions, your tastes.*

▶ *Set good habits in the early days. Consider all the ways you show your feelings to your partner, by holding hands, hugging or kissing and telling them about your day, and resolve to continue doing so even when the honeymoon period is over. Don't let the presence of children saying 'Yuck!' put you off.*

▶ *Once your relationship has settled into a comfortable routine, keep reminding yourself and your partner what drew you together, what attracted you to them, and the way you felt in the early days of your relationship. Focus on the positive aspects.*

▶ *Make a point of doing something every day for your partner, and thank them out loud for anything they do for you.*

▶ *Regularly see your own friends and do something that especially and specifically interests you to maintain your own individuality and social life. But share your thoughts, your ideas and your enthusiasms with your partner so you both keep in touch with this other side of yourselves, and never keep secrets.*

▶ *Be spontaneous. Relationships go stale and families get in a rut because it all becomes so predictable. You may feel you can't suddenly say 'I love you' because the children will hear, or throw everything into the car and go out for a picnic because the washing needs doing. Do it anyway.*

▶ *Make a big deal out of time together. Even if money is tight and you're only spending the evening in eating sausage and mash and watching TV, make it an event. Take steps to ensure you'll be on your own, dress up and splash on the cologne, turn the lights low and burn candles and use the best china.*

▶ *Regularly look at your relationship and ask yourself and your partner if you're satisfied and if not what you could do to improve things. If you feel it is healthy, look at what is making it work and keep on doing those things.*

Essential points to consider

▶ *Parents and step-parents need to look after themselves. If you don't, you won't have the resilience to care for the family.*

▶ *Remember the full cup of coffee; if yours is empty, you have nothing to share. Parents and step-parents need to fill their cup up regularly to have enough to go round.*

▶ *As well as being parents and step-parents you are also a couple. Adults in a stepfamily need to make time to tend their own intimate relationship.*

Caring for yourself and your partner

Most parents make a habit of looking after other people and often forget to look after themselves, or to allow others to care for them. This can be difficult in a stepfamily, where one of you may feel more involved in the private relationship than the other, who continues to focus on children. It's really important that both adults recognize that they need and deserve care too, and that they should take the time and effort to give themselves as much help as they are offering other people. Here are some helpful tips:

▶ *Be as generous and patient with yourself and your partner as you may be with the children.*

▶ *Have realistic expectations of yourself and what you can do.*

▶ *Recognize that other people's problems are their responsibility not yours. You can't fix everything nor should you try.*

▶ *Be positive with yourself and your family. Give support, encouragement and praise, and accept it in return.*

- ▶ *Don't get stuck in a rut. Change your routines as often as you can.*
- ▶ *Offload when you need to, but recognize the difference between complaining that makes you feel better, and complaining that just reinforces stress.*
- ▶ *Every day, focus on one good thing that happened.*
- ▶ *Make sure you have some time to yourself at least twice a week when you can be calm and at peace, to have bath, drink a cup of coffee, read a magazine or paper and no one interrupts you.*
- ▶ *Take control of and be responsible for your actions. Say 'I choose' rather than 'I should' or 'I ought to' or 'I have to' or 'I must'. If you don't choose to do these things, consider whether you should be doing them at all.*
- ▶ *Say NO sometimes – you can't do everything and you shouldn't be doing things you don't want to do. If you never say NO, what is your YES worth?*
- ▶ *Be clear and direct. If you choose not to do something, say you won't rather than making excuses.*
- ▶ *Say so if you can't cope. It's far better to ask for help and back off than make excuses and let people think you're offhand, distant or indifferent.*
- ▶ *Give yourself permission to have fun – often.*
- ▶ *Make time. There are only so many hours in the day, but that doesn't mean you can't have some time for yourselves. Often, the only reason you don't is because you feel you don't have a right to it. Make time by planning ahead, knowing it's essential for you and everyone else.*

THINGS TO REMEMBER

▶ *Being a step-parent can be a complex and tiring job. What often makes the difference between struggling or managing is the attitude you bring to the situation.*

▶ *A strong relationship is at the core of a functioning stepfamily. Be 'selfish' occasionally and look after yourself and your partner as well as looking after everyone else.*

▶ *Relationships need regular maintenance. Tending your relationship as well as your family should make your partnership able to withstand the stresses and pressures of stepfamily life.*

▶ *Have realistic expectations of what you can and cannot do. Plan, make time for yourselves and take control of and responsibility for your actions.*

▶ *Remember 'good enough' is the achievable goal, not perfection. Relax and enjoy your new family.*

IDEAS TO TRY

▶ *Using the suggestions in this chapter, draw up your own list of ways of looking after yourself. Divide them into 'daily treats', 'weekend specials', 'monthly indulgences' and 'occasional spoils'. If you need to stick the list on the family notice board and tick them off to make sure you take care of yourself, do so.*

▶ *Encourage everyone in the family to 'fill their cup' in this way, and accept encouragement to do so yourself.*

▶ *Make time for you and your partner apart from your family. Have dates, and keep track on a calendar or diary to ensure you don't let this slip.*

▶ *Use 'Please' and 'Thank you' regularly, to family members as well as outsiders.*

Taking it further

Family Live (formerly Parentline Plus) is the national charity that works for, and with, parents and step-parents. They have websites with plentiful information and message boards where parents can chat together, Parents Together groups, workshops and information leaflets.

Free, confidential, 24-hour helpline: 0808 800 22 22
Free textphone for people with a speech or hearing impairment: 0800 783 6783

Email, skype or chat online through the websites.
Websites: www.parentlineplus.org.uk but soon to be www.familylives.org.uk

Families Need Fathers is a registered charity providing information and support on shared parenting issues arising from family breakdown to divorced and separated parents. Support is provided through a national helpline, a website, a network of volunteers, and regular group meetings, held in a variety of locations.

Helpline: 0300 030 0363 (Monday–Friday 6p.m.–10p.m.)
Website: www.fnf.org.uk

Fatherhood Institute is the national information centre on fatherhood. They offer publications to support fathers and their families.

Main website: www.fatherhoodinstitute.org
Online community for fathers with help, advice, forums and features: www.dad.info

Gingerbread (now incorporating One Parent Families) provides a helpline with free information to lone parents on issues including benefits, tax, legal rights, family law and contact issues, child maintenance and returning to work. They are able to connect lone parents with other organizations and local groups.

Helpline: 0808 802 0925
Website: www.gingerbread.org.uk

Relate offers relationship counselling and life-skills courses through local Relate centres. Counselling is also available over the telephone.

Tel: 0300 100 1234 to find your nearest centre.
Website: www.relate.org.uk
Counselling by phone booking line: 0845 130 4016

Centre for Separated Families is the national charity that works with everyone affected by family separation in order to bring about better outcomes for children.

Coppergate House
16 Brune St
London E1 7NJ
Email: advice@separatedfamilies.org.uk
Website: www.separatedfamilies.org.uk

National Domestic Violence Helpline (run in partnership between Women's Aid and Refuge) provides a free telephone helpline for women experiencing physical, emotional or sexual violence in the home. The free, 24-hour helpline can refer to local refuges and emergency accommodation across the UK.

Helpline: 0808 200 0247
Website: www.womensaid.org.uk

National Association of Child Contact Centres promotes safe child contact within a national network of child contact centres. A child contact centre is a safe place where children of separated families can spend time with one or both parents and sometimes other family members. Details of local centres can be found on their website or by ringing them.

Telephone: 0845 450 0280 (Monday–Friday 9a.m.–1p.m.)
Website: www.naccc.org.uk

CAFCASS (Children And Family Court Advisory and Support Service) looks after the interests of children and young people involved in cases in the family courts ensuring their voices are heard. It helps families to reach agreement over arrangements for their children. CAFCASS only works with families on referral from the court but their website contains useful information, case studies, advice and contact links.

Website: www.cafcass.gov.uk

The Child Maintenance and Enforcement Commission (CMEC) is the non-departmental public body established to take responsibility for the child maintenance system in Great Britain. They give impartial information and support service to help parents make an informed choice about the maintenance arrangement best suited to their circumstances.

Website: www.childmaintenance.org

Child Maintenance Options provides impartial information and support to help both parents make informed choices about child maintenance. They offer practical information in areas linked to child maintenance, such as housing, employment and money. Child Maintenance Options is a service provided by the CMEC.

Freephone: 0800 988 0988
(Monday–Friday 8a.m.–8p.m. and Saturday 9a.m.–4p.m.)
Website: www.cmoptions.org

Children's Legal Centre offer information on all aspects of child law in England and Wales, particularly contact, parental responsibility and residence orders. A pre-recorded telephone service gives information on frequently asked questions on a wide range of topics. A website and email response service are also available.

For free legal advice on any topic relating to children, call the Child Law Advice Line (freephone) on 08088 020 008
Website: www.childrenslegalcentre.com

Citizens Advice Bureau is an independent organization providing free, confidential and impartial advice on all subjects to anyone. The address and telephone number of your local CAB can be found in the telephone directory. There is also advice online on their website.

Website: www.citizensadvice.org.uk
Advice online website: www.adviceguide.org.uk

Family Rights Group provides a specialist advice and information service for families in England and Wales, who are in contact with social services about the care of their children, and their advisers and supporters.

Helpline: 0808 801 0366 (Monday–Friday 10a.m.–12 noon and 1.30p.m.–3.30p.m.)
Website: www.frg.org.uk

ChildLine offers a free confidential helpline open 24 hours.

Address: ChildLine, Freepost NATN1111, London, E1 6BR
Freephone: 0800 1111
Website: www.childline.org.uk

It's Not Your Fault is a website for children and young people about divorce and separation, with useful information.

Website: www.itsnotyourfault.org

National Youth Advocacy Service provides advocacy services for children and young people up to the age of 25. They provide specialist help in children's rights, children in care, contact issues, education and youth justice. They have a network of advocates throughout the country and their own legal advice.

Free helpline for children and young people: 0800 616101
Email advice for children and young people: help@nyas.net
Website: www.nyas.net

The Site is a website for young people with information about a wide range of local services, as well as discussion forums.

Website: www.thesite.org.uk

Youth Access has a directory of youth advice, information, support and counselling services for young people across the UK. This can be found by ringing their referral line or by looking at the online directory on their website.

Referral information: 0208 772 9900 (Monday–Friday 9a.m.–1p.m. and 2p.m.–5p.m.)
Website: www.youthaccess.org.uk

'Parenting Plans – putting your children first, a guide for separating parents' is a booklet of questions that you could use to trigger discussion on issues such as day-to-day arrangements, holidays, health, money, and a section to guide you through what to do if you're finding it hard to agree. It is a very helpful outline for your discussions and agreement. Parent plans help you to think of all the things you will need to manage as parents living apart. You can download it from:

http://tinyurl.com/yavt5s4 or go to www.cafcass.gov.uk and click on 'Publications' then 'Leaflets for adults'.

Resolution – first for family law (the Solicitors Family Law Association) can give advice on any family dispute and with separation, divorce and new families, and encourage mediation and agreement rather than confrontation.

Address: PO Box 302, Orpington, Kent, BR6 8QX
Tel: 01689 820272
Website: www.resolution.org.uk

The Community Legal Service can help you find the right legal
information and advice to solve your problems. You can get help
through a network of organizations, including:

- ▶ *Citizens Advice Bureaux*
- ▶ *Law Centres*
- ▶ *many independent advice centres*
- ▶ *thousands of high street solicitors.*

They also provide leaflets on a wide variety of issues to do with
separation, divorce and stepfamilies.

Tel: 0845 345 4345
Website: www.communitylegaladvice.org.uk

Family Mediators Association can put you in touch with trained
mediators who work with both parents and children.

National helpline: 0800 200 0033
Website: www.thefma.co.uk

National Family Mediation is an umbrella organization for local
family mediation services and can provide details of local services
in the UK.

Telephone: 0117 904 2825 (Monday–Friday 9.30a.m.–3.30p.m.)
Website: www.nfm.org.uk

UK College of Family Mediators can help you to find a mediator.

Address: UK College of Family Mediators, Alexander House,
Telephone Avenue, Bristol, BS1 4BS
Tel: 0117 904 7223
Website: www.ukcfm.co.uk

Relationships Scotland

Website: www.relationships-scotland.org.uk

Cruse Bereavement Care promotes the wellbeing of bereaved people and enables anyone bereaved by death to understand their grief and cope with their loss. The organization provides counselling and support, information, advice, education and training services.

Helpline: 0844 477 9400
Young person's helpline: 0808 808 1677
Website: www.crusebereavementcare.org.uk

The British Association for Counselling and Psychotherapy can suggest a counsellor in your area.

Address: BACP, BACP House, 35–7 Albert Street, Rugby, Warwickshire, CV21 2SG
Tel: 0870 443 5219
Website: www.bacp.co.uk

The Institute of Family Therapy can help with family problems.

Address: Institute of Family Therapy, 24–32 Stephenson Way, London, NW1 2HX
Tel: 020 7391 9150
Website: www.instituteoffamilytherapy.org.uk

Separated Dads is a website containing articles and advice for dads living away from their children and offering a regular email newsletter.

Website: www.separateddads.co.uk

The Hideout is a site for young people worried about domestic violence.

Website: www.thehideout.org.uk

The Advisory Centre for Education (ACE) is an independent, registered charity, which offers information about state education in England and Wales for parents of school-age children. They offer free telephone advice on many subjects such as exclusion from school, bullying, special educational needs and school admission appeals.

General advice line: 0808 800 5793 (Monday–Friday 10a.m.–5p.m.)
Exclusion information line: 0207 704 9822 (24hr answer phone)
Exclusion advice line: 0808 800 0327 (Monday–Friday 10a.m.–5p.m.)
Website: www.ace-ed.org.uk

Parents Centre is an information and support website for parents on how to help with your child's learning, including advice on choosing a school and finding childcare.

Website: www.parentscentre.co.uk

Young Minds is the charity that is concerned about the importance of children's mental health; the importance of recognizing when a child is troubled and providing adequate support for these children before their problems escalate out of control. They provide a helpline and information for parents and young people.

Helpline: 0800 018 2138 (Mondays 10a.m.–1p.m., Tuesdays 1–4p.m., Wednesdays 1–4p.m. and 6–8p.m., Thursdays 1–4p.m., Fridays 10a.m.–1p.m.
Website: www.youngminds.org.uk

Grandparents' Association supports grandparents whose grandchildren are out of contact with them or who have childcare responsibilities for their grandchildren.

Address: Grandparents' Association, Moot House, The Stow, Harlow, Essex, CM20 3AG
Helpline: 0845 4349585
Website: www.grandparents-association.org.uk

The Child Exploitation and Online Protection (CEOP) Centre works across the UK and abroad to tackle child sex abuse wherever and whenever it happens. Part of their strategy for achieving this is by providing internet safety advice for parents and carers and offering a 'virtual police station' for reporting abuse on the internet.

Website: www.ceop.gov.uk

UK Parents Lounge has online forums for parents and step-parents.

Website: www.ukparentslounge.com

Parents.com has an online community for parents.

Website: www.parents.com

Dads UK runs a news and information website with online forums for dads with limited or restricted contact.

Website: www.dads-uk.co.uk

… and if all else fails, look at my own site: www.agony-aunt.com

Index

Image credits